Installing & Finishing DRYWALL

William Spence

Sterling Publishing Co., Inc.
New York

Disclaimer

Those using this book must realize that the information presented was secured from a wide range of manufacturers, professional and trade associations, government agencies, and various architectural and engineering consultants and that in some cases generalized or generic examples are used. Every effort was made to provide accurate presentations. However, the author and the publisher assume no liability for the accuracy or applications shown. As the author and publisher have no control over how the reader chooses to utilize the information presented in this book and cannot determine the reader's level of proficiency or physical condition, they are not responsible for mishaps or other consequences that result from the reader's use of the information herein. It is essential that appropriate architectural and engineering staff be consulted and specific information about products be obtained directly from the manufacturer.

Library of Congress Cataloging-in-Publication Data

Installing & finishing drywall / by Willaim Spence.

p. cm.

Includes index (p.).

ISBN 0-8069-3885-4

[Data on file]

Edited and Layout by Rodman Pilgrim Neumann

3 5 7 9 10 8 6 4 2

Published by Sterling Publishing Company, Inc.
387 Park Avenue South, New York, N.Y. 10016

Distributed in Canada by Sterling Publishing
c/o Canadian Manda Group, One Atlantic Avenue, Suite 105
Toronto, Ontario, Canada M6K 3E7
Distributed in Great Britain and Europe by Cassell PLC
Wellington House, 125 Strand, London WC2R 0BB, England
Distributed in Australia by Capricorn Link (Australia) Pty Ltd.
P.O. Box 6651, Baulkham Hills, Business Centre, NSW 2153, Australia
Printed in the United States

Sterling ISBN 0-8069-3885-4

Contents

Part II: Installing Gypsum Wallboard 41

Part III: Finishing 91

Preface

Drywall installation and finishing is a task undertaken by many who enjoy doing some of the work on their home—be it a repair or a new addition. It is also a service provided by skilled craftsmen. It requires strength, ability to plan and execute the plan, ethical attitudes toward proper installation, and highly skilled finishing ability.

This book provides a look at the basic materials, installation techniques, and finishing procedures. If these procedures and guidelines are carefully followed, a person can do a good job of installation and finishing. The craftsman will do the job much faster but the homeowner, while slow, can handle smaller projects.

Part 1 of the book alerts you to the importance of building codes and then illustrates the installation tools in common use. It gives details about the most commonly used drywall panels and fasteners and concludes with a simple method for estimating the materials needed.

Part 2 gets into the actual installation techniques and methods, including some special wall and ceiling covering problems. It concludes by showing some of types of trim and corner beads most frequently used, and explains how to install them.

Part 3 relates to finishing the walls and ceiling after the drywall has been installed. It alerts you to the common defects that might occur which require correction. The most frequently used finishing tools and materials are discussed, and the techniques for finishing joints, trim, and corner bead are covered in detail. Since textured ceilings are popular, an entire chapter is devoted to hand and spray texturing and other finishing techniques commonly used.

William Spence

Part I

Tools & Materials

Chapter 1

Building Codes & Inspections

Residential and commercial construction must meet the requirements of local building codes. A **building code** is a published code, established by the local government, that sets forth regulations for building practices, materials, and installations in order to protect the health, welfare and safety of the public. The architect is responsible for recording construction details so that the building meets the code. This includes all factors related to the installation and finishing of drywall. As the drywall contractor, it is imperative that your work proceeds as set forth by the architect; if areas appear to not meet local codes, you should discuss this with the general contractor.

Building Codes

There are a number of organizations that have written nationally recognized building codes. Local governments generally accept one of these as their code because the writing and updating is a huge task. The local government can establish additional code requirements if they choose.

The national building codes include:

BOCA — **B**uilding **O**fficials and **C**ode **A**dministrators International
4051 West Fossmore Rd.
Country Club Hills, IL 60478

CABO — **C**ouncil of **A**merican **B**uilding **O**fficials
5203 Leesburg Pike, Suite 708
Falls Church, VA 22041

ICBO — **I**nternational **C**onference of **B**uilding **O**fficials
20001 Walnut Drive South
Walnut, CA 91789

NCSBCS **N**ational **C**onference of **S**tates on **B**uilding **C**odes and **S**tandards
505 Huntmar Park Dr., Suite 210
Herndon, VA 22070

SBCC **S**outhern **B**uilding **C**ode **C**ongress International
900 Montclair Rd.
Birmingham, AL 35213-1206

In addition these organizations sponsor codes for other parts of the building, such as plumbing, mechanical, and electrical codes.

A typical national building code will have an entire section related to gypsum board and plaster. It will include such things as nailing requirements, storage of gypsum board prior to construction, the quality of the gypsum board used, special applications as to shear walls and fire walls, the quality of the joint compound, and installation requirements. Following are the standards frequently used to assure quality:

Gypsum Board Materials & Accessories

Material	Standard*
Gypsum sheathing	ASTM C79
Gypsum wallboard	ASTM C36
Joint reinforcing tape and compound	ASTM C474; C475
Nails for gypsum boards	ASTM C514
Steel screws	ASTM C1002; C954
Water-resistant gypsum backing board	ASTM C630

* Standard developed by the American Society for Testing and Materials

BUILDING INSPECTION

The local government will have a department responsible for inspecting buildings under construction. You should remember that the drywall covers up the electrical system, the plumbing system, and a lot of the mechanical system. Before you start to work, be certain the general contractor has had all of these systems inspected. You do not want to cover up anything until the inspections have been complete. One way to tell is to check the on-site building inspection sheet. It is posted on the site for all to see. The building inspectors sign it when an inspection, such as electrical, has been completed and the work is found to be according to code (*see* 1-1).

BUILDING PERMIT

Contractor ______________________________

Issued ____________________ Permit No. ____________________

Lot ____________ Address ______________________________

Nature of Work ______________________________ Unit ____________

BUILDING INSPECTIONS

Footing [ ] Slab [ ] Insulation [ ]

Foundation [ ] Framing [ ] Final [ ]

Heating Inspections **Plumbing Inspections** **Electrical Inspections**

Rough [ ] Sewer [ ] Rough [ ]

Gas Pipe [ ] Rough [ ]

Village of Pinehurst

NORTH CAROLINA

NOTE: This Permit, With A Set Of Plans Attached, MUST Be Displayed At The Address Shown Above, During The Entire Period Of Construction. Please Give One Working Day's Notice On Inspections Needed.

1-1 This building permit, issued by the local government, must be posted on the job-site. (Courtesy Village of Pinehurst, North Carolina)

Building Inspectors

Since your local building inspectors are more familiar with the codes than you probably are, if you can visit with them during an inspection or call them with questions you can learn a lot about how they read and interpret the code and what they expect when they come on the job. Most inspectors hope the job is finished correctly so they can approve it and move on to the next job. They get no pleasure out of having to reject a job and make a return visit. They can also make suggestions about how to correct a defect or do the job better next time.

When checking the drywall, the inspector looks for things like the proper placement of the drywall panels, adequate nailing, and if the required firewall covering has been hung.

Chapter 2

Installation Tools

Tools you will need to hang gypsum board are few, but should be of the highest quality. Speed is important and quality tools will result in a faster and higher-quality result. For installation you will need measuring and layout, cutting, nailing, screwing, lifting, and hole cutting tools and some type of bench or platform.

Measuring & Layout Tools

You will use various measuring tools to mark the length and width of panels and layout angles.

TAPE MEASURE

A tape measure of good quality, usually 12 to 25 feet long, is required. Longer tapes are not needed because these cover the distances normally required and are not as large and heavy as longer tapes. Measuring tapes are used a great deal and are subject to hard wear and bending. Two types are available. One is a standard metal tape and the other is an electronic tape. The electronic tape has a digital readout which makes it a lot easier and faster for you to use (*see* 2-1 and 2-2).

2-1 (Above) A standard steel tape. (Courtesy L. S. Starrett Company)

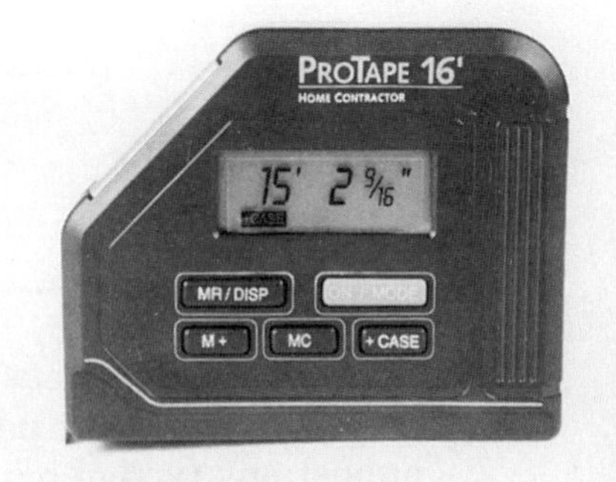

2-2 (Right) This device measures with a steel tape and has a digital readout. (Courtesy Seiko Instruments, USA, Inc.)

T-SQUARE

The drywall T-square (*see* 2-3) is used to lay out cuts on the surface of the panel. These can be 90-degree cuts and angles. In addition it can be used as a guide for cutting the panel with a utility knife, as shown in 2-4. (*See* Chapter 5 for additional information.)

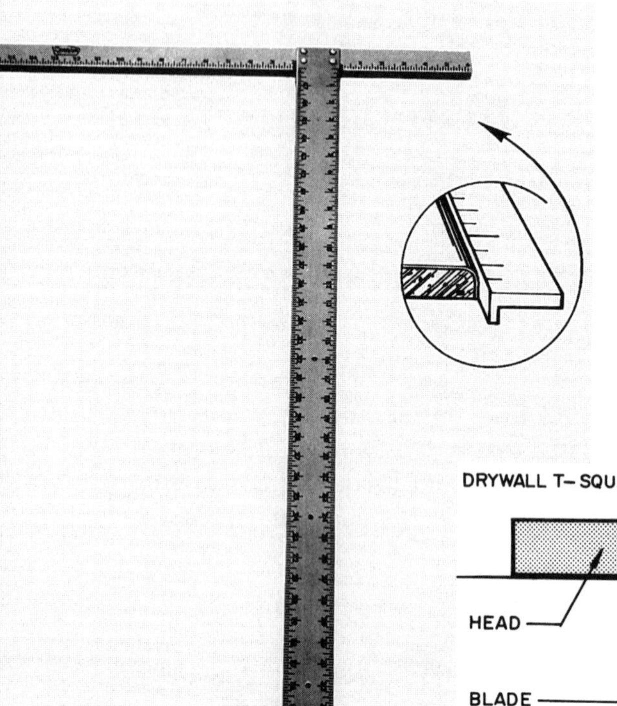

2-3 (Outside left) This drywall T-square has a 48-inch-long blade—for measuring, laying out angles, and as a guide for cutting panels. (Courtesy Goldblatt Tool Company)

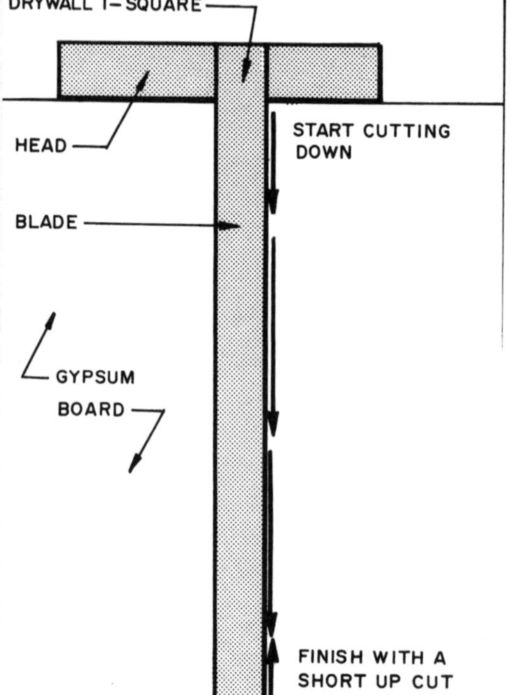

2-4 (Left) The T-square is used as a guide when cutting the drywall panel. (Courtesy Kraft Tool Company)

LEAD PENCIL

A soft lead pencil is best for marking on the gypsum panels. It should be kept light. Never use ballpoint pens. If any of the line shows after taping, it will bleed through almost any type of paint put over it.

CUTTING TOOLS

Cutting gypsum board is very hard on the tools. They must be designed for this purpose. You will find that using a saw designed to cut wood does not stay sharp very long. Following are the most frequently used tools.

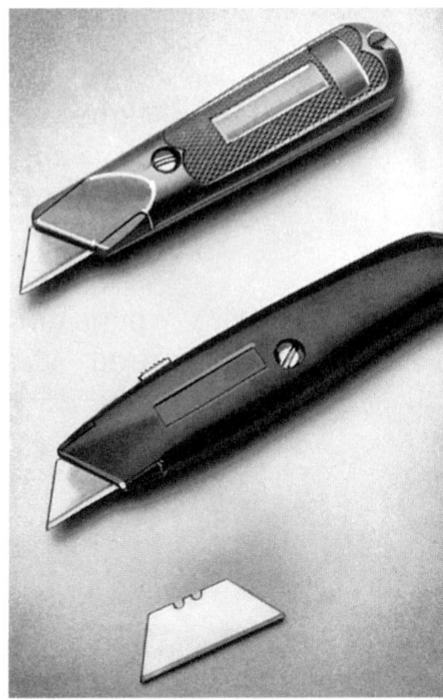

2-5 A utility knife is an excellent tool for scoring drywall. (Courtesy Kraft Tool Company)

UTILITY KNIFE

The utility knife is an inexpensive but sharp cutting tool. Most come with a supply of replaceable cutters in the handle, and additional cutters can be purchased at your hardware store. Do not use a dull blade. It can lead to a slip and a cut hand or leg (*see* 2-5).

SAWS

A drywall saw (*see* 2-6) is used to make straight cuts, and the drywall keyhole saw (*see* 2-7) can make curved cuts and various openings in the panel, as for an electrical outlet box. The tip of the keyhole saw is very sharp and is used to penetrate the panel so a cut can be made. Place the tip against the panel and rotate it, cutting a hole through it. Then begin a sawing action to form the opening desired.

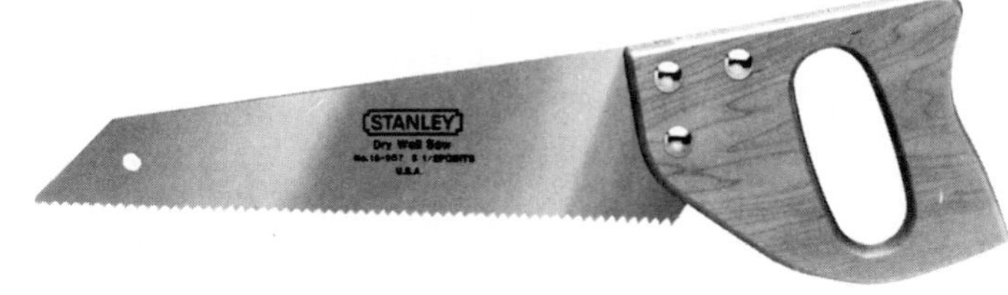

2-6 (Middle right) The drywall saw is hardened and tempered for long wear. (Courtesy Goldblatt Tool Company)

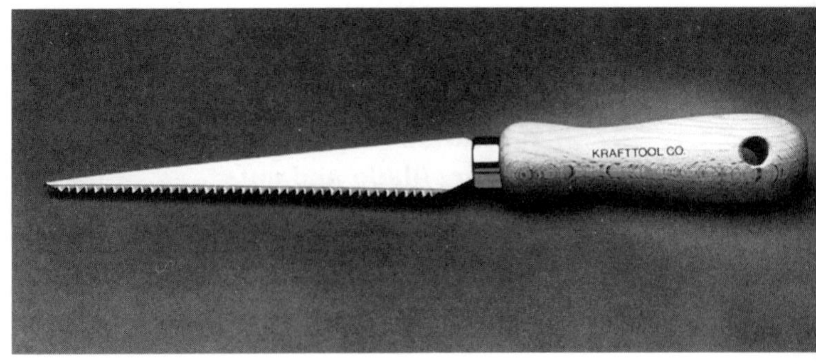

2-7 (Below right) The drywall keyhole saw has a sharp point, permitting it to pierce the wallboard when making internal cuts. (Courtesy Kraft Tool Company)

In addition to the two handsaws that are standard equipment when hanging drywall, it will useful to have on hand an electric saber saw (*see* 2-8). This basic power handtool can become indispensable for making quick and accurate cuts in wallboard. The up-and-down blade action is especially good for making internal cuts, both straight and curved, that need to be precise

2-8 (Above) The electric saber saw rapidly cuts wallboard and is especially good for making internal cuts.

CIRCLE CUTTER

A circle cutter is used to score through the paper and into the gypsum (*see* 2-9). The pivot is inserted into the panel at the center of the hole. The cutting wheel is moved out a distance equal to the radius of the circle and is rotated about the center as it is pressed into the panel. It should cut the paper and score the gypsum core. After removing the circle cutter, knock out the scored circle with a hammer. Use your utility knife to smooth out and clean up the hole on the rear of the panel.

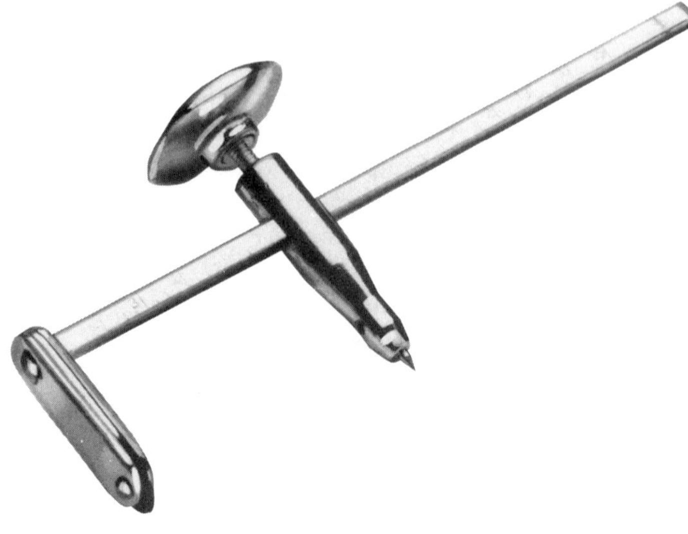

2-9 (Right) The circle cutter has a hardened steel cutting blade and cuts through the face paper to score the gypsum core. (Courtesy Kraft Tool Company)

RASPS

Various types of rasp are used to smooth the rough edge of a panel after it has been cut. The most effective is the perforated-blade type of surface forming tool (*see* 2-10). These rasps are available in a range of sizes. The blade is removed and replaced when it becomes dull.

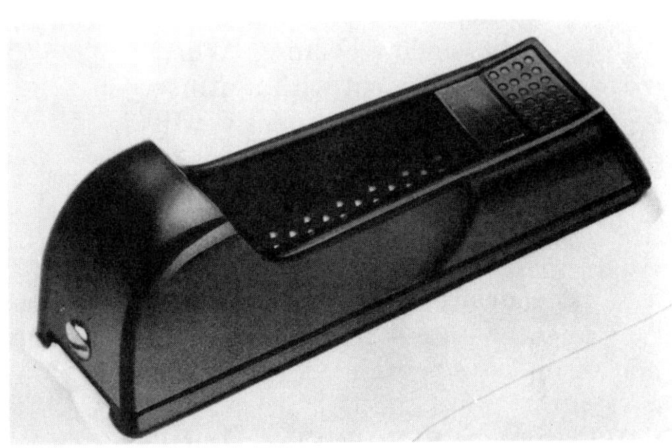

2-10 (Right) This is one of a wide variety of rasps that can be used to smooth the rough edges of the wallboard. (Courtesy Kraft Tool Company)

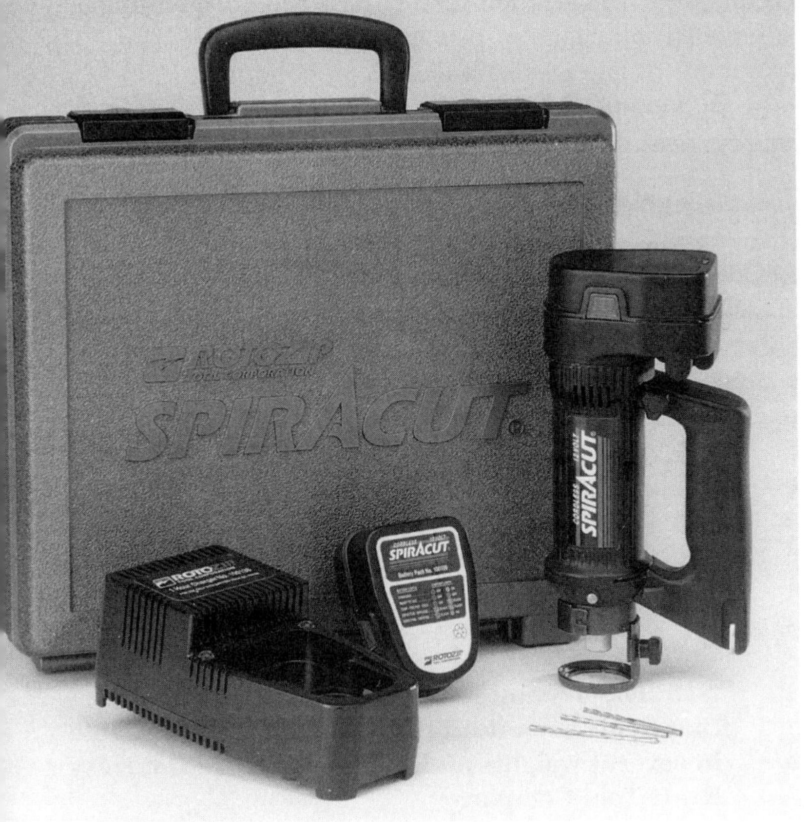

ROUTER

A drywall router—also refered to as the power hole saw—is used to cut openings in the panel. The center of the hole, such as for an electrical outlet box, is marked. The drill bit enters at this point and is moved until it hits the side of the box. It is then guided around the sides,, cutting away the gypsum board as it moves (*see* 2-11). (*Refer to* Chapter 5 for additional information.)

2-11 (Left) This battery-powered hole saw uses a variety of spiral bits to penetrate and cut openings in drywall, wood, wood composites, plastics, vinyl siding, and laminaters. (Courtesy Rotozip Tool Corporation)

STRIPPER

A gypsum board stripper is shown in 2-12. It is used to cut long narrow strips of gypsum board such as are often needed around a door or window opening. When these are cut with a utility knife they frequently will crack. The handle serves as a guide and runs along the edge of the panel. The cutter is set in the distance desired. The maximum width is 4 1/2 inches.

2-12 The drywall stripper is used to cut long, narrow strips of wallboard. (Courtesy Kraft Tool Company)

Nailing & Screwdriving Tools

You have the choice of manual- or power-operated nail and screwdriving tools. Power-operated tools drive nails and staple much faster than when a hammer is used. Screws are always driven with some type of power screwdriving tool.

DRYWALL HAMMER

The drywall hammer has its face rounded to create a dimple depression in the drywall as the nail is set. This depression is filled with joint compound to cover the nail head. The face is serrated with grooves at a 90-degree angle to help keep it from slipping off the head of the nail. The blade end has a dull rounded edge. It is used to pry and jack the wallboards into the desired position. It has a notch which is used to pull nails (*see* 2-13).

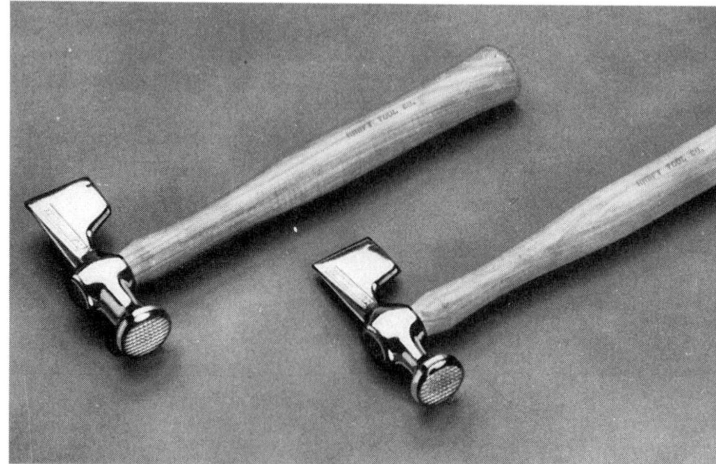

2-13 The drywall hammer has a serrated face that helps keep it on the nail. They are available in several weights and handle lengths. (Courtesy Kraft Tool Company)

ELECTRIC SCREWDRIVER

An electric screwdriver (also called a screwgun) is used to drive drywall screws through the panel into wood and metal studs (*see* 2-14). It has a magnetic screw-holding tip and an adjustable nosepiece. The nosepiece is used to adjust a clutch. The clutch controls the amount of torque available to drive the screw. This is adjusted so that the clutch will release and stop the driving of the screw when it has reached the proper degree of tightness. This involves setting it so the head of the screw is just below the surface of the panel but has not torn the paper or crushed the gypsum core.

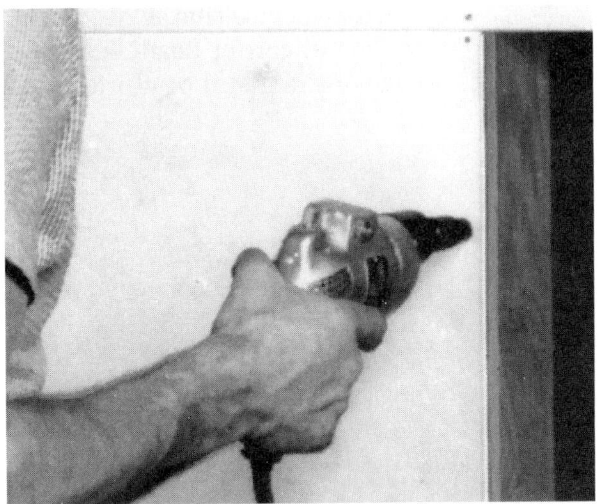

2-14 Screws are driven with an electric screwdriver. (Courtesy National Gypsum Company)

In 2-15 is an automatic screwdriving attachment that fits most electric screwdrivers. It has a series of 50 screws on a collated strip that automatically positions them in the chuck for rapid driving.

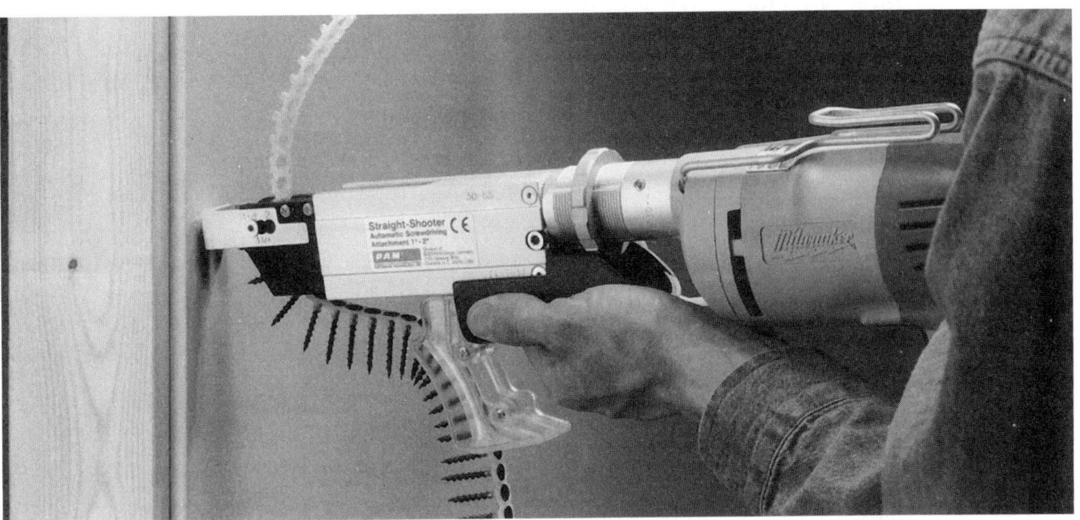

2-15 This electric screwdriver is equipped with a strip collated screw system that enables the gypsum board installer to quickly position and install the screw. It has a lock-in calibrated depth control. (Courtesy PAM Fastening Technology, Inc.)

CLINCH-ON TOOL

Another device that is used in some areas is the clinch-on tool (*see* 2-16). It fits over the metal corner bead, is struck with a mallet, and forces metal teeth to crimp the edge of the metal bead into the drywall.

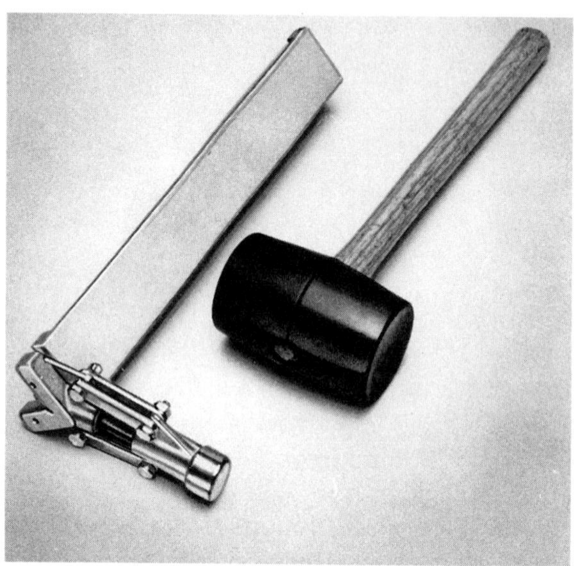

2-16 The clinch-on tool is placed against the metal corner bead. The protruding face is struck with a mallet, forcing the prongs to pierce the bead and bend metal prongs into the drywall. (Courtesy Kraft Tool Company)

2-17 Power staplers are available that can drive a wide range of staple sizes and wire diameters. (Courtesy Airmark/Airy Sales Corporation)

STAPLERS

Various types of staplers are used to attach corner beads. They must be powerful enough to drive the staple through the gypsum panel and into the stud (*see* 2-17). They may be either manually activated or air-powered.

POWER NAILERS

Some types of air-powered nailers can be used to hang gypsum board. They are operated by pressing the tool firmly against the panel and squeezing the trigger. They will not work unless the tool is held firmly against the work. You have to adjust it until the nail is driven firmly in place, producing the required dimple in the surface of the panel.

Lifting Tools & Working Platforms

Much of the work you will be doing will be above the floor level—which means working on some form of trestle or scaffold. The danger of falls is a constant problem and adequate working platforms are mandatory.

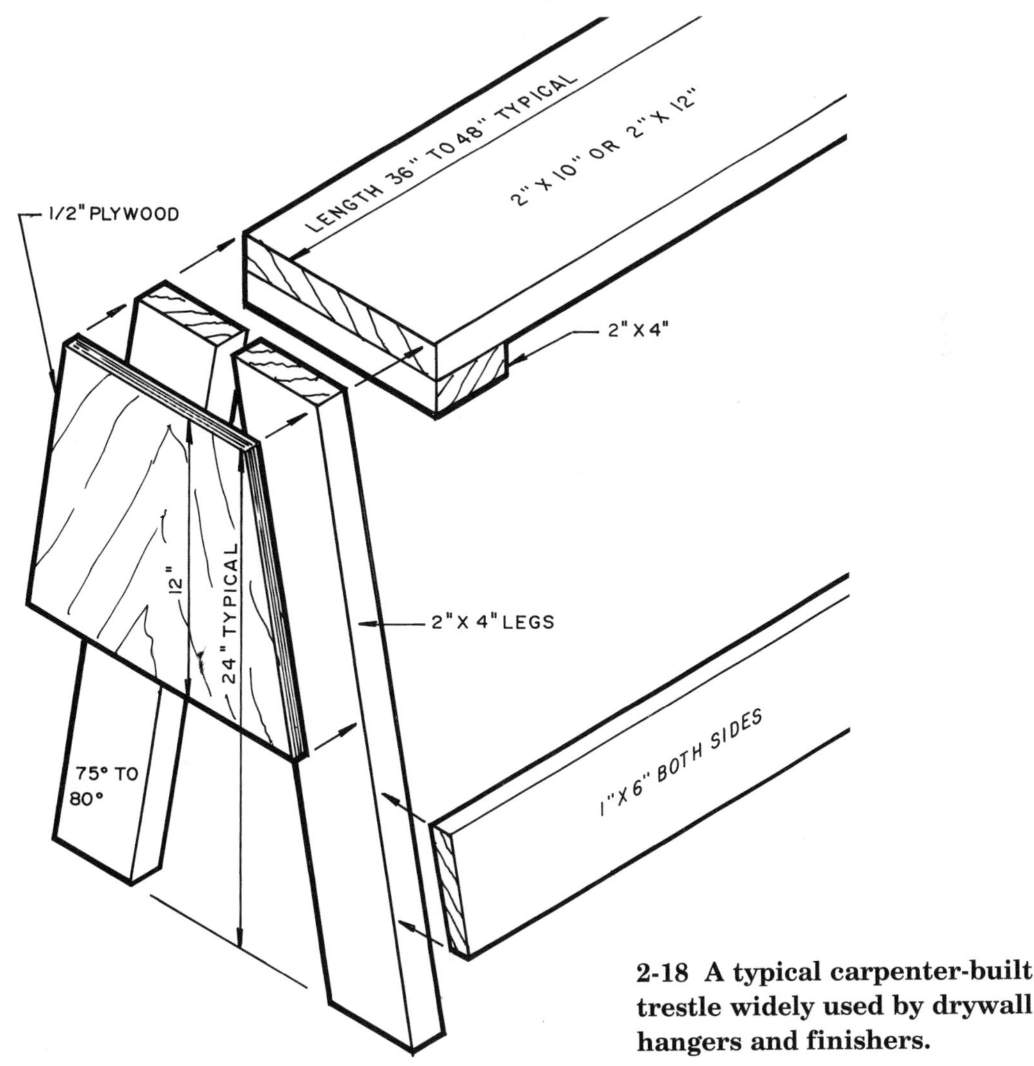

2-18 A typical carpenter-built trestle widely used by drywall hangers and finishers.

TRESTLES AND SCAFFOLDS

Much of the work in residential building involves ceilings from 8 to 12 feet high. The installer and finisher on 8-ft. ceilings can work from a platform about 2 ft. above the floor. Such a platform may be simply a carpenter-built trestle (*see* 2-18).

2-19 Heavy-duty commercial scaffolding must be used to hang and finish drywall on high walls and cathedral ceilings.

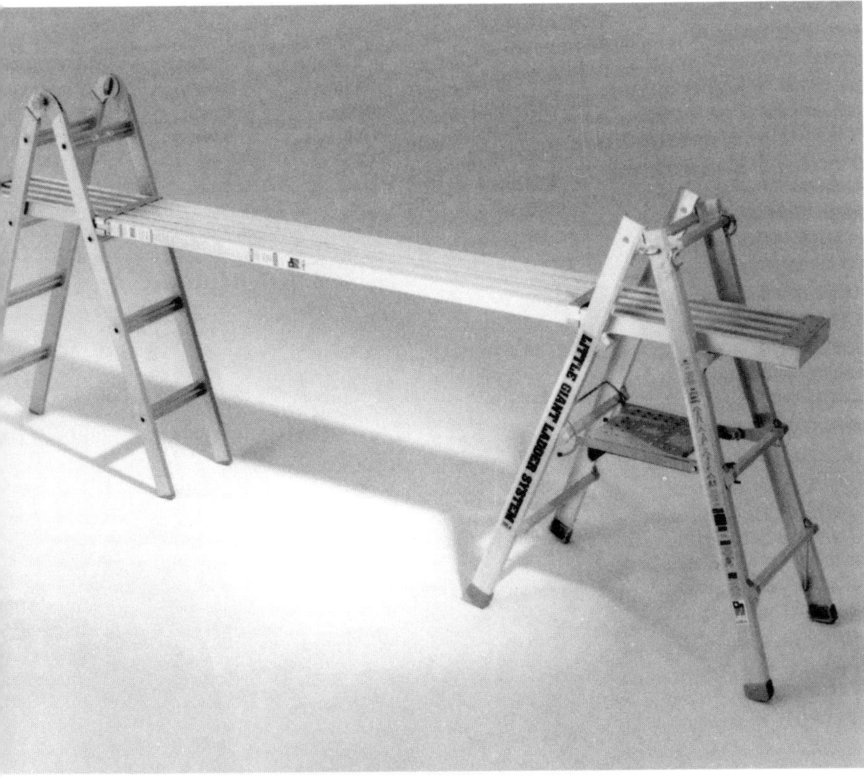

2-20 (Left) These ladder-type trestles permit the height of the scaffold board to be adjusted as needed. (Courtesy Wing Enterprises, Inc.)

In commercial buildings it is often necessary to erect a full scaffolding. It is best to use a manufactured product (*see* 2-19). They are easily set up and taken down and will meet the regulations established by the Federal Government under the Occupational Safety and Health Act (OSHA). OSHA has manuals available detailing the requirements for various scaffolding devices.

For residential jobs, aside from the carpenter-built trestle, the installer could also use metal manufactured trestles (*see* 2-20) or a commercial portable scaffold.

STILTS

Stilts are worn by the finish applicator; they give him full mobility and the height needed to reach normal ceilings. It takes some practice to get used to walking on them (*see* 2-21). They can be adjusted for different heights.

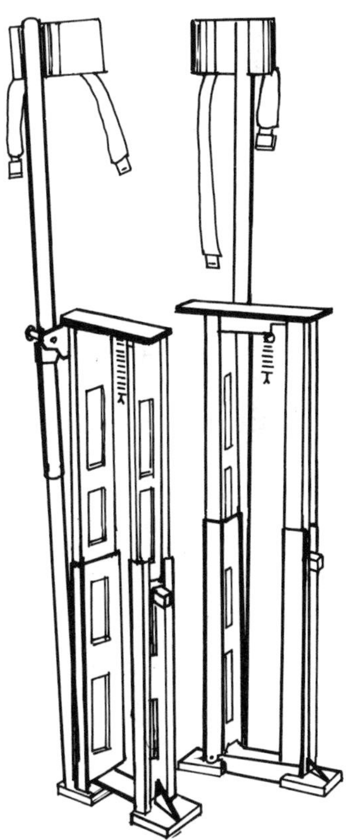

2-21 (Above) Stilts can be used to reach the ceiling and upper walls instead of scaffolding. The applicator has the mobility to move about as required.

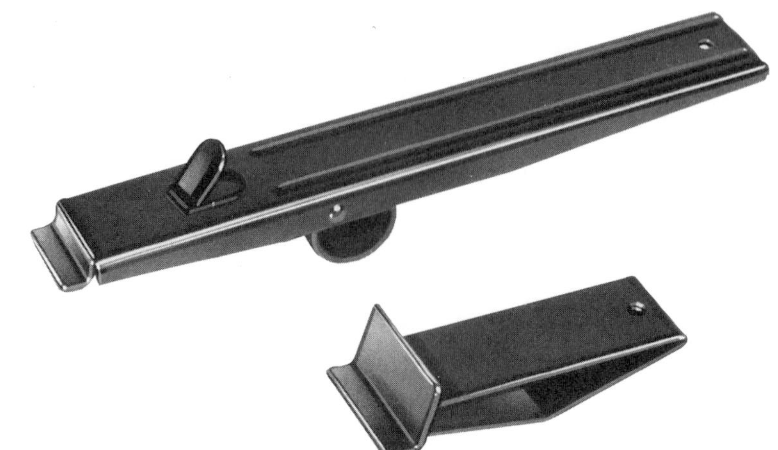

2-22 A drywall lifter will lift and hold the bottom panel in place while you nail it. (Courtesy Kraft Tool Company)

LIFTING TOOLS

The two commonly used devices to assist in lifting and placing panels are the drywall lifter and the panel lifter. The drywall lifter is placed under the edge of the gypsum panel as it leans against the wall and rests on the floor. The tail is pushed down, raising the panel an inch or so until it butts against the top wall panel already installed (*see* 2-22). Keep the lifter near the center of the panel so that both ends will rise evenly. The panel lifter will hold the entire gypsum panel, raise it up against the wall or ceiling, and then hold it there while it is being nailed (*see* 2-23).

2-23 Full panels can be lifted into place on the wall or ceiling with a panel lifter. (Courtesy Telpro, Inc.)

Chapter 3

Drywall Panels & Fasteners

Gypsum drywall panels have been in use for over 60 years and have become the standard interior wall and ceiling finish material. In addition they have exterior applications, are a major fire-retardant material, and are used to control the flow of sound through walls, floors, and ceilings.

Gypsum wallboard is installed dry, which has led to calling it drywall. Drywall is easier to install and costs less than plaster walls, which require a base material plus several layers of wet plaster.

The panels are formed with a gypsum core between layers of a specially formulated paper. On the face is a strong smooth-surfaced paper that will be finished with paint, wallpaper, or some other material. The back has a strong natural-finish paper. The paper is folded around the long edges of the panel and the ends are square-cut and smooth, revealing the gypsum core.

The fire-resistant properties of gypsum wallboard are due to the fact that gypsum will not burn and the water in it is released as steam, enabling it to remain intact until all the water has been removed. The panel then fails because the gypsum has been calcined (roasted).

The gypsum panel, while resisting fire, also reduces the passage of heat to the other side of the panel. This reduces the possibility that wood on the back side of the panel will ignite. Fire-resistant wall designs are available from various manufacturers. One- and two-hour fire ratings are common (*see* 3-1). A special drywall product, type-X gypsum panels, is designed for areas where a high fire resistance is mandated by building codes.

SINGLE LAYER — WOOD STUDS

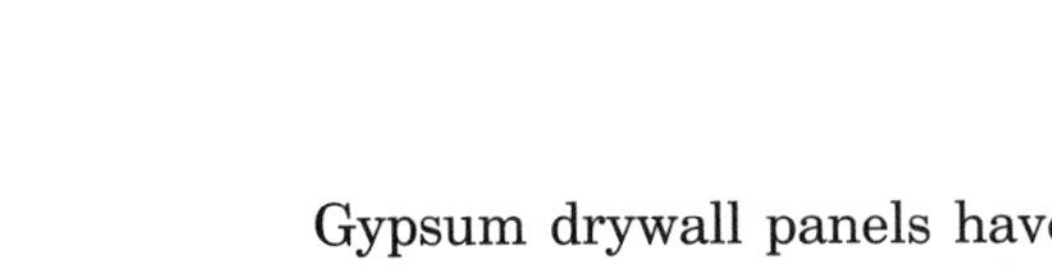

	FIRE RESISTANCE (HOURS)	SOUND TRANSMISSION CLASS
1/2" TYPE X	1	30 – 34
5/8" TYPE X	1	30 – 34

DOUBLE LAYER — WOOD STUDS

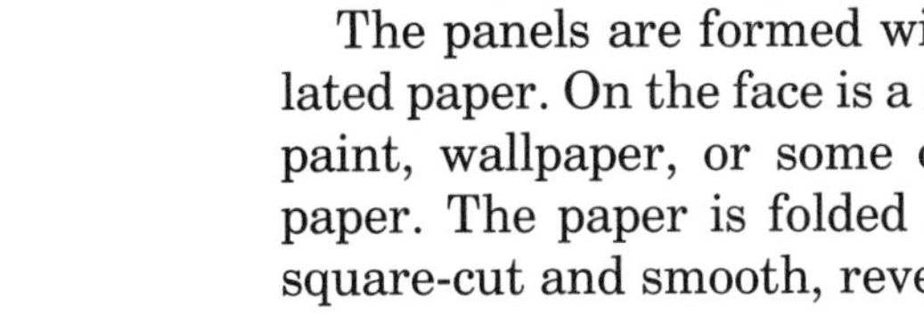

	FIRE RESISTANCE (HOURS)	SOUND TRANSMISSION CLASS
5/8" TYPE X	2	50

3-1 Fire resistance ratings for several frequently used gypsum drywall installations

The gypsum core is composed of a mineral rock called gypsum. The basic mineral is calcium sulfate, chemically combined with water to become crystallized. The rock is mined, crushed, and ground to flour finess. It is calcined (roasted) which drives off some of the chemically combined water as steam. The calcined gypsum is then mixed with water and sandwiched between two sheets of specially manufactured paper—forming the gypsum wallboard panel.

Gypsum drywall panels are sold two to a package. They are held together with a tape edge. This is stripped off, separating the two panels. These double panels are quite heavy. Two 1/2 in. panels will weigh 109 pounds and two 5/8 in. panels weigh 147 pounds.

Gypsum Wallboard

There are many types of gypsum wallboard available. Manufacturers have catalogs giving detailed technical information about the properties and uses of each. The following types are frequently used. Specific details will vary depending upon the company manufacturing the panels. General technical information is shown in 3-2.

3-2 Data for various types of gypsum wallboard.

Type	Thickness (in.)	Width (ft.)	Length (ft.)
Regular	1/2, 3/8, 5/8	4	6–16
Type X (fire-resistant)	1/2, 5/8	4	6–16
Moisture-resistant	1/2 reg., 5/8 type X	4	6–16
Flexible	1/4	4	8 & 10
High-strength ceiling	1/2	4	6–16
Predecorated	1/2	4	8, 9 & 10

REGULAR DRYWALL

Regular panels have a paper covering on each face and the long edges. These edges have a taper which makes it easy to tape the joint and get a flush finish (*see* 3-3). When hanging these panels, the long tapered edges are always placed together and the square ends are abutted. Square ends are harder to finish.

Following are typical uses of regular drywall:

1/4 in. and 3/8 in.—remodeling, two layer installations, and curved walls
1/2 in. and 5/8 in.—all interior walls and ceilings

TYPE X FIRE-RATED DRYWALL

These panels have a specially formulated gypsum core that contains additives that enhance the fire resistance qualities. They are used on ceilings and walls where codes specify the need for fire resistance greater than that provided by regular panels. Examples are walls between apartments or the garage wall joining the house. It should be mentioned that this material is fire-resistant for a specified number of hours and is not considered fireproof.

MOISTURE-RESISTANT DRYWALL

Moisture-resistant drywall is used on walls and ceilings in areas where there will be higher than average moisture, such as a bath or kitchen wall where tile will be applied. It typically has a green color and is available with a regular or type X core. The core, face paper, and back paper of moisture-resistant panels are treated to resist the effects of high humidity and moisture. They are usually extended beyond the area to be tiled. They have a tapered edge. The area not covered with tile can be taped and finished using normal materials. The area covered with tile relies on the tile adhesive to cover the nails, seal the edges, and treat the corners.

Moisture-resistant drywall is not to be used in areas with direct exposure to water or excessively high moisture, as in a sauna. Cementitious tile backer board is used in these areas.

CEILING DRYWALL

A high-strength 1/2-in.- and 5/8-in.-thick gypsum panel is available for use on ceilings. It has a special treated core that helps the panel resist sagging over time.

FLEXIBLE DRYWALL

A 1/4-in.-thick drywall panel with heavy paper faces is available that is designed to bend around concave and convex walls. The long edges are tapered. It bends better in the long direction, so is best installed with the long edge perpendicular to the wall studs. It is also used on curved ceilings and other such surfaces.

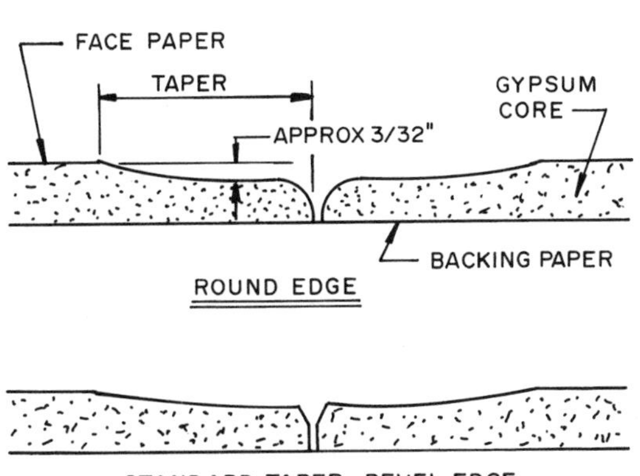

3-3 Two of the types of tapered panel edges commonly available.

PREDECORATED DRYWALL

These panels are covered with some type of decorative material,such as a fabric or vinyl, and do not require additional finishing. The panel edges may be tapered or square and the joints are covered with moldings supplied by the manufacturer. The panels may be installed using nails colored to blend in with the colors on the panel.

GYPSUM SHEATHING PANELS

Gypsum sheathing panels are fire-resistant panels with a water-resistant core. They are enclosed with a specially treated water-repellent paper on both sides and on the long edges. They are used as sheathing where the fire rating of the wall exceeds that possible with other types of sheathing, such as plywood sheathing. Local codes specify these requirements. The panels are also widely used on multi-story commercial buildings and with curtain wall construction.

They can be covered with almost any commonly used siding such as brick, wood, aluminum, and vinyl.

Drywall Nails

The two basic types of nails used to secure drywall to wood studs are the annular ring nail and the cement-coated nail. The annular ring nail holds the best and reduces the tendency for nails to pop out through the finished wall. Nails may have flat or concave heads that are thin at their outer rim. Special colored nails are used to secure predecorated panels. They have a very small head and are supplied by the drywall manufacturer (*see* 3-4).

You should be certain to use the proper length nail. Annular ring nails must penetrate the stud at least 3/4 in. and smooth nails 7/8 in. Type X gypsum panels require longer nail penetration—typically 1 1/8 in. to 1 1/4 in. for one-hour fire-rated wall assemblies.

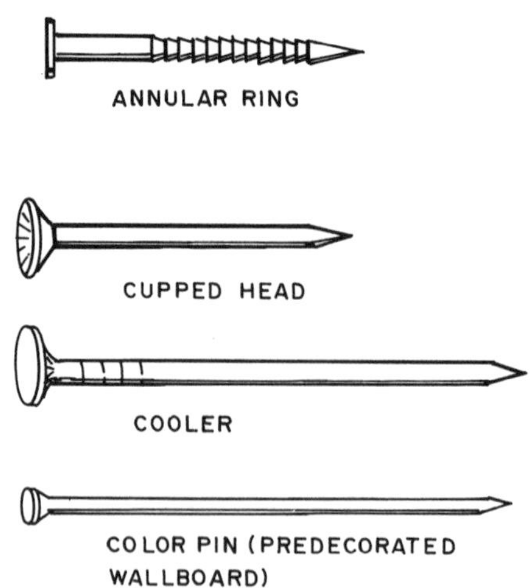

3-4 Nails commonly used to secure gypsum panels to wood framing.

Drywall Screws

Drywall screws have greater holding power than nails and are preferred by many contractors. They will have fewer pop-outs—resulting in fewer call-backs for further repairs.

For most purposes the bugle-head screw is used (*see* 3-5). It is power driven and produces a uniform, controlled penetration of the panel.

The types available are:

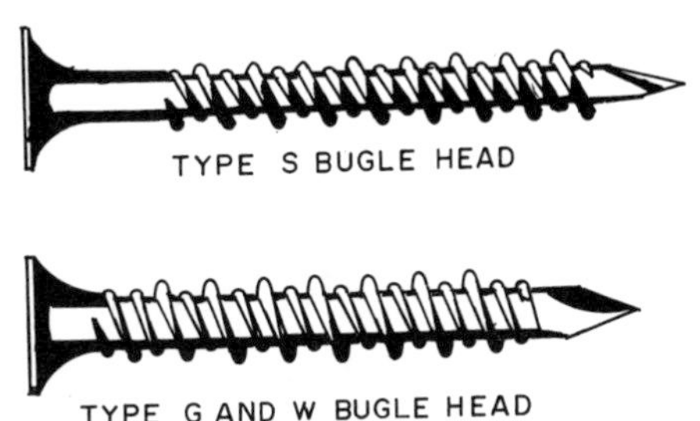

3-5 Two of the most commonly used drywall screws. Choose the proper screw type for use on wood or steel framing and gypsum backer panels.

Type-W
Used to secure the gypsum panel to wood framing.

Type-S
Used to secure the gypsum panel to steel studs. They are a self-drilling, self-tapping fastener.

Type-G
Used to secure gypsum panels to gypsum backing or base material. They should be long enough to penetrate the base panel at least 1/2 in.

Staples

Staples are used to secure gypsum panels to wood studs only when the panels are the base layer in multi-ply construction. They must have at least a 7/16 in. crown and be made from 16-gauge, flattened, galvanized wire, and have spreading points (*see* 3-6). They must penetrate the wood framing at least 5/8 in.

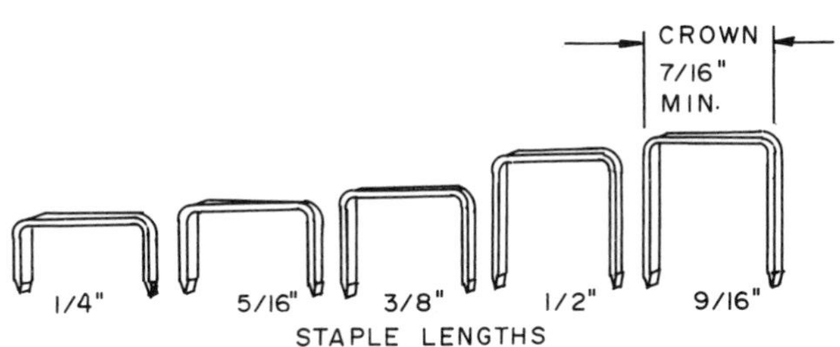

3-6 The most commonly used sizes of staples for securing gypsum panels to wood framing in multi-ply construction.

3-7 Adhesives are sold in cartridges and extruded by pressure from a plate in the gun.

ADHESIVES

Adhesives are used to bond the gypsum panel to the framing, masonry, or concrete substrate (*see* 3-7). You can also use them to bond the top panel to the base panel in a two-panel construction. If you are installing rigid foam insulation panels or sound-deadening panels, they can be bonded to the base material with drywall adhesive. A few nails are used to hold the panels in place as the adhesive cures.

Chapter 4

Estimating Drywall Materials

Whether the job is big or small, it is necessary to estimate the amount of materials needed. It is better for you to get a little extra and be able to complete the job without having to run back to the building supply dealer for additional items. In addition to a material estimate, try to make a realistic estimate on the time that will be required to complete the job.

Commercial installers have to figure material and labor costs so that they can give a firm bid to the general contractor. In addition to relying on their own experience, installers have available a number of commercial estimating publications that give material and labor cost factors.

A Simplified Estimating Plan

The following sections present an approach to a simplified estimating plan that can be used by the person who wants to do a small job, such as a room addition. A brief explanation of the factors that must be considered for large commercial applications completes this chapter.

HOW MUCH WALLBOARD?

For a small job, such as a single room, it is advantageous to decide how you are going to place the panels and the sizes you will use on each wall. Remember, plan as though any openings (doors, windows) are covered. The cut-out material for these is waste.

When planning the panel layout, you should consider two main factors—cost and time. Wallboard panels 8 and 12 feet long are widely available. The 12-foot length costs more than the 8-foot length but can cover the wall faster and often eliminates end joints. If you can cover a wall with a 12-foot panel (such as for a 10-foot-long wall) it is faster and costs less than using 8-foot material because of the time saved, especially when taping.

The same technique can be applied to the ceiling. Look at the example room shown in 4-1. This room is 10 x 16 feet. The ceiling layout will require two 12-foot panels and two 8-foot panels. This permits the end butt joints to be staggered and at least 4 feet apart. End butt joints should never line up.

A layout for the 10-foot wall is shown in 4-2. Two possibilities are given. The one using 12-foot panels is the best because it has no end joints. The small waste caused by cutting off the end of the panel is negligible. To find the number of panels simply count them for the ceiling and each wall.

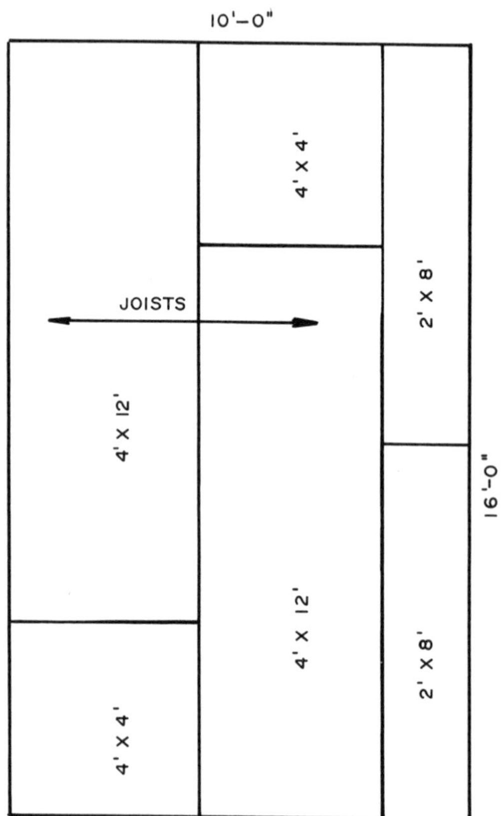

4-1 **A good ceiling layout uses the longest panels possible and staggers end joints.**

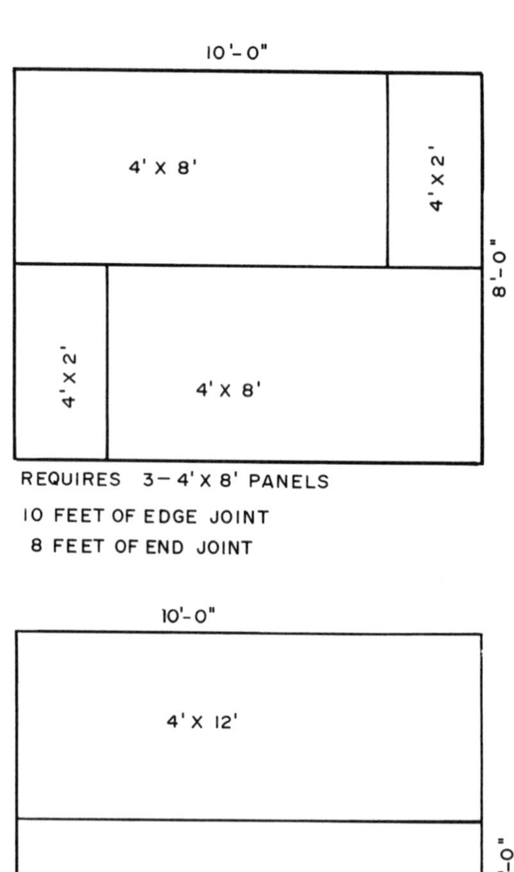

4-2 **Two possibilities for a short wall; it is best covered with long panels—even though some drywall is cut off and wasted. The loss due to waste is small. The savings for not having to tape two end joints is large.**

A layout for the 16-foot wall is shown in 4-3. Again, I give two possible arrangements. The one using 12-foot panels has fewer feet of end butt joints and would be preferable even if the cost for the panels is greater. Taping is difficult, time consuming, and costly because of the labor charges.

I suggest you make a wall and ceiling layout as I did in illustrating these points. It only takes a few minutes and is well worth the time.

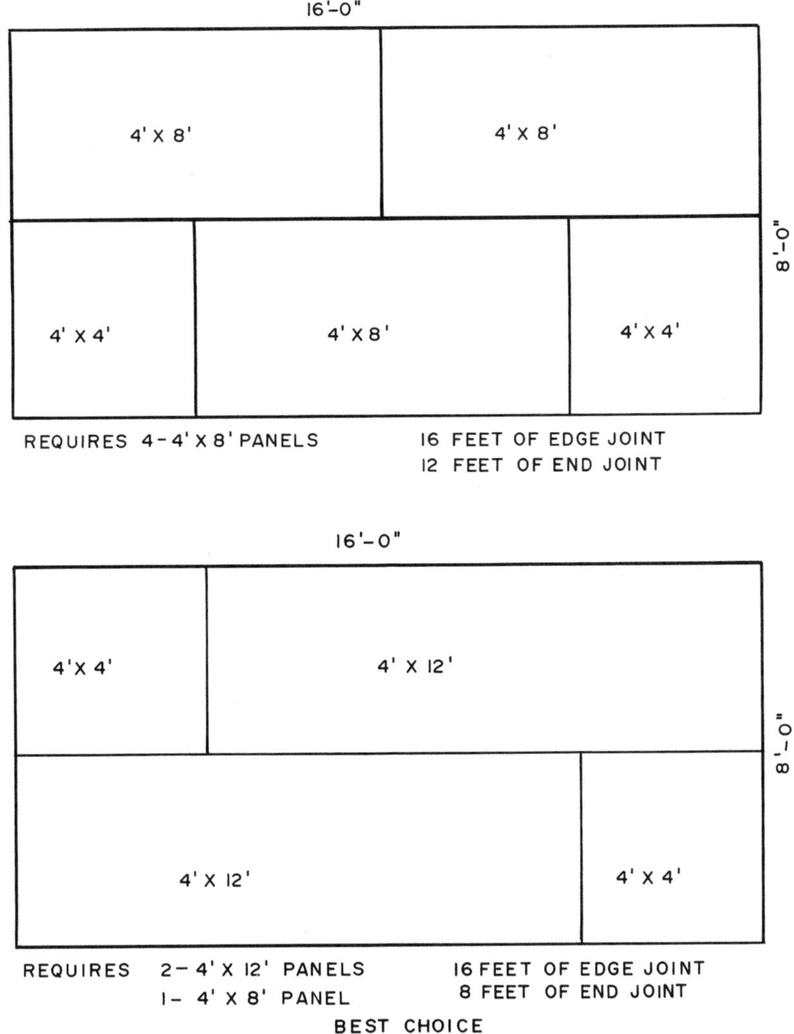

4-3 Two possible panel layouts for a medium-long wall. Notice that the use of longer panels eliminates one end joint.

HOW MANY FASTENERS?

A simple way to do this for a small job is to use the nail count per panel. These numbers are in 4-4. Multiply the number of nails in each size panel by the number of panels. If you figure there are about 300 nails per pound, you can divide the total number of nails needed by 300 to get a close estimate of how many pounds of nails you will need. I suggest buying three pounds (as I recommend in 4-8), because you will drop and lose quite a few nails. In general it takes about three pounds of nails per 1000 sq. ft. of drywall.

4-4 A typical way to estimate the number of nails that you may need, based on the panel size.

	Number of Nails per Panel	
	Single-Nailed	**Double-Nailed**
4' x 8' panel	39	54
4' x 12' panel	54	78

(Number of nails per pound approx. 300)

Example problem—(*Refer to* 4-1 through 4-3)—single-nailed.

	No. of Panels	Nails per Panel	Total Nails
4' x 8' panels	5	39	195
4' x 12' panels	10	54	540
			735 nails
			Buy 3 pounds of nails

HOW MUCH JOINT TAPE?

Since you now know the placement of the gypsum wallboard panels, you can add up the number of lineal feet of tape required for each wall and the ceiling. Tape is usually available in 100-foot rolls. Another way is to figure about 380 lineal feet of tape per 1000 sq. ft. of drywall.

HOW MANY CORNER BEADS?

Corner beads are made in 8-foot lengths, so buy one for each outside corner. Do not plan to use short pieces because they create an end butt joint, which is difficult to get flat and cover with tape and joint compound.

HOW MUCH JOINT COMPOUND?

For a small room a 5-gallon bucket of joint compound will usually be enough. It is available in 1- and 2-gallon buckets, which can be helpful if you need just a little to finish. As a rule of thumb, figure 1 gallon per 90 sq. ft. of wall area.

COMMERCIAL ESTIMATING

The following information gives a brief look at what a commercial drywall installer might do to prepare a bid and figure the materials to order for delivery to a job.

To estimate the amount of needed materials needed on a large job, calculate the area of the ceilings and walls in all the rooms, halls, closets, garages, and other spaces to be covered. To do this find the length of each wall. which when added together gives the perimeter length. These distances can be found on the architectural drawings. Multiply the perimeter by the wall height to get the **square feet of wall area**. Multiply the length by the width of the ceiling to get the **square feet of the ceiling**. An example is given in 4-5.

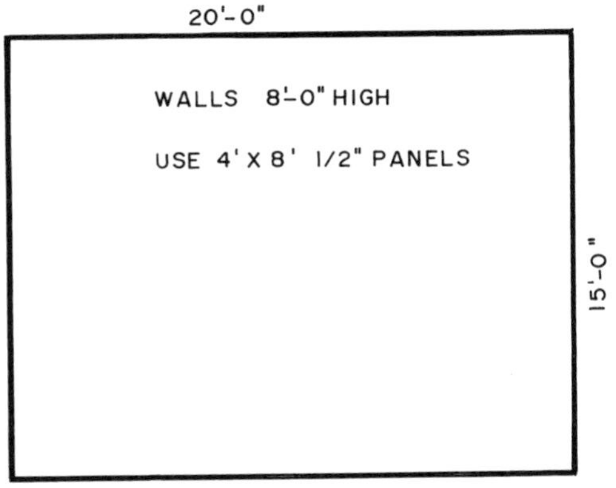

20'-0"
WALLS 8'-0" HIGH
USE 4'X8' 1/2" PANELS
15'-0"

4-5 An example of estimating the materials needed for a room. This example uses 4 ft. x 8 ft. panels. Figure a better layout and panel size and refigure the quantities.

Ceiling	20 x 15 =	300 sq. ft.
Walls	(20+15 +20+15) x 8 =	560 sq. ft.
Total		860 sq. ft. **of drywall surface**

No. of 4' x 8' panels	= 860 x 0.03125	= 26.9	(order 28)
Pounds of 1 3/8" nails	= 860 x 0.0050	= 4.3	(order 5 lbs.)
Tubes of adhesives	= 860 x 0.0020	= 1.7	(order 2)
Rolls of tape	= 860 x 0.00167	= 1.4	(order 2)
Five-gallon joint-compound buckets	= 860 x 0.00100	= 0.9	(order 1)

Follow this estimating procedure for each area to be covered. Do not allow for wall openings. To find the number of panels needed—and the amount of tape, joint compound, and nails that will be required—multiply the total square feet by the estimating factors presented in 4-6.

4-6 Estimating factors for the installation and finishing of gypsum wallboard.

Material	Factor	Gives
4' x 8' panel	0.03130	no. of panels
4' x 12' panel	0.02087	no. of panels
1 3/8" annual ring nails (single-nailed)	0.0054	pounds of nails
adhesive	0.00209	tubes of adhesive
tape	0.00170	no. of rolls
joint compound	0.00105	no. of five-gallon cans
joint compound (for textured ceiling)	0.00255	no. of five-gallon cans

(Reproduced with permission from *Carpentry Estimating*, by W.P. Jackson, Craftsman Book Company, 6058 Corte del Cedro, Carlsbad, CA 92009)

To find the number of hours that are estimated for installing and finishing the drywall, various companies supply extensive tables giving standardized times for performing various tasks. A brief abstract of part of one of these tables is in 4-7. It gives the estimated minimum time, average time, and maximum time factors.

4-7 Man-hour estimating factors* for drywall nailed or screwed wood framing.

Activity		Man-hours per square foot
1/2" drywall		
	ceiling	0.009
	walls	0.008
Taping & finishing		
	minimum	0.006
	average	0.008
	maximum	0.009
		Man-hours per lineal foot
Installing corner bead		
	minimum	0.025
	average	0.029
	maximum	0.042

*These are for illustration purposes only. Contact an estimating organization for accurate figures for your area.

(Reproduced with permission from the *1995 General Construction Costbook*, Building News, 3055 Overland Ave., Los Angeles, CA 90034)

In 4-8 another example is presented that is based on the same room that was used in 4-5. Notice how the total square feet of drywall required for each activity is multiplied by the estimating factor to find the approximate quantities of man-hours required.

4-8 Man-hour installation and finishing estimates.

Installing 1/2" wallboard				
	Ceiling	300 sq. ft. x 0.009	=	2.7 hours
	Walls	560 sq. ft. x 0.008	=	4.5 hours
Taping and finishing				
		860 sq. ft. x 0.008	=	6.9 hours
	Total			14.1 hours

(Reproduced with permission from the *1995 General Construction Costbook*, Building News, 3055 Overland Ave., Los Angeles, CA 90034)

Part II

Installing Gypsum Wallboard

Chapter 5

Installation Skills & Techniques

Drywall panels must be measured, cut, pierced, drilled and thennailed, screwed, or bonded to framing with an adhesive. Both wood and metal framing could be involved. The following material will show you how to work with the gypsum panels as you install them to the framing.

Measuring

Accurate measuring of the framing to receive the panel as well as accurate measuring and marking the panel for cutting is critical. The old saying "Measure twice, cut once" certainly applies here.

Measuring the framing will reveal if it is out of line or not square. If it is not possible to cut the panel to compensate for this, the framing must be corrected. (*Refer to* Chapter 9 for correcting techniques.) All markings on drywall panels should be with a soft lead pencil. Do not use a ballpoint pen because if any of the ink shows on the wall after hanging, it will bleed through the joint compound and latex paint. It will sometimes even show through a layer of joint cement.

Chalk lines can be used to mark long cuts. Locate each end of the line on the mark, rub chalk on the line, then lift it slightly and let it snap against the surface. The line must be very tight and lifted straight up a very small amount. Long wood and metal straightedges are also available.

Cutting Drywall Panels

The easiest way to cut a panel is to cut through the **good face paper** and into the core. Then bend the panel, breaking the core (*refer to* 5-1 on page 44). Finally, cut the back paper. Long cuts running the length of the panel can be marked with a chalkline or straightedge and cut freehand.

There is available a steel tape that has an adjustable edgeguide with a tip that will hold the blade of a utility knife. Set the tape on the line to be cut, press the

5-1 (Right) The steps to cut a gypsum wallboard panel. (Courtesy United States Gypsum Company)

5-2 (Below) The T-square can be used to guide the utility knife to make a straight cut.

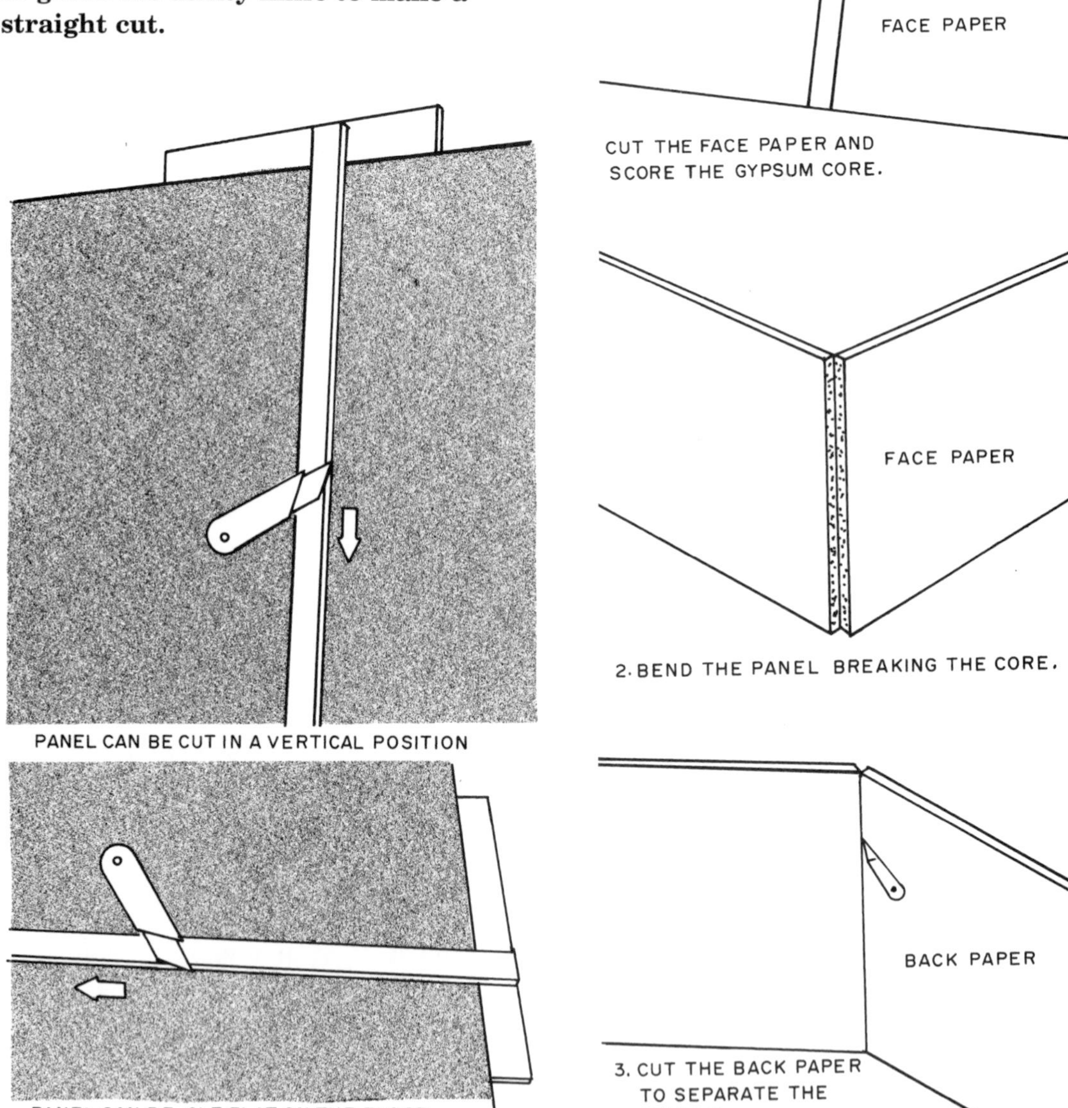

knife into the panel, and move it down the length of the panel. This cuts the paper and scores the core. Bend the panel to snap the core and cut the back paper.

When a straight edge is important, use the drywall T-square (*see* 5-2). Hold the head tight against the edge of the panel. Run the utility knife along the edge. If the panel is in a vertical position, place your toe against the bottom of the blade to keep

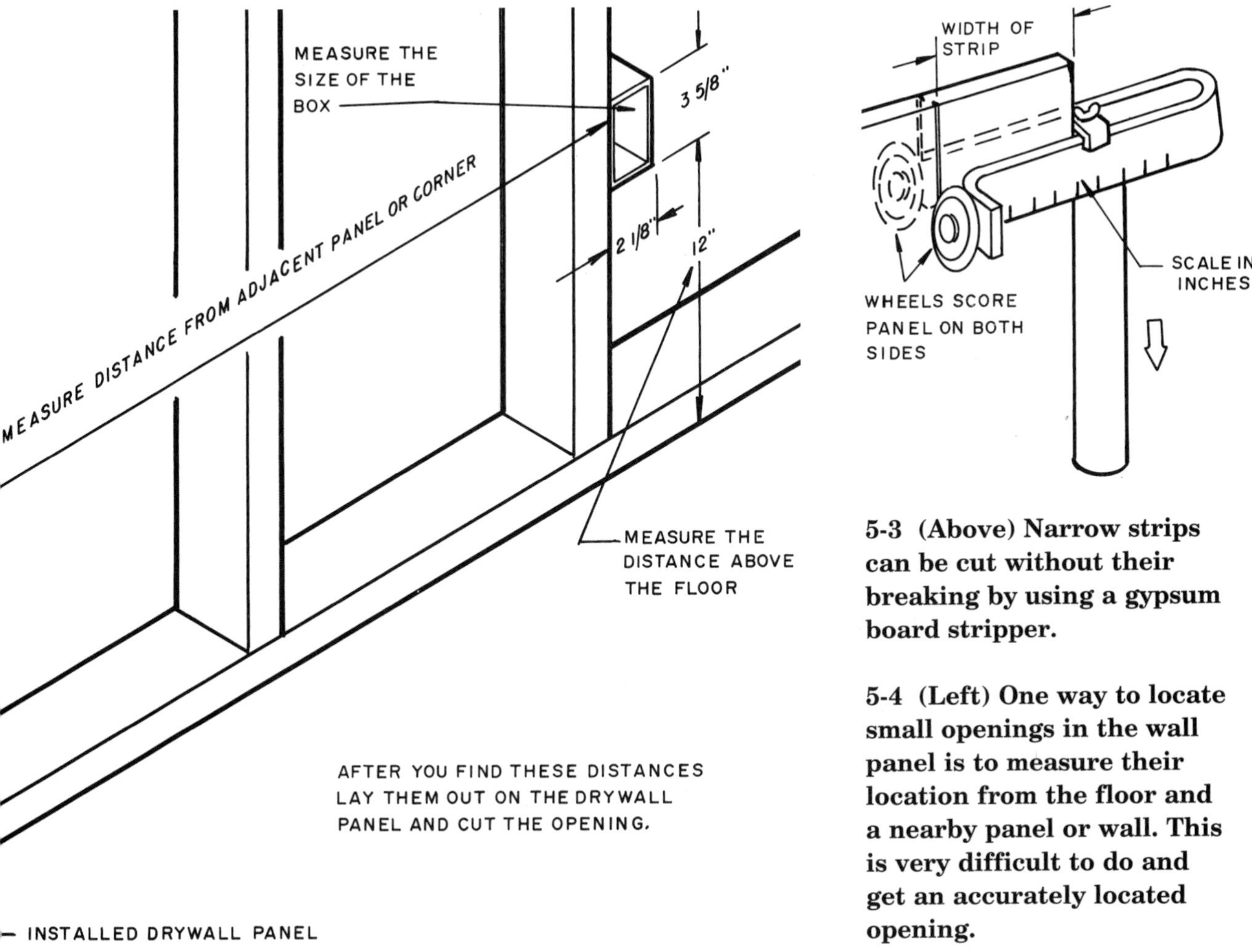

5-3 (Above) Narrow strips can be cut without their breaking by using a gypsum board stripper.

5-4 (Left) One way to locate small openings in the wall panel is to measure their location from the floor and a nearby panel or wall. This is very difficult to do and get an accurately located opening.

it from moving. Some prefer to cut the panels in a horizontal position. After the edges are cut they must be smoothed with a rasp or coarse sandpaper.

Long, rather narrow strips can be cut using a gypsum board stripper. Set the cutter the width of the strip wanted. Run the handle along the edge of the panel pressing hard enough to score the core. Since it has two cutters (one on each side) both sides of the panel are scored. After scoring, carefully bend the strip to break it loose (*see* 5-3).

LOCATING SMALL OPENINGS IN THE DRYWALL PANEL

It is necessary to cut openings in the panels for electrical outlets, pipes, recessed cabinets, and other such protrusions. There are several ways to locate these openings. One is to measure very accurately the location by measuring up from the floor and over from an adjacent panel or a wall (*see* 5-4).

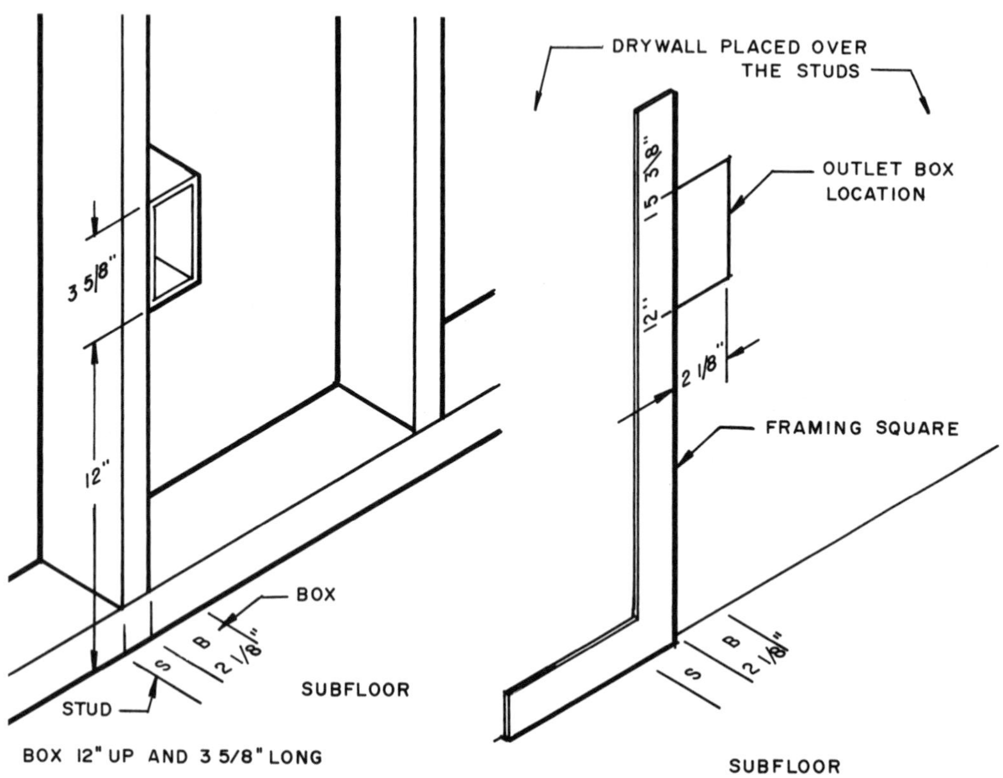

5-5 You can get the location of the opening by lightly tacking the wallboard to the wall, measuring the location, and cutting through the wallboard carefully, enlarging the opening until the panel slips over the outlet.

This is very difficult because the walls and installed panels are often not quite square or level. There is little room for error when locating an exposed opening, such as an electrical box. You must have a gap less than 1/4 in., because this is all the outlet plate will cover.

Another method is to cut the panel to the size required. Coat the outlet box with chalk, position the panel in place on the wall, and press it against the box. Cut on the chalk outline left on the back of the panel.

Another technique is to mark the location of the box from the stud on the floor. Measure the height it is above the floor (*see* 5-5). Then place the wallboard in place on the wall and tack it to the studs—just enough to hold it in place. Using the measurements you just made, mark the location on the face of the wallboard and cut from the face side.

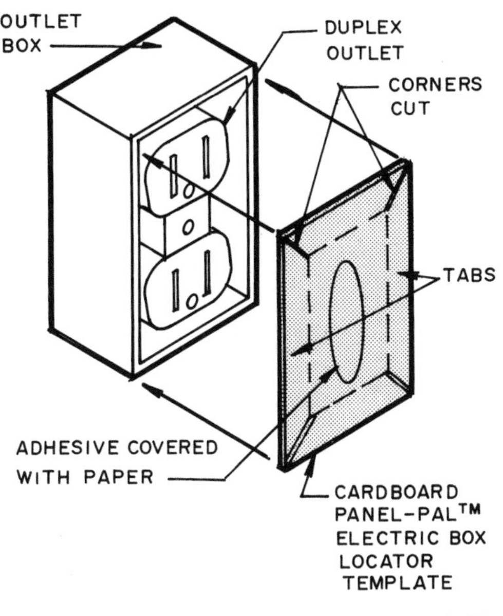

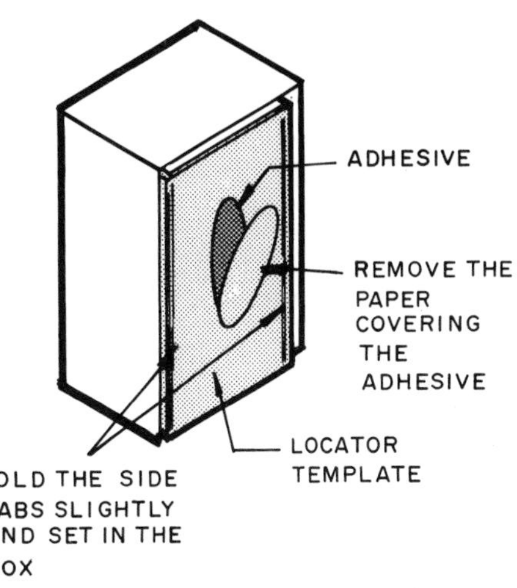

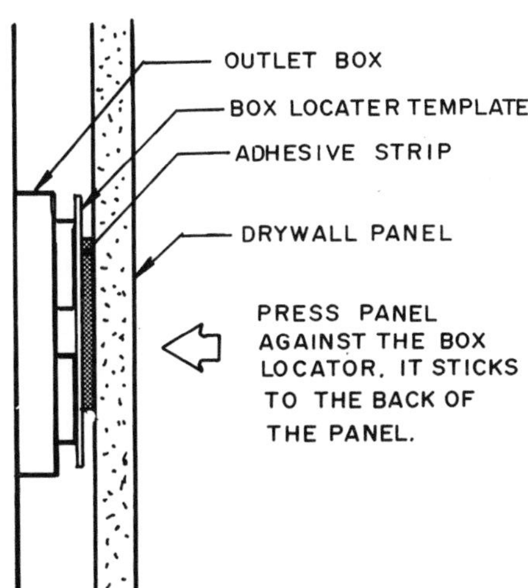

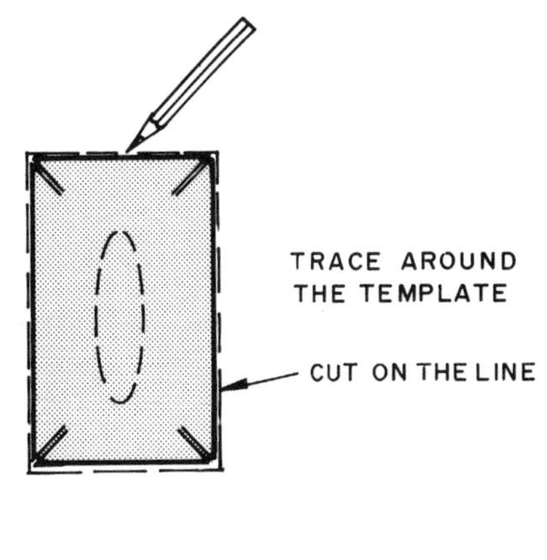

5-6 This commercially available locator template lets you quickly locate electrical boxes. (Courtesy Poly-Tex, Inc.)

Another technique is to use a commercially available electric box cutout locator. It is a template that clips to the box. The gypsum panel is set in place and pressed against the locator, which has an adhesive face. It sticks to the panel and you trace around it, thus locating the cuts for the box (*see* 5-6). The template can be reused many times.

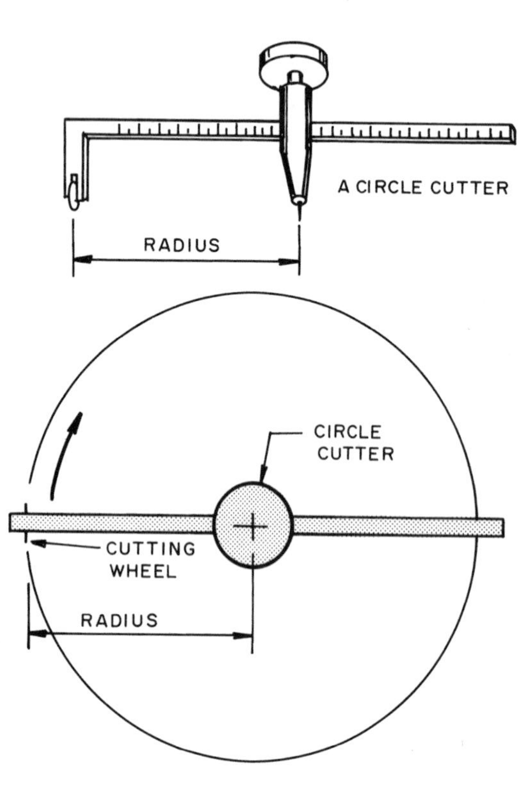

5-7 A circle cutter scores the gypsum core, enabling the circled area to be knocked loose with a hammer. Then cut the paper on the back, freeing the round piece.

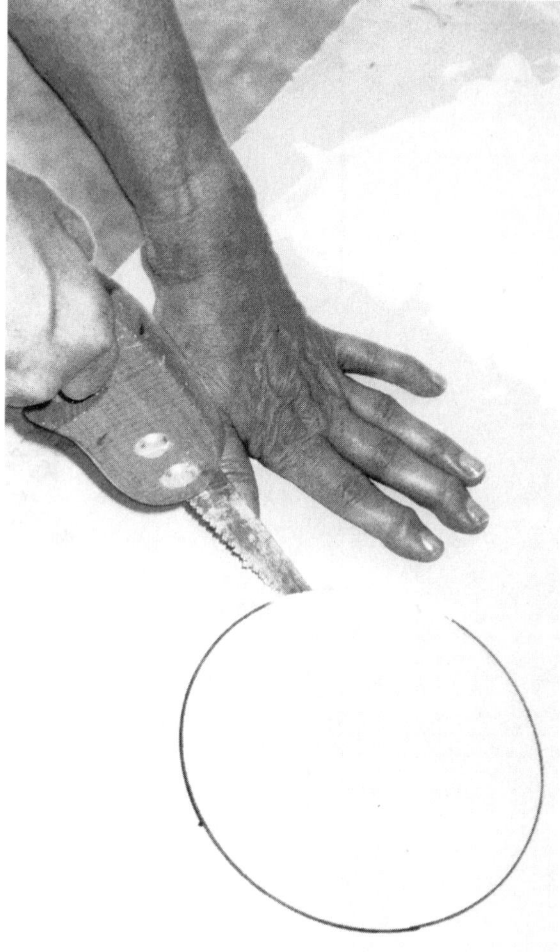

5-8 Circles and other shaped openings can be cut with a keyhole saw.

After the holes are located they can be cut several ways. Round holes can be cut with a drywall **circle cutter** like the one shown in Chapter 2 (*see* 5-7). The pivot is placed on the center of the hole and the cutter is set a distance equal to the radius from it. The paper and core are scored and this round section is knocked out with a hammer. A knife is used to smooth up the back paper and core.

Circular holes can also be cut with a **keyhole saw**. Locate and mark the circumference of the hole. The saw has a sharp tip that is placed against the drywall and rotated, drilling a hole through it. The teeth of the saw then hit the core and cut along the line, marking the hole (*see* 5-8). If the saw does not have the cutting tip, you will have to drill a hole through the panel, insert the saw in it, and make the cut.

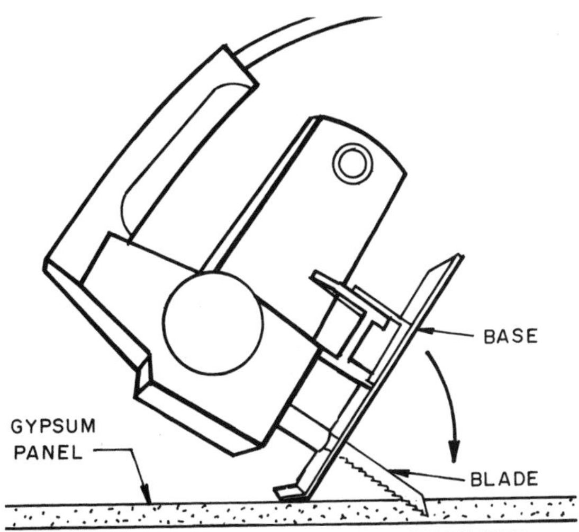

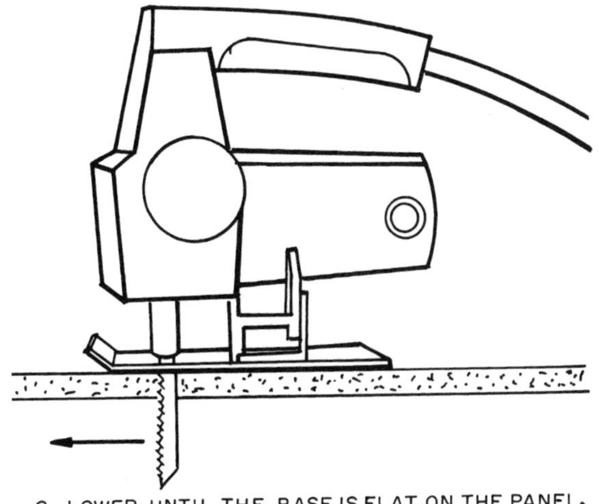

5-9 A saber saw can plunge-cut a hole in the gypsum panel and cut any shape of opening desired.

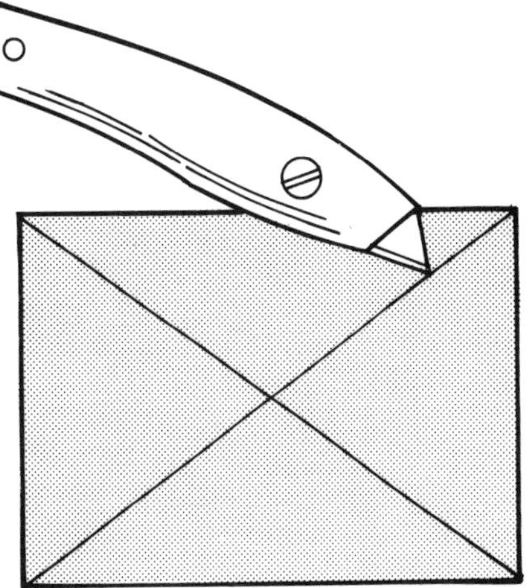

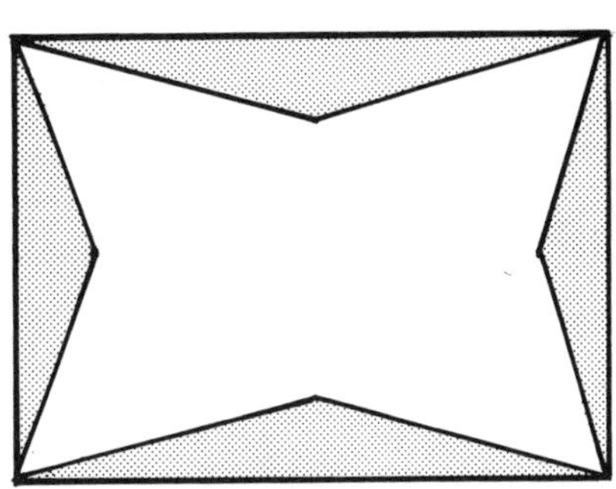

5-10 Holes can be cut by scoring the edges and several diagonals. Knock back the pieces and trim the paper on the back.

A power **saber saw** can be used instead of the keyhole saw. The end of the blade will cut through the panel if you tilt the saw and slowly lower it into the panel. This is called plunge cutting (*see* 5-9).

Holes can be cut by scoring the outline with a knife and cutting across the diagonals (*see* 5-10). Then tap out the pieces and cut the back paper smoothing up the core on the back. Always mark and cut from the finish side of the panel.

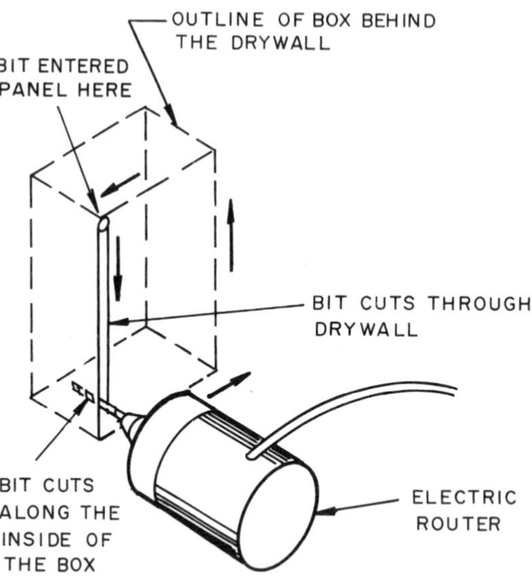

5-11 Holes can be cut using a router and a special bit designed to penetrate and cut the gypsum, forming the opening.

Holes can also be cut using a power router with a special bit. It is inserted through the panel and then is moved along the inside surface of the electrical box (*see* 5-11).

A tool designed to penetrate and cut holes in gypsum, plywood, reconstituted wood panels, plastic panels, aluminum, ceramic tile, and plaster is shown in 5-12. It uses a special Spiracut Bit that will plunge through the drywall and make clean cuts as it is being moved clockwise around the marked opening.

5-12 This power tool, Spiracut, will plunge-cut through the material and then cut a hole of any size or shape with a special bit. Notice the electrical outlet and heat duct openings cut by this machine. (Courtesy Rotozip Tool Corporation)

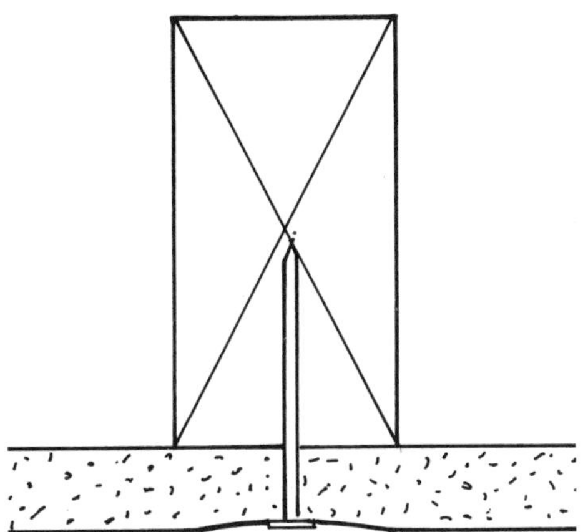

5-13 The nail head is set in a slight dimple so it can be covered with joint compound.

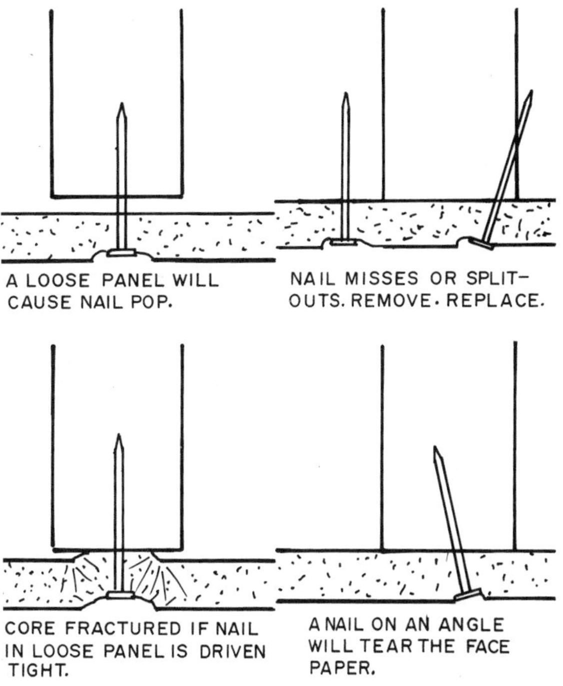

5-14 Examples of improper nailing that will eventually lead to nail pops and panel damage.

Rectangular holes can also be cut using the keyhole saw or electric saber saw. Use the same procedure as described for circular holes (*refer to* 5-8 and 5-9).

Attaching Panels with Nails

Nails are the most commonly used method to attach gypsum drywall panels to wood studs. Both cement-coated and annular-ring nails are used. (*Review* the information on nails and the selection of the proper sizes in Chapter 3.)

The nail must be set so it holds the panel firmly to the stud, and the head should be set slightly below the surface in a small dimple. The paper facing should not be broken (*see* 5-13). This provides a space for the joint compound to conceal the nail. The face of the hammer is curved to form this dimple. Power nailers can be adjusted so they have only enough of a blow to seat the nail, produce a dimple, but not tear the paper or break the gypsum core.

Improper nailing is probably the main cause for nail pops and other problems after the job is finished. Among these are nails that are not set in enough to hold the panel to the stud, a nail that misses the stud, a nail driven when the panel was not tight against the stud (rupturing the core), and nails driven on an angle, which breaks the face paper (*see* 5-14). In addition twisted or warped studs, studs out of line, and inadequate backing cause problems in the future. Remove any nails that are improperly driven (*refer to* 5-15 on page 52).

NAILING PATTERNS

Gypsum panels can be either single-nailed or double-nailed. Double-nailing produces a better job. In some cases, as in a firewall, building codes specify double-nailing. The use of annular-ring nails also improves the installation.

Single-nailed patterns are shown in 5-16 and double-nailed patterns are shown in 5-17.

Following are recommended procedures to follow for nailing gypsum panels.

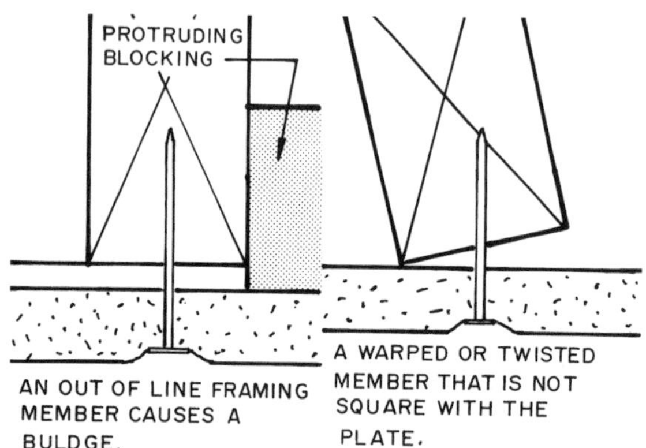

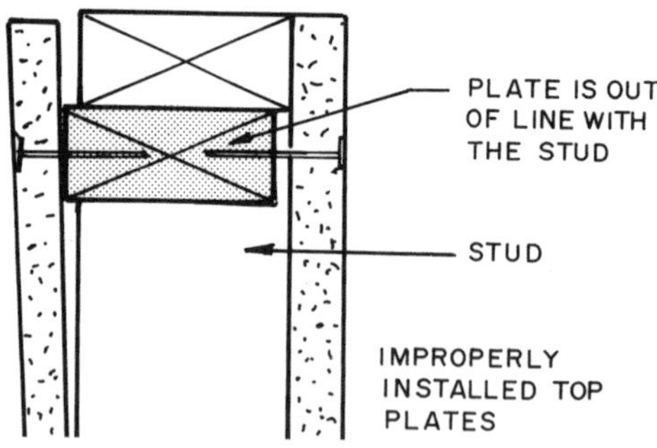

5-15 (Left) Defective framing will cause damage to the panel surface over time.

5-16 (Below) The nails on single-nailed gypsum panels are spaced 7 to 8 inches apart in the field and along the edges. They are not less than 3/8 in. in from the edges and ends of the panel. Nail in the field first and work toward the edges.

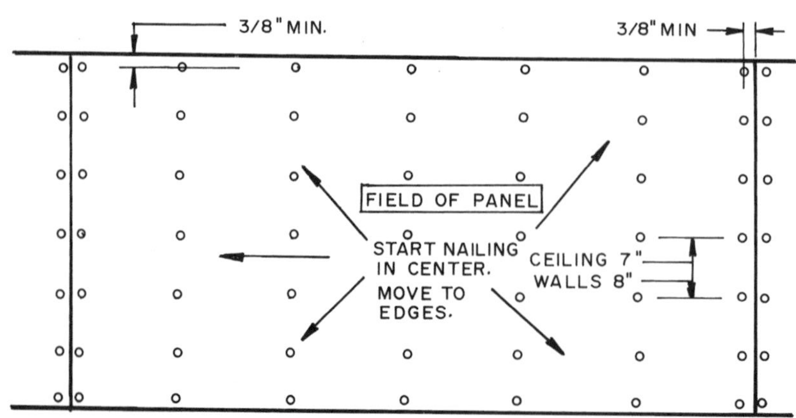

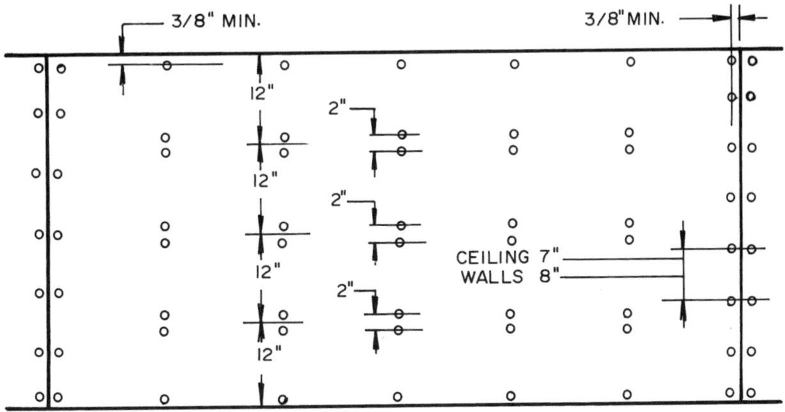

5-17 (Above) To double-nail a panel first drive one set of nails in the field, ends, and edges of the panel. Then go back and place the second series of nails in the field.

5-18 (Right) Double nailing minimizes the possibility of nail-pop. (Courtesy National Gypsum Company)

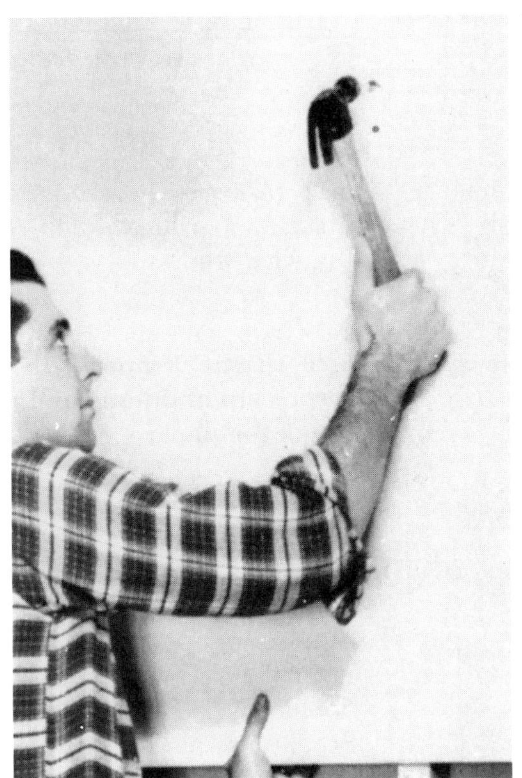

Recommended Procedures

1. Begin nailing from the edge of the panel that butts one already in place. Nail all nails on each stud (perimeter and/or those in the field of the panel) as you move across the panel. **DO NOT** nail the perimeter first and then nail the field.

2. Locate the nails on butting edges or ends opposite each other.

3. Drive the nails at least 3/8 in. in from the ends and edges of the panel.

4. Press the panel hard against the stud before setting the nail.

5. Keep the shank of the nail perpendicular to the panel.

6. Set the head of the nail in a shallow dimple, but do not break the face paper or crush the gypsum core.

7. Space nails on the perimeter 7 in. O.C. on ceilings and 8 in. O.C. for walls and 12 in. O.C. in the field for both installations. Ceilings should be double-nailed. You should note that double nailing minimizes nail-pop (*see* 5-18).

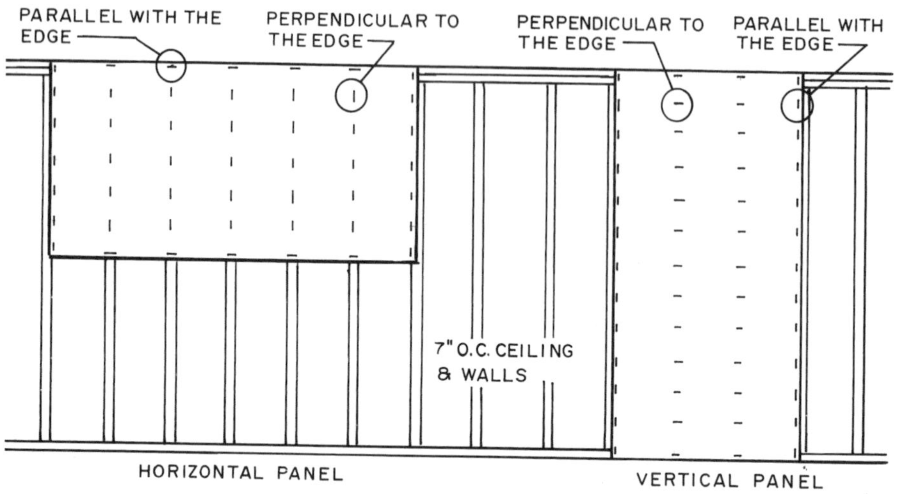

5-19 (Above) The proper way to attach a gypsum panel to wood framing with staples.

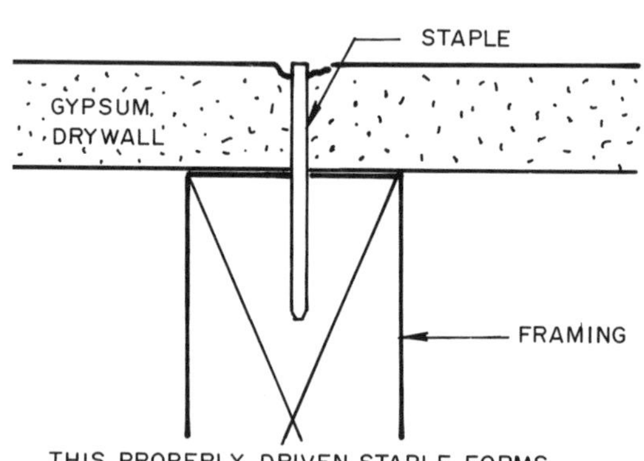

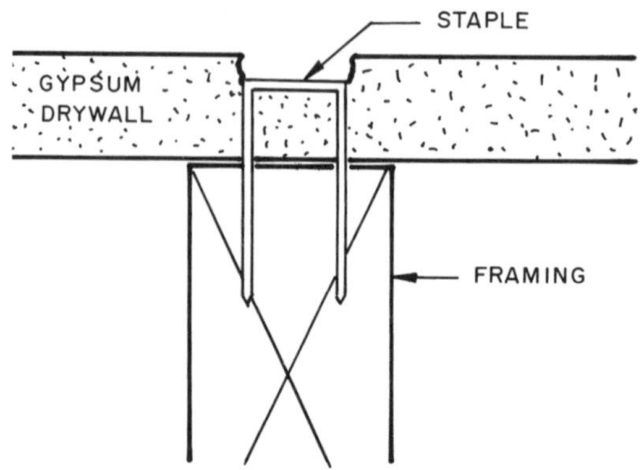

5-20 (Right) Properly driven staples form a slight dimple and do not break the paper.

Attaching Panels with Staples

Staples are used only to attach the base layer panels to wood framing when a double-layer construction is to be used. Staples are placed with the crown perpendicular to the gypsum board edges except where the edges fall on supports. Here they are installed parallel with the edge of the panel (*see* 5-19).

Adjust the stapler to set it to staple in a shallow dimple as shown in 5-20. It should not cut through the face paper and go into the gypsum core. Staples are spaced 7 in. O.C. on ceilings and on sidewalls.

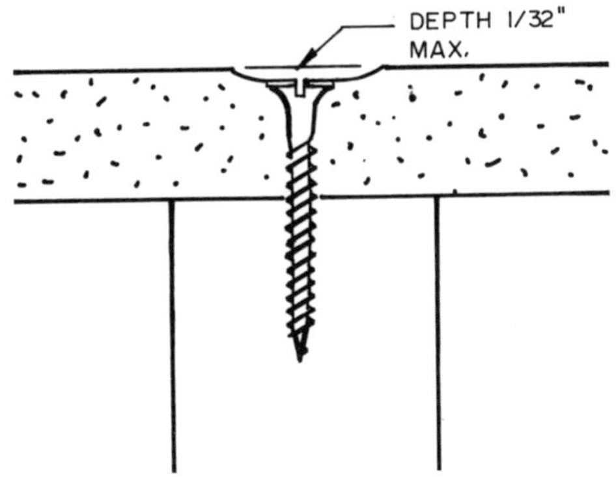

5-21 (Left) The proper depth to drive a screw.

5-22 (Below) When screws are used to mechanically attach a single layer of gypsum board to wood framing spaced 16 in. O.C., space the ceiling screws 12 in. O.C. and those in wall panels 16 in. O.C.

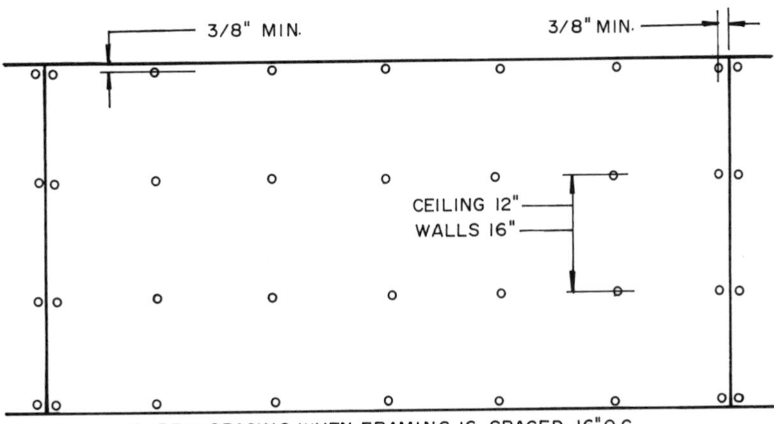

Attaching Panels with Screws

Screws are used to attach panels to wood and metal studs. You can find information on screws and screwguns in Chapters 2 and 3. They are installed with an electric screwgun that has a magnetic chuck and an adjustable screw-depth control. The screw head should be slightly below the surface of the panel (*see* 5-21). Be certain to drive the screw perpendicular to the face of the panel and firmly into the stud. If it misses the stud or is on an angle, it should be removed and another properly driven.

Install the screws as described for nails by beginning on the end that butts another panel and working across the panel, installing perimeter and field screws as you go. Recommend placement for a single-screw application is shown in 5-22. On ceilings you should space screws not more than 12 in. O.C., and 16 in. O.C. on walls when the framing is 16 in. O.C. If the framing is 24 in. O.C. space the screws not more than 12 in. O.C. on ceiling and walls.

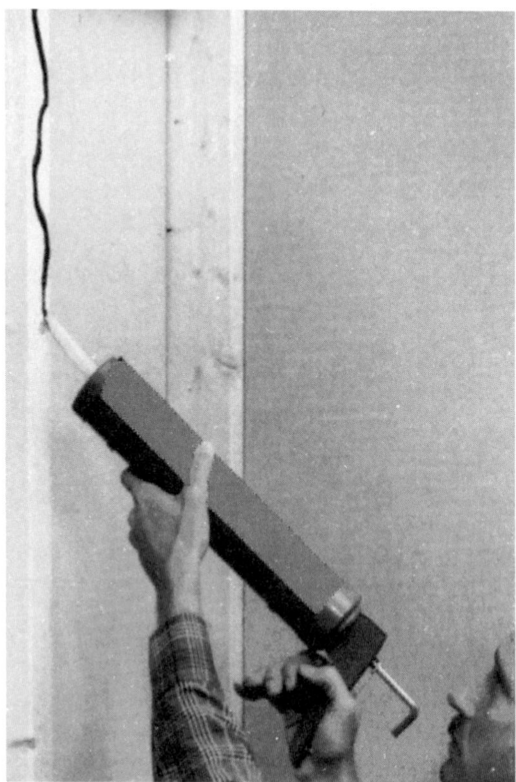

5-23 (Left) Adhesive is applied to the studs from a cartridge held in a caulking gun. (Courtesy National Gypsum Company)

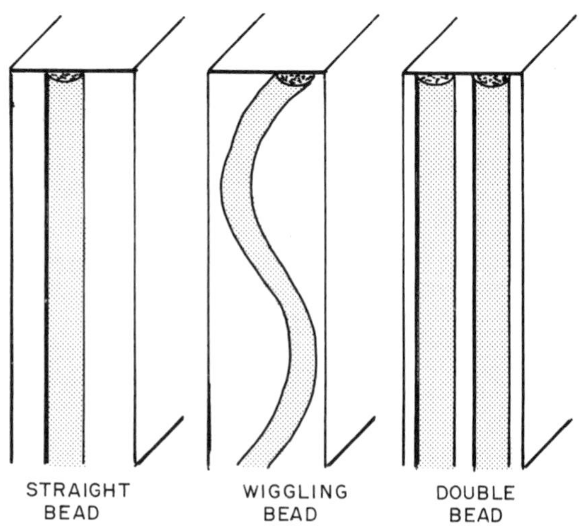

5-24 (Below) Methods for applying adhesive to studs.

Attaching Panels with Adhesive

Adhesives are applied to the stud in addition to nailing or fastening with screws. It helps bond the panel to the studs, reducing nail pops. The use of an adhesive will reduce the number of nails or screws required. Consult manufacturers' data for detailed recommendations.

Adhesive is applied to the studs from a cartridge that is placed in a caulking gun as shown in 5-23. The adhesive is applied in a continuous 3/8 in. bead in the center of the framing in the field of the panel. When two panels butt on a member, two beads can be laid, although some prefer to lay a wiggling bead as shown in 5-24. When the panel is pressed against the framing and nailed or screwed, the adhesive spreads out, covering most of the face of the framing (*see* 5-25).

Be certain to read the directions on the adhesive cartridge before you buy it to be certain it can be used for drywall installation. Do not apply to surfaces that are dirty or have oil or other contaminating materials. In cold weather keep the room heated above 50 degrees F (10 degrees C) and in the summer do not use if the room temperature exceeds 100 degrees F (38 degrees C). Observe the open time (time it is in place before a panel is applied) on the cartridge so that it has not started to set before the panel is applied. Do not tape the joint for 48 hours after application. Remember, adhesives are flammable, so be cautious about fire and provide adequate ventilation in the room.

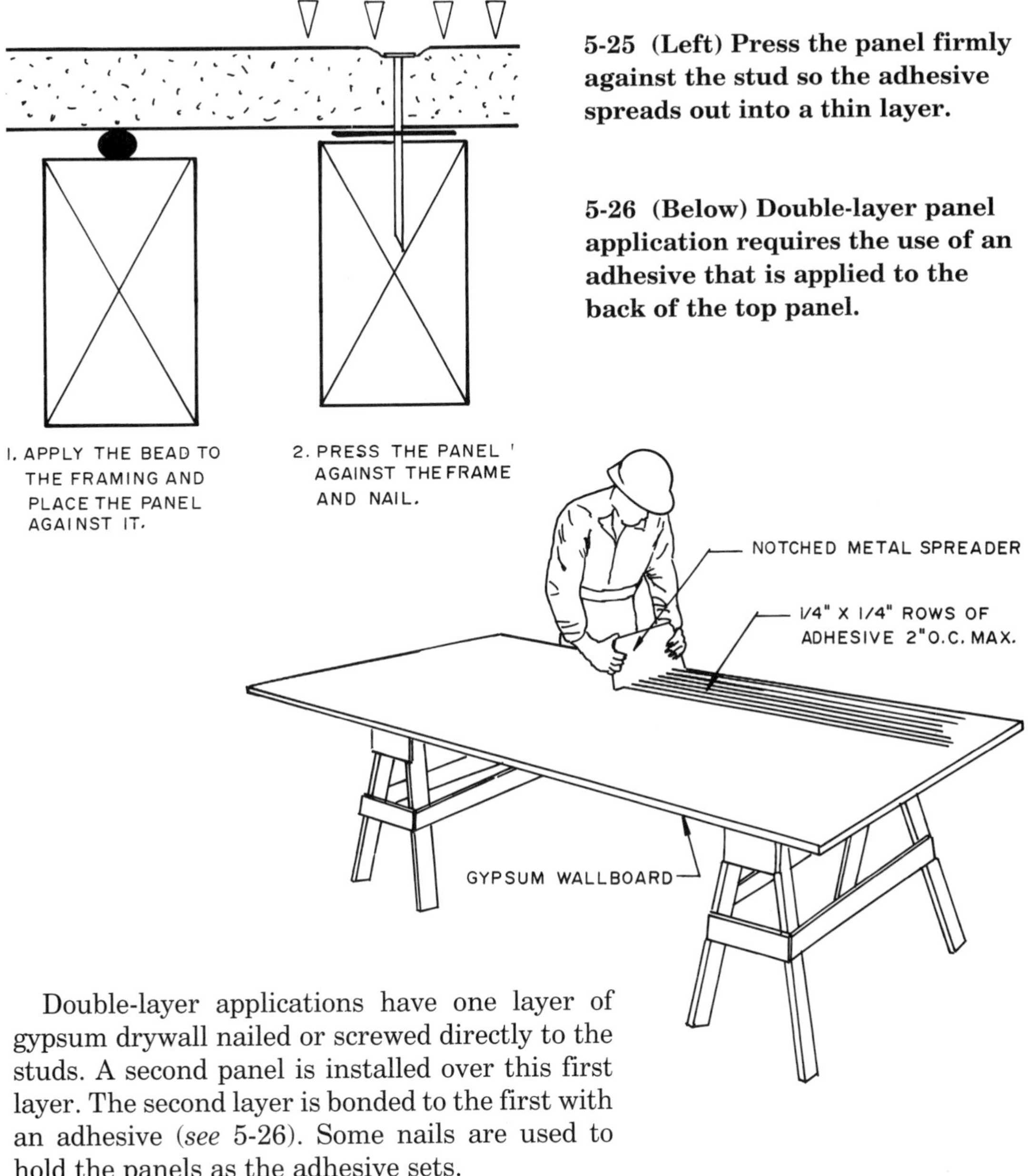

5-25 (Left) Press the panel firmly against the stud so the adhesive spreads out into a thin layer.

5-26 (Below) Double-layer panel application requires the use of an adhesive that is applied to the back of the top panel.

Double-layer applications have one layer of gypsum drywall nailed or screwed directly to the studs. A second panel is installed over this first layer. The second layer is bonded to the first with an adhesive (*see* 5-26). Some nails are used to hold the panels as the adhesive sets.

Chapter 6

Gypsum Wallboard Installation

Hanging gypsum wallboard is a hard job. It requires lifting heavy panels and holding them in place while they are secured to the framing. It must be done correctly or the finishing operations will be more difficult and problems will occur in the years after the job was finished. It involves planning, measuring, cutting, placing, and fastening.

Before You Start to Work

Before installing the gypsum wallboard you should check the framing to see if any corrections are needed. The ceiling joists may not be on the same plane or some studs may be bowed or out of line. The carpenters may have failed to install the needed nailing blocks on the top of the wall framing or where walls meet. All corrections should be made before starting to install the drywall. Some suggestions for handling various defects are in Chapter 8.

This chapter is concerned with the placement and installation of the panels of wallboard. Specific techniques—such as cutting and fastening panels—can be found in Chapter 5.

Some Things to Remember

1. Install the gypsum wallboard to the walls after the ceilings have been covered.

2. Use the longest panels possible to minimize the number of end joints.

3. Install gypsum wallboard so that the edges and ends are secured to framing except when they are at right angles to the framing members. If the framing members are spaced wider than allowed by code for the panel to be used, install blocking at each joint.

4. Hold the wallboard tight against the framing while driving nails or screws.

5. Cut the gypsum wallboard so it fits easily into the space without binding against the other panels.

6. Match similar edges. Abut a tapered long edge to another tapered long edge. Butt a square-cut end to another square-cut end.

7. Whenever possible span from one side of the room to the other with a single-length panel.

8. If there are butt joints, try to have them occur near the walls. They are more noticeable if they occur in the center of the room.

9. Stagger end joints.

10. Drywall board joints should not occur at the sides of openings, such as a door opening. Plan the joint to occur near the center of the opening.

11. Begin fastening the panel in its center and work toward the edges.

12. Set the heads of fasteners just below the surface of the panel but do not tear the paper or crush the core.

13. Remove and replace all incorrectly installed fasteners.

14. Be certain mechanical and electrical outlets, such as an electric box, are installed so they project out from the framing a distance equal to the thickness of the drywall.

15. Check to see that framing has been installed to support heavy items, such as lighting fixtures. The drywall should never be used to support loads.

16. Have a helper to lift, hold, and nail the panels.

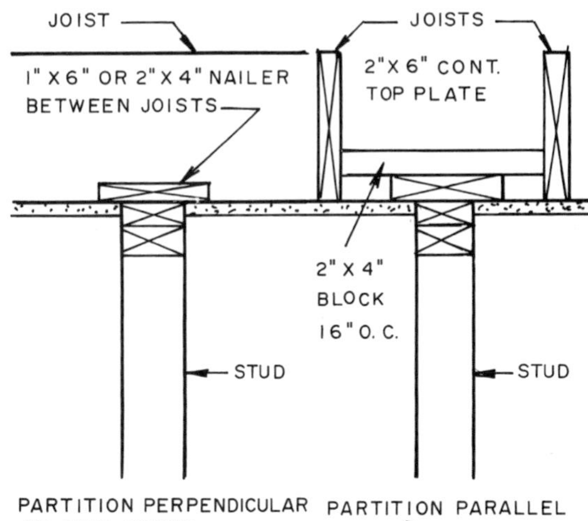

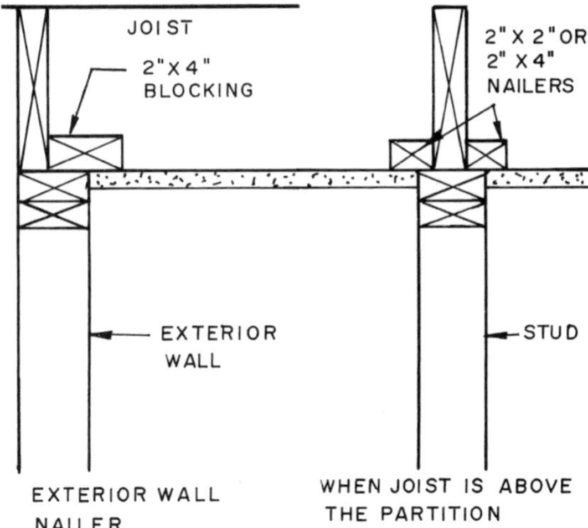

6-1 Some of the ways nailers are installed on top of the partition.

Preparation for Nailing Drywall

The carpenters framing the building should make provision for surfaces needed to back up the drywall for nailing. At the ceiling, blocking or a wide top plate can be used to nail the edges of the ceiling panel (see 6-1).

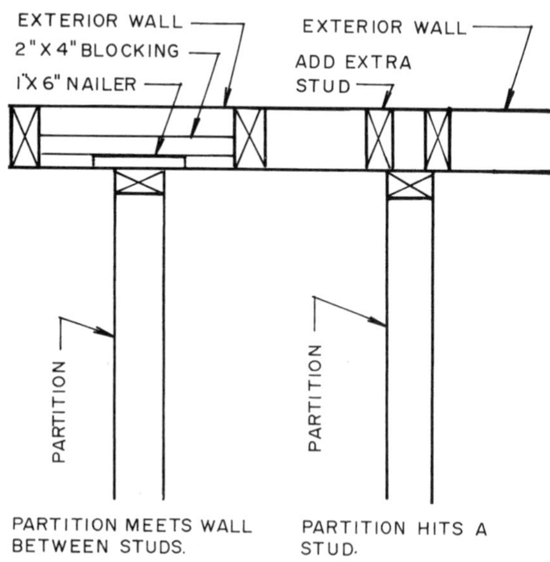

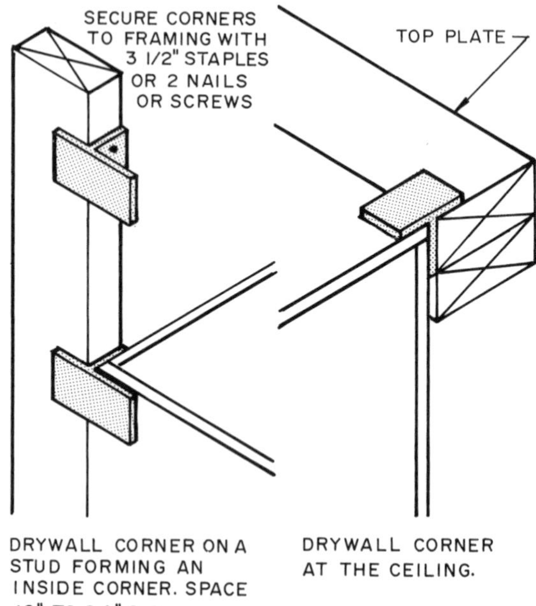

6-2 Two ways to provide nailers at the points where two partitions meet.

6-3 Drywall clips can be used to support the edges of drywall panels instead of using wood nailers.

When interior partitions meet or butt the exterior wall, there are several framing methods that can be used to provide a nailing surface (*see* 6-2). In addition there are clips available that are nailed to the studs and serve to hold the end of the wall or ceiling panel (*see* 6-3). These are typical of the way the drywall contractor should find the framing when arriving on the job.

Installing the Ceiling

The gypsum wallboard is installed on the ceiling first. Then the walls are covered. The panels are installed on the ceiling with their **long edge perpendicular** to the joists. The ends should rest on the center of a joist. The panels should be cut to fit to each other with very little space between them. A space of 1/16 in. is considered satisfactory. Use the longest panels possible and keep end joints away from the center of the room when possible.

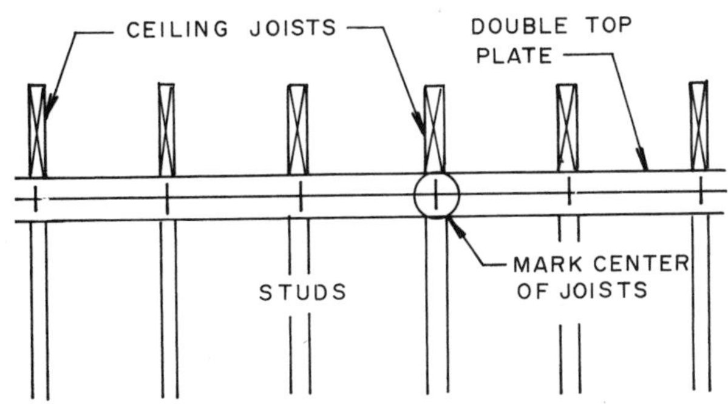

6-4 Mark the center of each ceiling joist on the top plate so its location is known after the ceiling panel is placed against the joists.

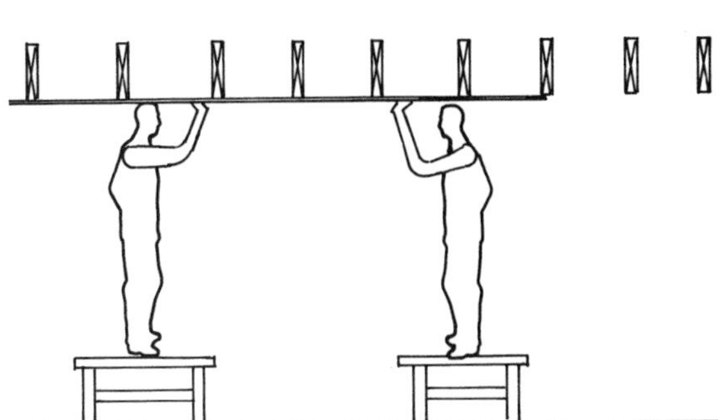

6-5 It takes two persons to raise and hold a ceiling panel for nailing.

When the ceiling panels are lifted into place, the location of the joists at the wall is lost. Therefore mark the center of each joist on the top plate as shown in 6-4.

It takes two people to lift, hold, and nail a ceiling panel. They should have their trestle or other device in place so they can lift the panel, step on the trestle, and press the panel to the joists. It is then slid into place. Many installers hold the panel with their heads while they drive the first few nails (*see* 6-5). You can nail a temporary support to the wall studs to support the edge of the panel being installed next to the wall (*see* 6-6).

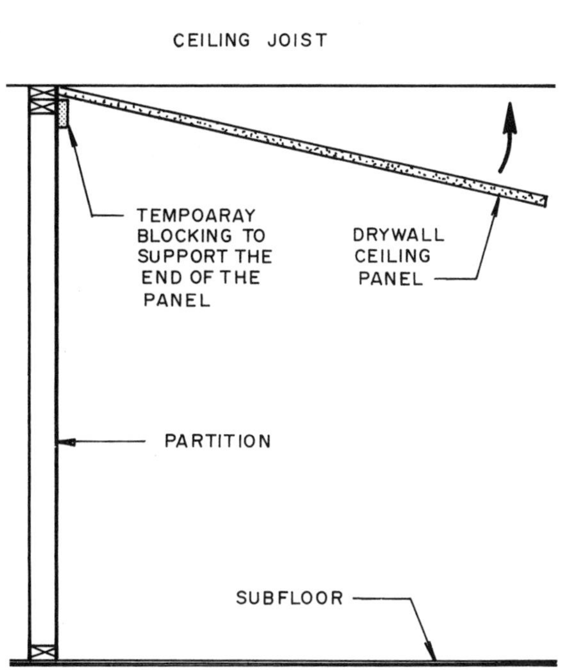

6-6 (Left) A temporary support block can help hold one end of a ceiling panel as it is raised next to a wall.

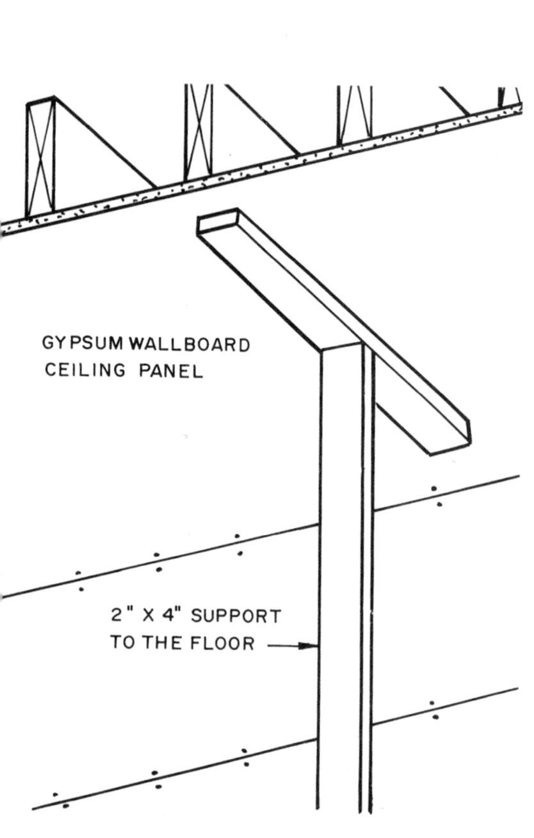

6-7 T-braces made from 2 x 4 in. stock can help support the ceiling joist as it is being nailed.

6-8 This mechanical lifter makes it easy to raise and hold panels for nailing. (Courtesy Telpro Inc.)

A T-brace is used by some to help hold the panel in place. The panel can be raised by someone on a trestle or step ladder while the braces are set in place. These are made to suit the height of the ceiling. The top surface of the brace should be smooth so it does not damage the face of the panel (*see* 6-7).

Another lifting device is shown in 6-8. This mechanical lifter can place panels on flat and cathedral ceilings.

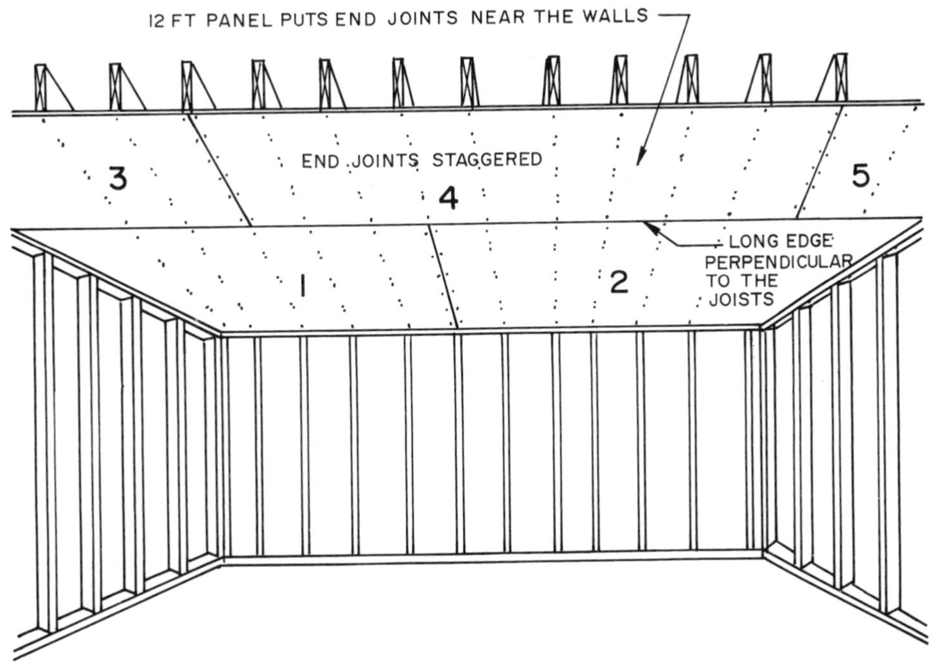

6-9 Install panel 1 in a corner and finish that row across the room. Plan to use a 12-ft. panel in the center of the next row to get the end joints near the wall. When all panels are installed go back over them and check for loose spots, torn paper, and other defects that should be repaired.

LOCATING THE PANELS

Begin by installing one panel in the corner of the room (*see* 6-9). Be certain it does not extend past the center of the joist on which the end rests. Trim as necessary to fit in place. Then install the second panel. Depending on the room size, it may have to be cut to length. The edge of the board does not have to fit tight to the top plate. A space of 1/8 to 1/4 in. will be covered by the wall panel and allow room for possible expansion. Continue across the room.

Now measure and cut the first piece for the second row. Be certain you keep the end joint several feet away from the first joint. Continue this process keeping the end joints staggered. If it is possible, use full-ength panels (such as a 12-ft. panel in rooms up to 12 ft. wide). This will give a ceiling with no end joints.

Remember to locate and cut out any openings required, such as for an electrical box for a light or ceiling fan.

NAILING THE CEILING PANELS

Begin nailing in the center of the panel and work toward the edges. This enables the installer to get the panel flat against the joists and prevents possible bowing, which can occur if the perimeter is nailed first. The ceiling panel may be either single- or double-nailed. Whenever possible, it is always best to double-nail. Detailed patterns for fastening with nails and screws are explained in Chapter 5.

Gypsum wallboard manufacturers recommend that the edges of ceiling panels next to the wall not be nailed. This allows for movement between the wall and joists. Since the wall panels butt up against the ceiling panel, it is supported by them. This is called a floating angle (*see* 6-10).

Ceiling panel running perpendicular to the joists may be installed with adhesive and nails. Apply a 3/8-in.-wide bead of adhesive to the joists as shown in Chapter 5. Space the nails 16 in. O.C. on each end of the panel and 24 in. O.C. along the ceiling joists on the panel field.

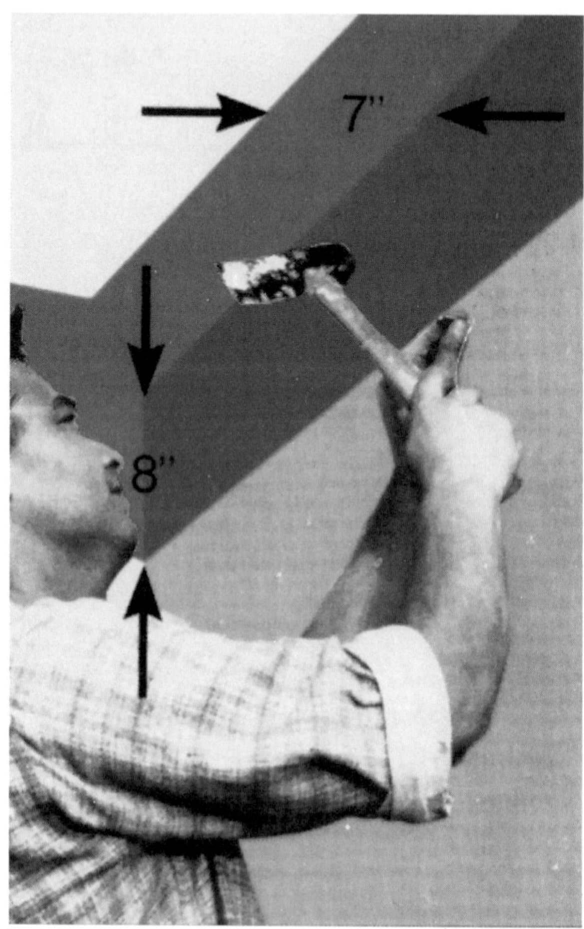

6-10 No nails are to be in the edge of the ceiling panel, creating what is referred to as a floating angle. (Courtesy National Gypsum Company)

INSTALLING SINGLE-LAYER WALL PANELS

After the framing has been checked and corrected for straightness, the wall panel installation can begin. Remember to check the insulation. It should be stapled to the inside of the studs, not to the face.

The first decision you must make is whether to install the panels horizontally or vertically. If the ceiling is 8 ft. high, horizontal installation will produce fewer joints. However, they can be installed vertically if you wish. The horizontal method is best if single panels can cover the wall from one side of the room to the other. This produces only an edge joint and no end joints.

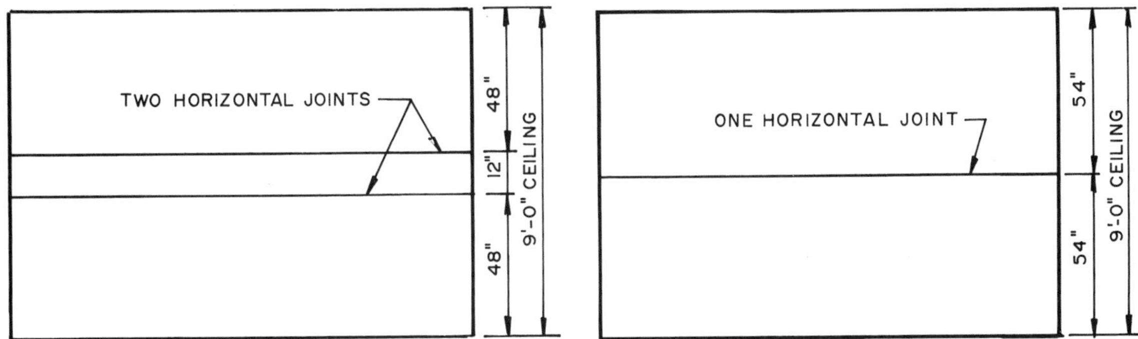

6-11 Use a wider panel whenever it will eliminate one edge joint. If you use the 48 in. width, many installers prefer to place the narrow strip next to the floor.

If ceiling heights are over 8 ft., apply the panels vertically or use a special 54-in.-wide panel (*see* 6-11). This eliminates a wide fill-in strip and a lot of extra, difficult taping and finishing. This is especially useful for 9-ft. ceilings. Most prefer to put the narrow strip down by the floor.

Begin by installing the top panels. After the top row is completed around the entire room, you can place the lower row (*refer to* 6-13 on page 66). Be certain to stagger the end joints. The lower panels can be lifted a few inches into place with the drywall lifter shown in Chapter 2 (*see* 6-12).

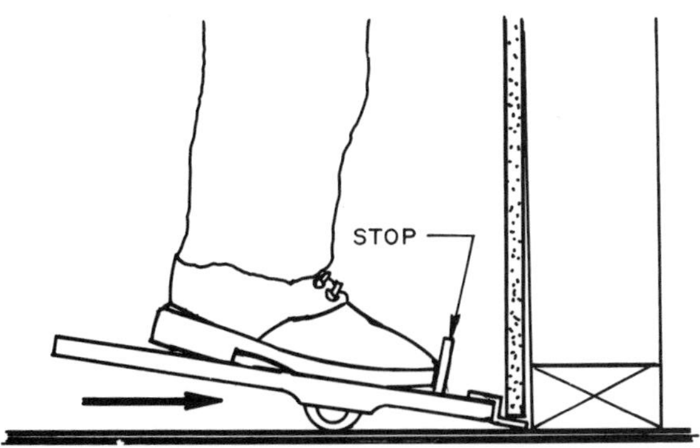

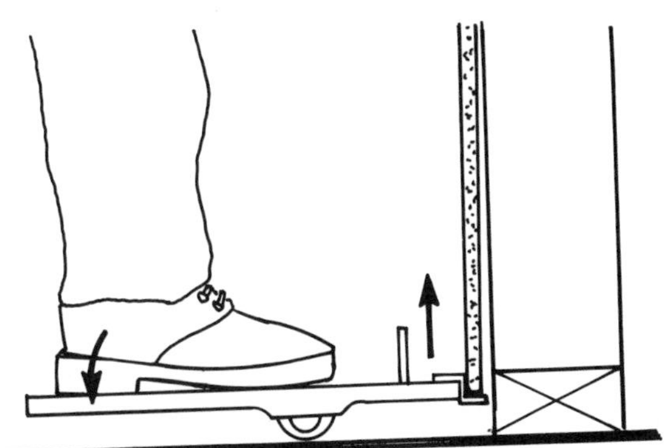

6-12 A drywall lifter will help raise the bottom panel an inch or so, leaving both hands free to fasten the panel to the framing.

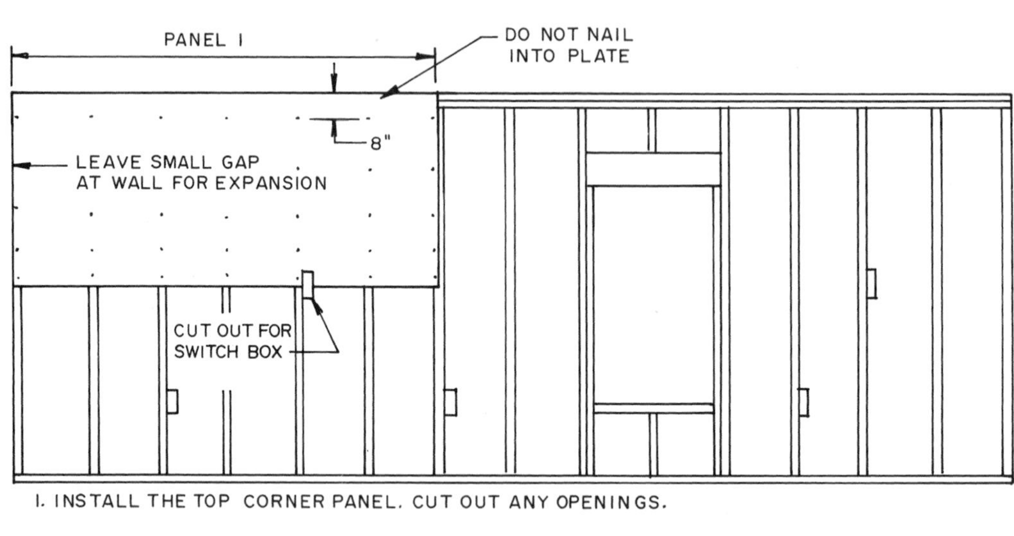

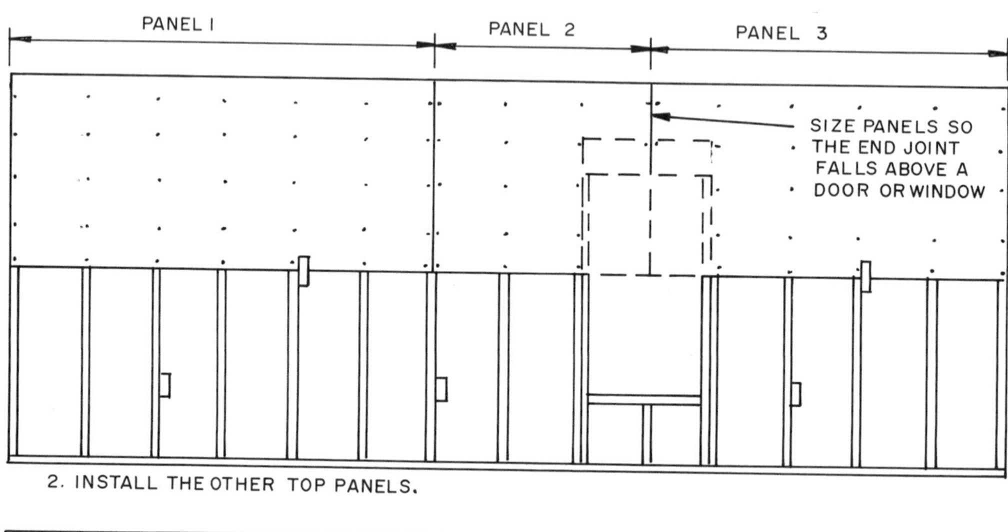

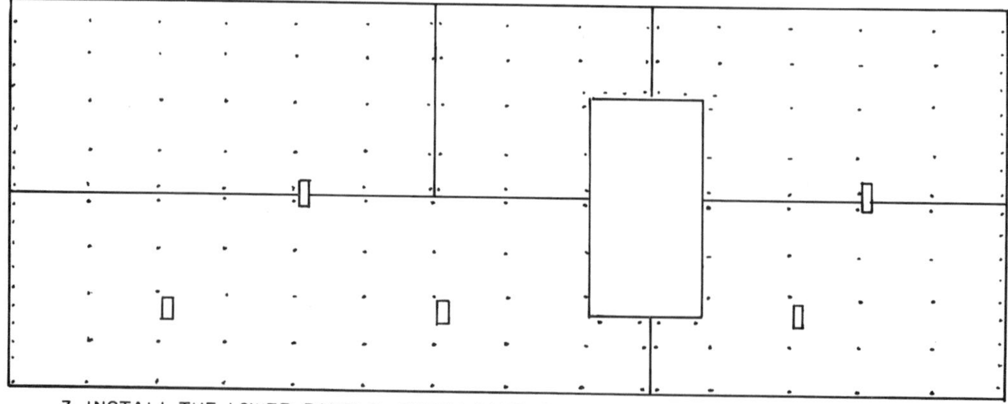

6-13 When hanging a wall, begin by installing the top row of panels. Complete each row before you hang the row below it.

You must never allow an end joint to occur by the corner of a wall opening. The stresses here will cause the wall to eventually crack. Plan the panels so the joint occurs near the center of the opening as shown in 6-13. The carpenter should have placed studs and cripples every 16 or 24 in. so that the nailing surface is there. Do not nail the panel to the header over the opening.

Remember to locate and cut the openings for light switches, outlets, as well as plumbing and mechanical system requirements.

NAILING THE WALL PANELS

Single-nailed application requires that the nails be spaced 8 in. O.C. on the edges and in the field of the panel. When double-nailing, space the nail 12 in. O.C. in the field and 7 in. O.C. on the perimeter. Instructions for securing panels with nails, screws, and adhesives are in Chapter 5. It is always best to double-nail a panel.

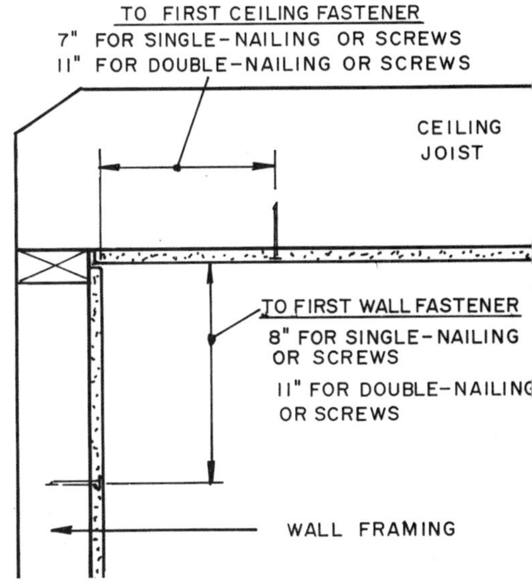

6-14 Typical floating interior-angle construction.

FLOATING INTERIOR-ANGLE CONSTRUCTION

Floating interior-angle construction is a method used to reduce cracking and nail pops caused by stresses that develop at wall-to-wall and wall-to-ceiling intersections. You do not install fasteners on one of the panels at each interior angle. The panels need wood backup blocking just the same as if they were to be nailed. When a wall panel meets a ceiling panel, the last fastener in the ceiling panel should be 7 in. from the wall for single nailing and 11 in. for double nailing (*see* 6-14). When nailing the wall panels near the ceiling, the top fastener should be 8 in. from the ceiling for single nailing and 11 in. for double nailing.

The nailing of wall panels forming an interior corner is shown in 6-15. The fasteners are omitted in the panel that is behind the butting panel. The butting panel is nailed in the usual manner.

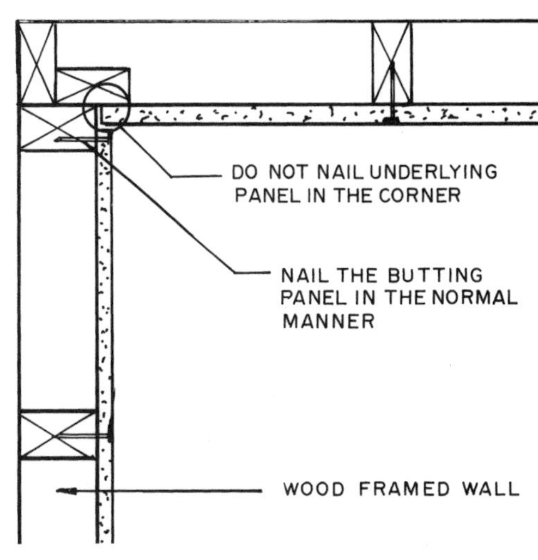

6-15 Omit the fasteners on one of the panels in order to form interior corners.

COPING WITH TRUSS RISE

The bottom chord of roof trusses can arch upward if the moisture content in the top and bottom chords is different. This causes cracks between the ceiling and the wall. The typical taped ceiling-wall corner is not strong enough to resist the stress and will not move, so it cracks. This can be overcome by using one of the techniques in 6-16.

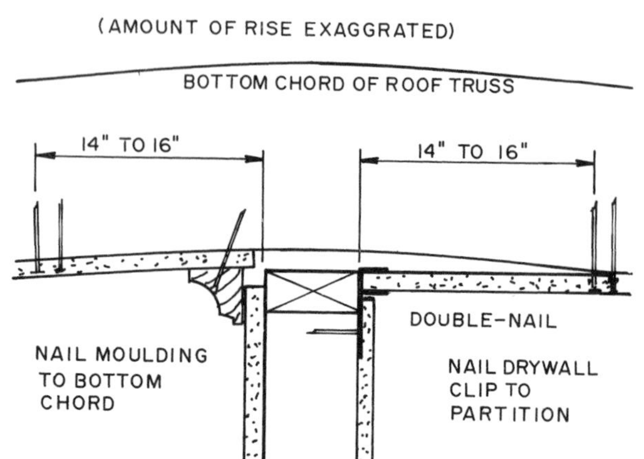

6-16 (Above) Either of these techniques permit the bottom chord of the truss to rise without causing a major crack in the drywall at the ceiling.

INSTALLING DRYWALL ON HIGH WALLS

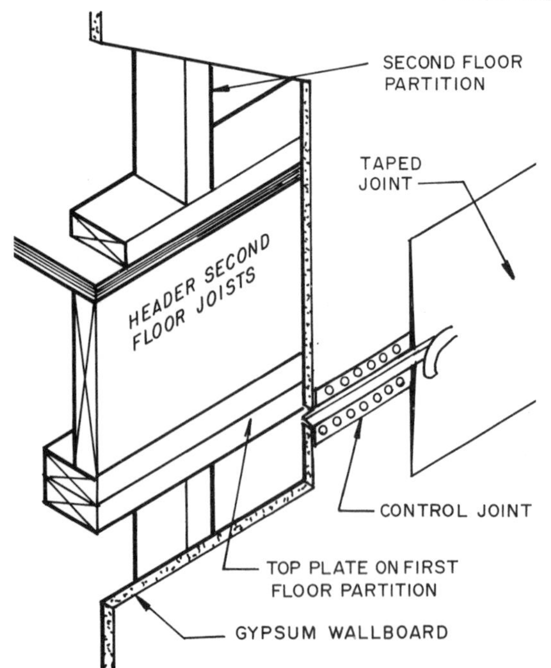

6-17 (Above) When installing high walls, place an expansion joint just below the second floor joist header.

When the wall exceeds one floor in height it is recommended that a horizontal control joint be installed between the gypsum panels along the line created where the first floor studs butt the double top plate (*see* 6-17). The gypsum panels should not be nailed to the side face of joists or headers. Consider the use of 54-in.-wide panels if it will reduce the number of edge joints.

The control joint (*see* 6-18) permits some movement of the gypsum panels on both floors. It has a 1/4 in. open slot that is covered by tape. After the joint has been installed and finished with joint compound, this tape is pulled off, leaving a small recess.

6-18 (Right) The control joint has a tape over the groove. It is pulled away after the joint has been finished with joint compound.

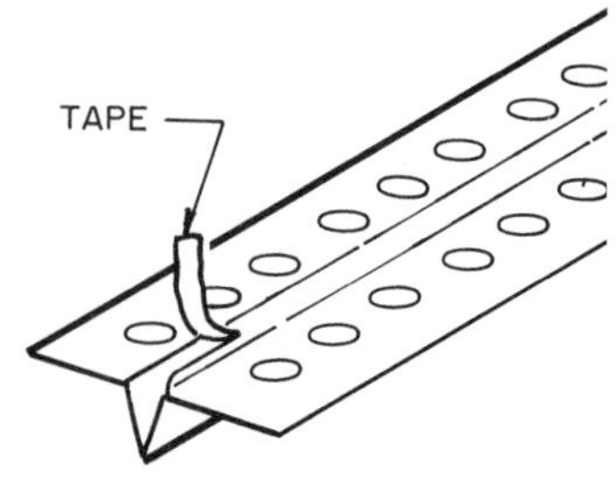

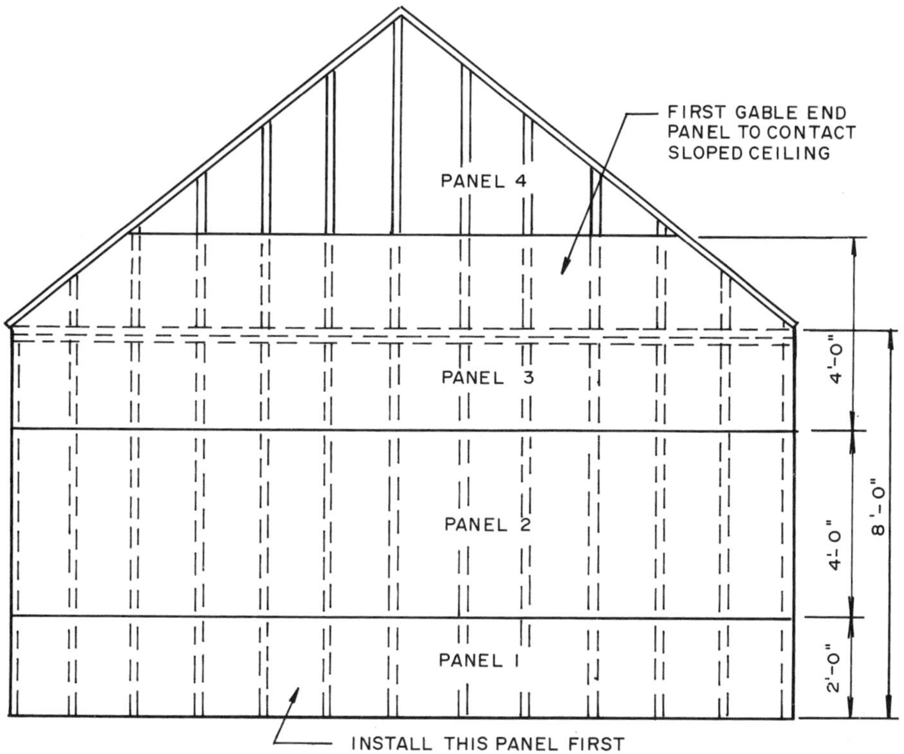

6-19 This is a suggested way to plan a panel layout for hanging a gable end with a cathedral ceiling.

It is recommended that control joints be used in ceilings over 2500 sq. ft. and in walls over 30 ft. in length. They are secured to the gypsum wallboard with 9/16 in. staples or nailed every 6 in. along each flange.

Installing Drywall on Gable Walls

Cathedral ceilings are popular—which means you will have to hang drywall on gable walls. This calls for careful measuring of the length of the panel so it ends on a stud and laying out out the angle on the end to match the roof slope. It may be economical to install extra studs for the end of panels on the gable end so the full length of the panel can be used. This will often eliminate one end joint.

Start by installing the panels from the floor. You want the first panel that touches the ceiling to have part of its end vertical and the rest sloped (panel 3) to fit the ceiling. While designs may vary it is typical to start an 8'–0" wall with a 24-in.-wide panel (panel 1), followed by a 48-in. panel (panel 2) as shown in 6-19. This makes the third row meet the requirements just mentioned. It goes without saying that you will have installed the ceiling panels before doing the gable end.

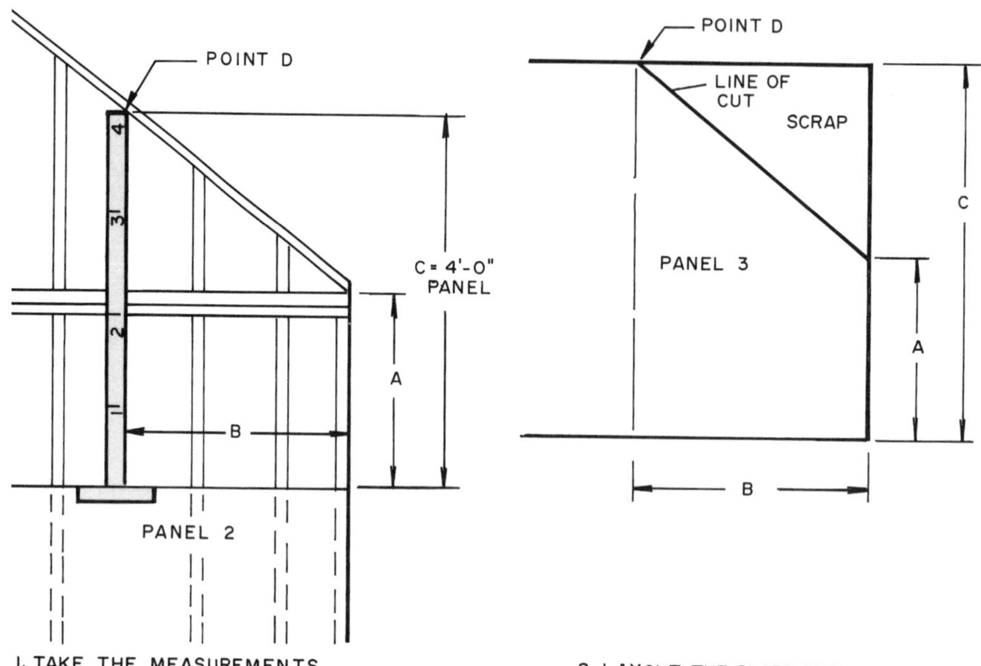

6-20 These are the steps to follow to locate the cut of the end of the panel that butts the sloped ceiling.

To lay out the first sloped panel (panel 3) place the T-square on the top of the wall panel as shown in 6-20. Slide it until the end touches the drywall ceiling. Measure distances A and B. Measure these on the panel and cut the angle. Then measure the length and mark and cut if necessary so the end rests on a stud. The other pieces can be laid out in the same manner, except the entire end will slope.

Installing Drywall on Stair Walls

A stair wall will contain the first floor studs, header, joists for the second floor, and the second floor studs. Begin the first panel at the ceiling. While the sizes will vary—some depending on the height of the wall—you want to avoid having an edge joint occur at the top plate of the first floor wall. It is likely there will be more movement here and it's best if you cover it over with a solid panel. Refer to 6-21 and you will see a typical situation. If using 54 in. wide panels helps reduce the number of edge joints by all means do so. As the drywall gets low enough to hit the stair, the

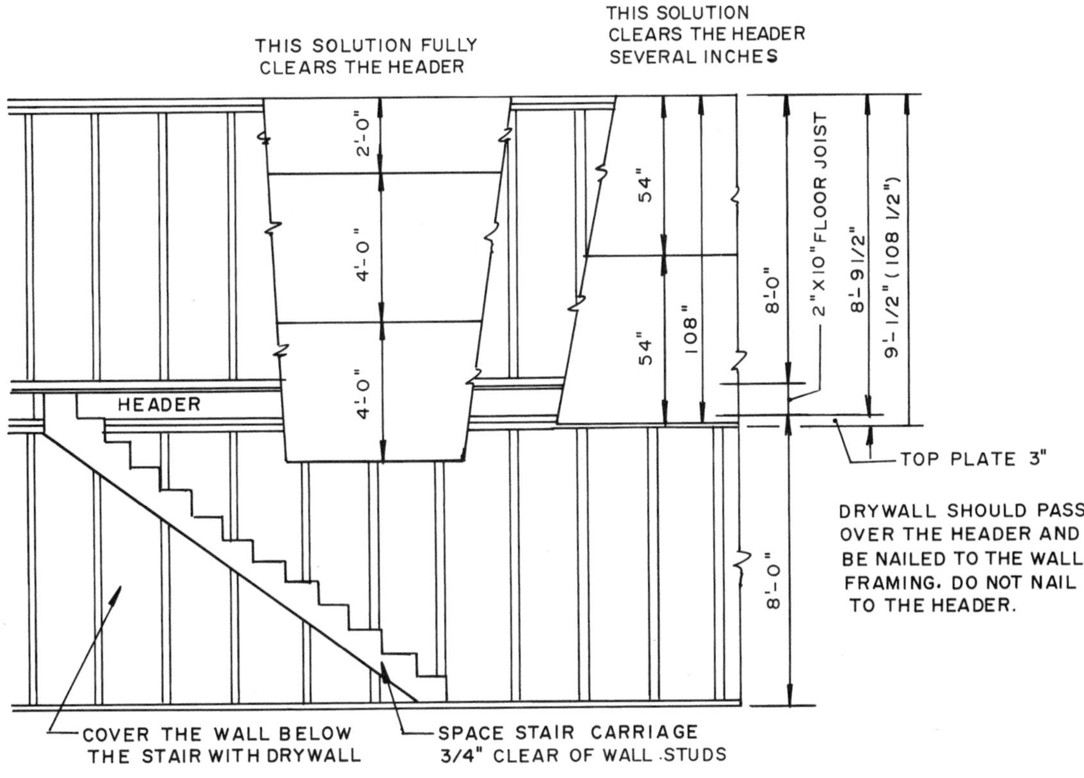

6-21 Two possible ways to hang the wall on a stair. The panel should pass over the header of the second floor and not be nailed to it.

end may be cut on the angle of the stair but generally is run to the floor behind the stair stringer. The stair stringer rests against the drywall and the finish stringer is nailed over the drywall (*see* 6-22). If the stair stringers are installed before the drywall, the carpenter will usually set the wall stringer out ½ in, to allow the drywall to fit behind it.

Refer back to the recommendations for using an expansion joint. The line of the top of the first floor top plate is a typical location on a high wall such as this.

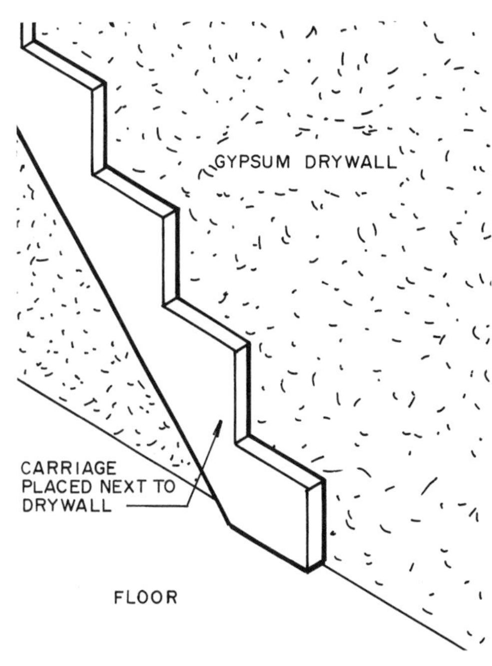

6-22 (Right) Typically the drywall is run behind the stair carriage and onto the floor.

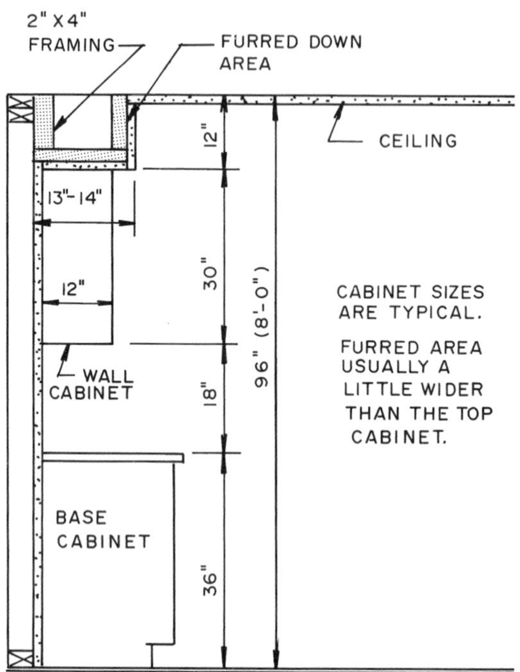

6-23 Typical sizes for kitchen cabinets. These produce a 12-in. furred-down area at the ceiling.

Installing Drywall on Furred-Down Areas

The ceiling is often furred down above kitchen cabinets, as well as built-in cabinets in the living room, bathroom, and other areas of the house. The carpenter will have constructed the framing which goes above the cabinets. Your job is to hang the wall up to the furred-down area and then cover this area. If it is a kitchen, most of the wall will be covered with the base cabinet and the wall cabinet. Usually the wall cabinets will have a back, so the drywall behind them is not seen. The base cabinets usually are open on the back. Remember, also, that there are a string of electrical outlets located just above the counter top and often a telephone outlet. A typical situation is shown in 6-23.

A good way to begin is to install a panel on the wall below the furred-down area (*see* 6-24). This will produce one edge joint near the floor. Remember to cut holes for the plumbing and electrical outlets. Complete covering the wall before you cover the furred-down area.

Now cover the bottom of the furred down area. Usually it is wider than the wall cabinets, so a clean sharp corner is needed. And finally cover the remainder, check for loose nails or torn paper, and you are ready to finish as shown in 6-25.

6-24 (Right) Hang the wall below the furred-down area before you cover it with drywall. This design puts the horizontal joint behind the base cabinets.

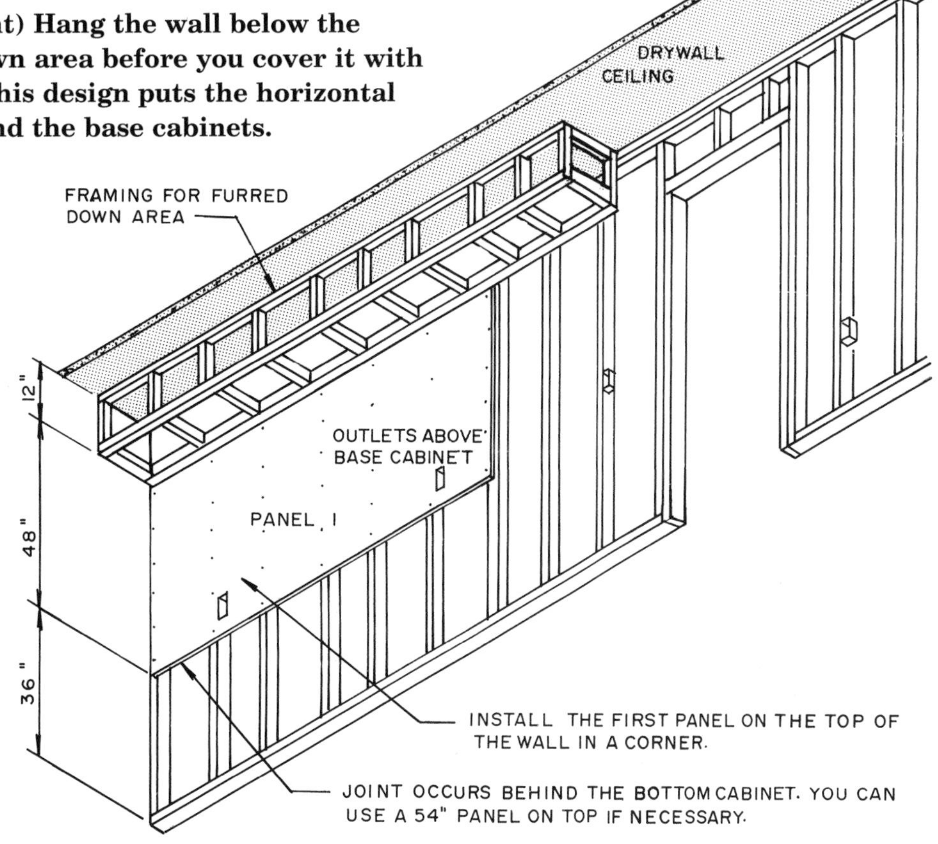

6-25 (Below) After the wall has been covered, hang the drywall on the furred-down area.

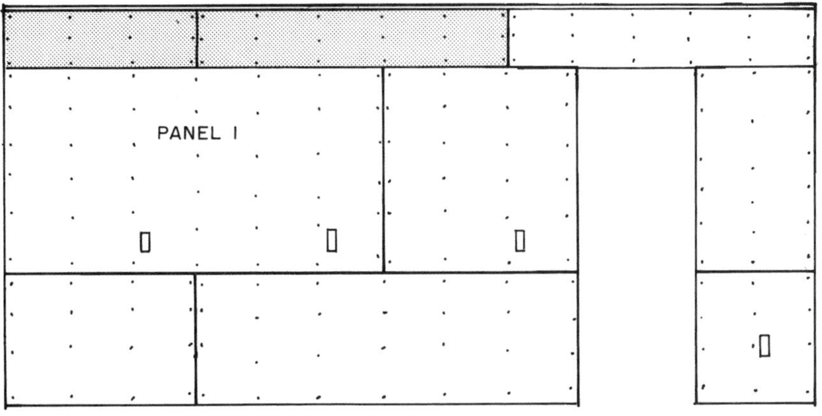

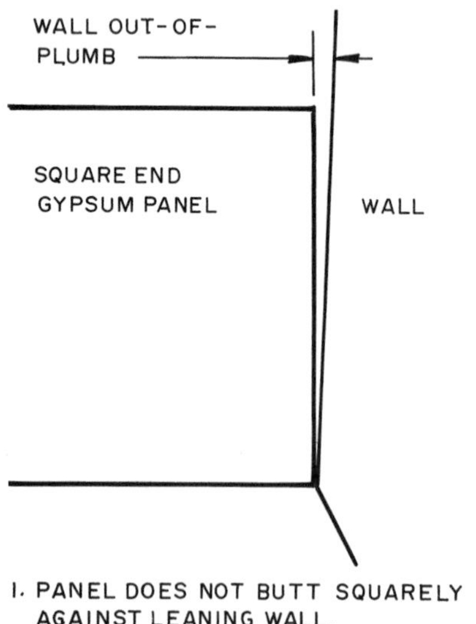

6-26 These are the steps to follow when a panel butts a wall that is out of plumb.

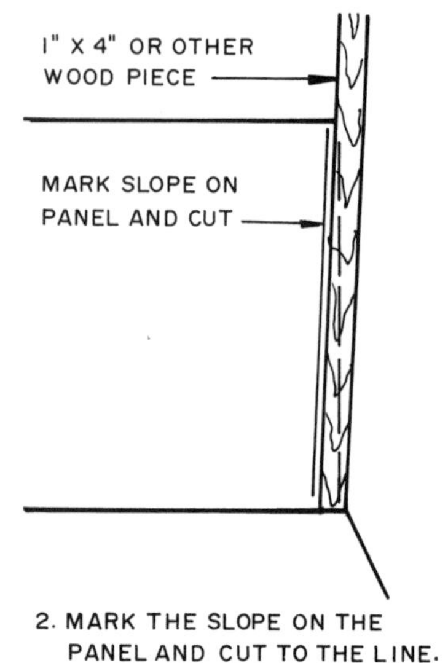

Hanging to an Out-of-Plumb Wall

When a wall is out of plumb, the square end of the butting panel will not meet it properly. To handle this place the panel against the wall, and place a board, such as a 1 x 4, against the out-of-plumb wall. Mark along the edge, locating a line that is parallel with the wall. After cutting this sloped end measure and cut the length of the panel (*see* 6-26).

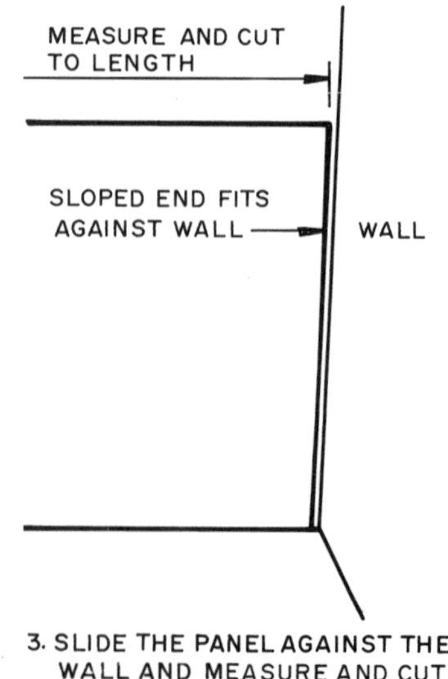

6-27 Double-layer construction requires that the long edge of the panels in each layer be perpendicular to each other.

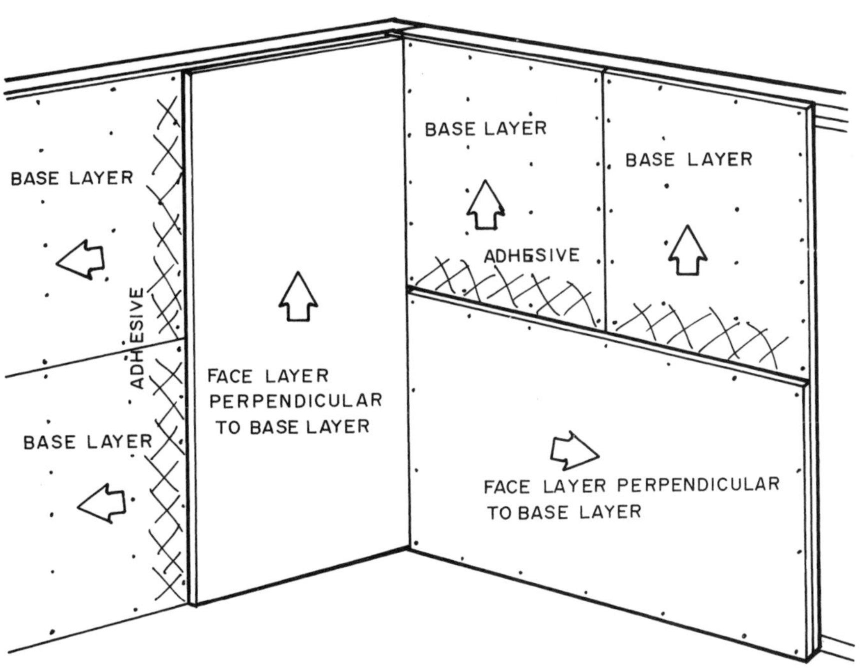

Double-Layer Wallboard Installation

Double-layer installation provides additional fire protection and reduces the amount of sound that can pass through the partition. The first layer is nailed or screwed to the framing using the same spacing as single-layer. The base may have the long joints vertical or horizontal. The face layer must have the long joints perpendicular to those on the base layer (*see* 6-27). The face layer is bonded to the base with adhesive and fastened with enough fasteners as needed to hold it tight as the adhesive sets. (*See* Chapter 5 for information on nails, screws, and adhesive.)

Installing Drywall on Curved Walls & Arches

It takes careful work and planning to hang curved walls and arches. First of all the carpenter should have properly prepared the framing. The space between wall studs and other framing material is very important. If the space is too great, the wall will have a series of flat surfaces.

HANGING CURVED WALLS

It is recommended that you use a special 1/4-in. flexible gypsum panel designed for curved surface installation. This is a two-layer installation with a second 1/4 in. panel overlaid on the first. Typical bending radii for 1/4-in. High-Flex wallboard, manufactured by National Gypsum Company, are given in 6-28. Consult the manufacturer of the product you will be using for specific technical data.

6-28 Minimum bending radii for 1/4" High-Flex wallboard.

	Lengthwise		Widthwise	
Application	**Bend radii**	**Max. stud spacing**	**Bend radii**	**Max. stud spacing**
inside (concave) dry	32"	9" o.c.	20"	9" o.c.
outside (convex) dry	30"	9" o.c.	15"	8" o.c.
inside (concave) wet	20"	9" o.c.	10"	6" o.c.
outside (convex) wet	14"	6" o.c.	7"	5" o.c.

(Courtesy National Gypsum Company)

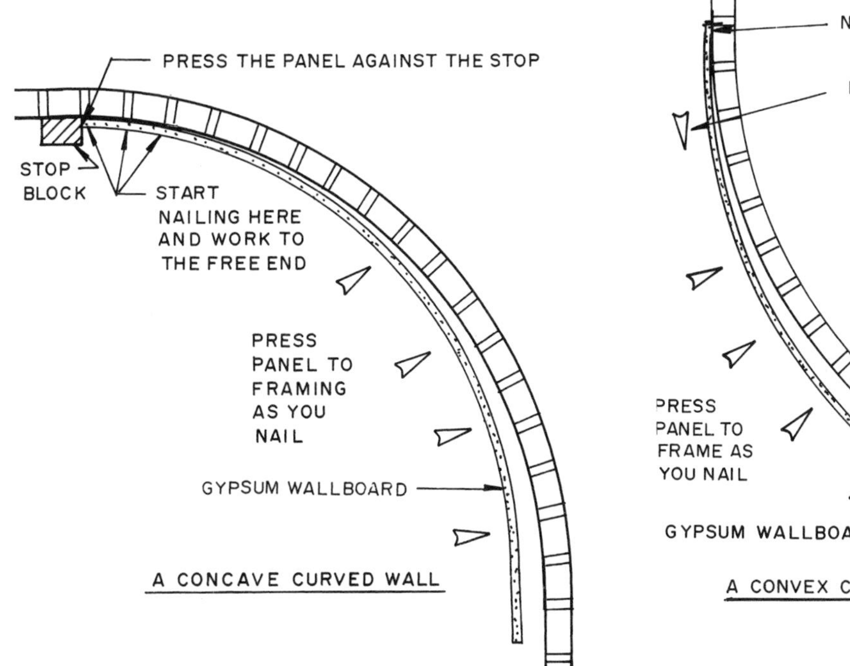

6-29 A concave curved wall is nailed starting on one end and you work toward the free end, keeping the panel tight to the framing.

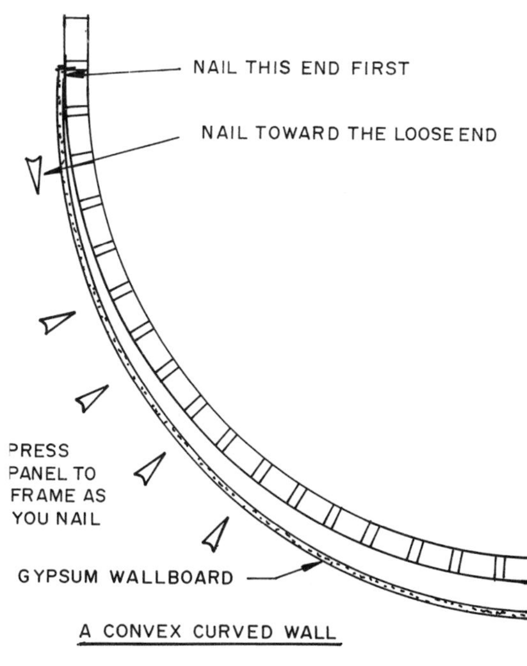

6-30 A convex curved wall is nailed at one end and pressed to the frame as you nail toward the free end.

This product is significantly more flexible if installed with the long edges in the vertical position. For instance, notice in 6-28 that when applied widthwise (width perpendicular to the studs) the minimum bend radii are considerably smaller. Critical to a good job is the spacing of the studs, also shown in 6-28. When fastening the panels they must be held in firm contact with the framing member as the fasteners are being driven.

When covering **concave surfaces,** place a wood stop at one end of the curve and press the panel against it from the other edge. This helps bow the panel to the wall. Start installing the fasteners from the end against the stop (*see* 6-29).

When installing on **convex surfaces,** first nail one end to the framing with nails or screws. Then push the panel against the framing nailing toward the loose end (*see* 6-30).

This product may require wetting if smaller radii are required or if the temperature is lower than 65 degrees F (18 degrees C) and the humidity is below 45 percent. Apply 10 to 15 ounces of clean water per side with a paint roller or a spray. Permit it to soak 10 to 15 minutes before bending.

6-31 Minimum bending radii of gypsum board.

Minimum bending radii of dry gypsum board.

Board thickness		Board applied with long dimension perpendicular to framing		Board applied with long dimension parallel to framing	
in.	mm	ft.	m	ft.	m
1/2	12.7	20(1)	6.1	—	—
3/8	9.5	7.5	2.3	25	7.6
1/4	6.4	5	1.5	15	4.6

(1) Bending two 1/4" pieces succesively permits radii shown for 1/2" gypsum board.

Minimum bending radii of wetted gypsum board.(1)

Board thickness —in.	Min. radius —ft.	Length of arc —ft.(2)	No. of studs on arc and tangents(3)	Approx. stud spacing —in.(4)	Max. stud spacing —in.(4)	Water required per panel side—oz.(5)
1/4	2	3.14	9	5.50	6	30
1/4	2.5	3.93	10	5.93	6	30
3/8	3	4.71	9	7.85	8	35
3/8	3.5	5.50	11	7.22	8	35
1/2	4	6.28	8	11.70	12	45
1/2	4.5	7.07	9	11.40	12	45

(1) For gypsum board applied horizontally to a 4" partition.
(2) Arc length = 3.24R/2 (for a 90-degree arc).
(3) No. studs = outside arc length/maximum spacing +1 (rounded up to the next whole number).
(4) Stud spacing + outside arc length/no. of studs –1 (measured along outside of runner).
(5) Wet only the side of board that will be in tension. Water required per board side is based on 4' x 8' sheet.

(Courtesy United States Gypsum Corporation)

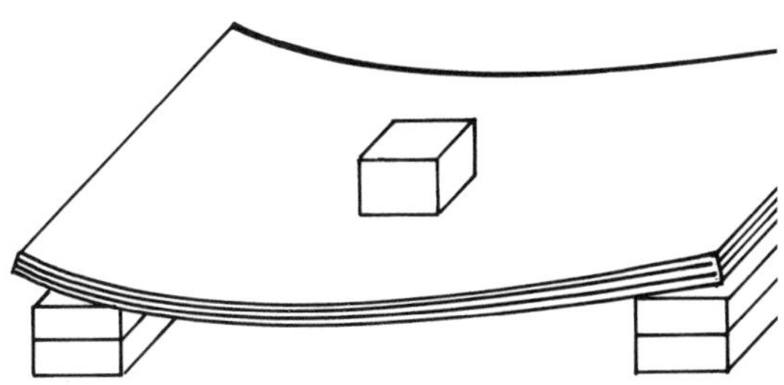

6-32 **(Above) Some permanent bow can be placed in panels by holding up the ends and placing a weight in their center.**

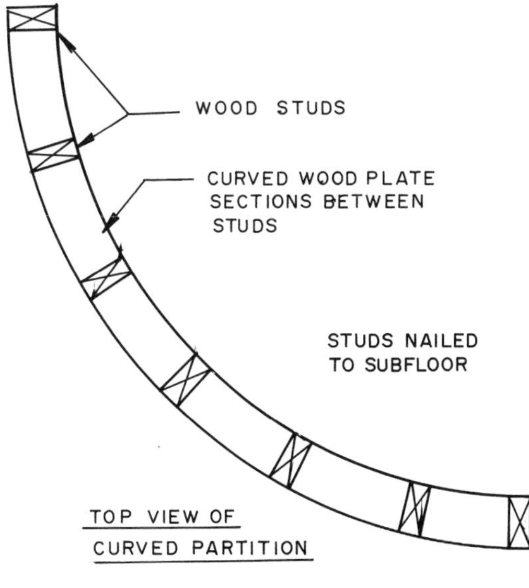

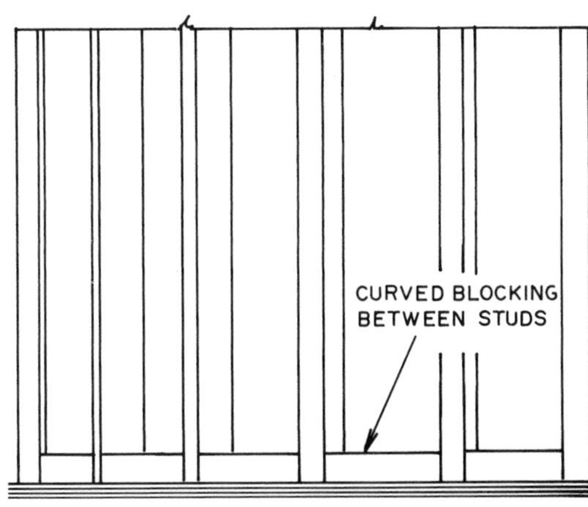

When regular gypsum wallboard is used on curved walls, the radii possible are much larger than those with flexible panels. Examples of bend radii are given in 6-31.

When standard gypsum panels are to be used, they can have a natural bend introduced by placing the ends on two objects with a weight in the center. Leave like this for a day or two. This natural bend will help when placing them on the wall (*see* 6-32).

Another technique is to dampen the back of the panel. Roll on the water with a paint roller. However, this is a bit difficult because too much water will cause the paper to loosen and then, when dry, form blisters. Let the wet panels set about an hour before installing them. Allow to dry at least 24 hours before taping.

Either wood or metal studs can be used for curved walls. When wood is used, the studs are nailed to the floor and curved wood blocking is nailed between them, serving as a bottom plate (*see* 6-33). When metal studs are used, the bottom runner is made to bend to the desired radius and the metal studs are set in the runner.

Install the panels in the same manner as other walls. Using screws can be a big help in stabilizing the installation. Be careful in nailing or screwing, because the panel will not necessarily always be flat against the stud. Nail into the edge of the stud touching the panel.

Place the fasteners no farther than 12 in. O.C. Be certain to stagger the joints on the second layer away from those on the first layer. If possible use panels that are long enough to make the curve without end joints. It is best to avoid end joints; end joints in a curve are very hard to finish.

Joints on curved walls are finished with paper tape and three coats of joint compound.

6-33 **(Left) A curved wall with wood studs can be framed by keeping them close together (*refer to* 6-28 and 6-31). Cut curved wood blocking and nail between the studs.**

6-34 Arches form a dramatic interior design feature.

INSTALLING ARCHES

Arches are widely used for interior partition openings and add a grace and beauty to the partition and the room (*see* 6-34). It is important that the carpenter properly frame the arch so an adequate nailing surface is available (*see* 6-35).

There are several materials used to cover arches.

Regular gypsum board can be used. However, it will not bend around the arch unless it is scored every 1/2, 3/4, or 1 in. on the back. The smaller the arch, the closer together the score marks. As the panel is nailed in place the score marks open, allowing the panel to round the arch (*see* 6-36).

The use of 1/4 in. **High-Flex gypsum** board permits most arches to be covered by simply bending the panel around the arch. Start fastening in the center and work toward each end. It can be lightly wetted as explained earlier, if the arch is small (*see* 6-37). Both the regular and High-Flex panels require the edge to be covered with a corner bead.

6-35 The carpenter will frame the arched opening with plywood panels and wood blocking.

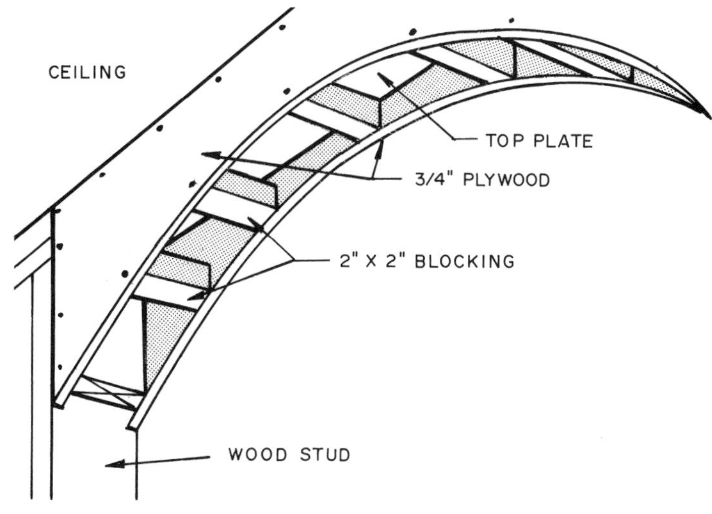

6-36 Regular gypsum wallboard will usually have to be scored on the back before it will bend around an arch.

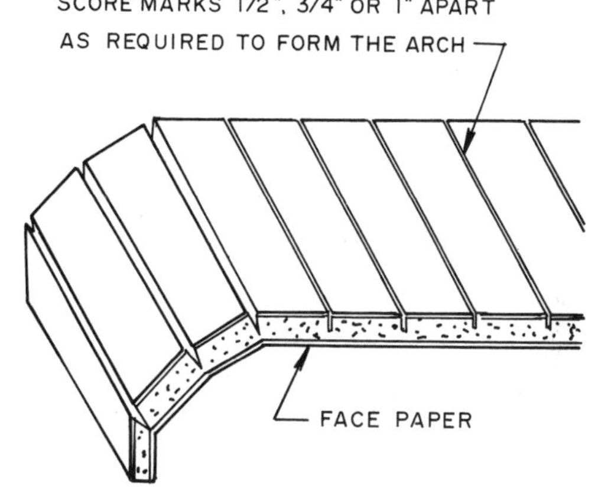

6-37 High-Flex gypsum wallboard will bend around arches as small as 30 in. when dry and 20 in. when wet.

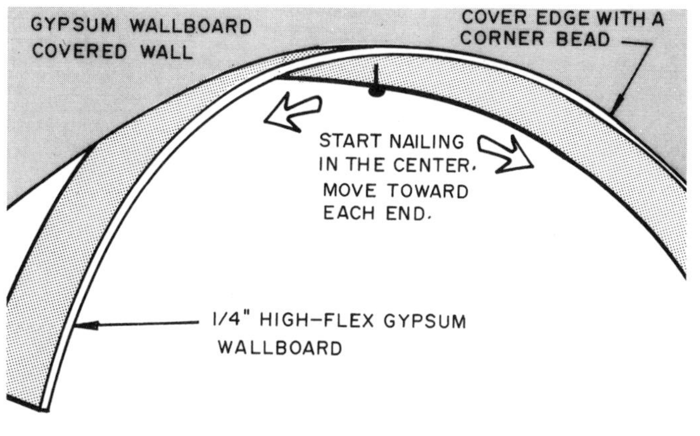

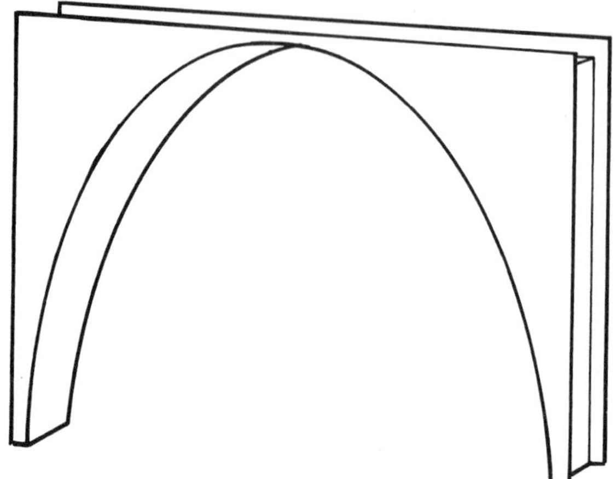

6-38 (Above) This arch form slides over the drywall walls and up into the arched area.

Another product is **plastic arch forms.** They are available in a variety of curved shapes (*see* 6-38). They are slid up over the gypsum wallboard and nailed in place. The edge is taped and finished with joint compound. Corner bead is not needed (*see* 6-39).

A fourth product is an **archway cap.** It is a vinyl covering with the flanges scored, permitting it to bend around the arch and be nailed through its flange. The flange is then taped and finished in the normal manner (*see* 6-40). The surface exposed on the interior of the arch is primed ready to be painted.

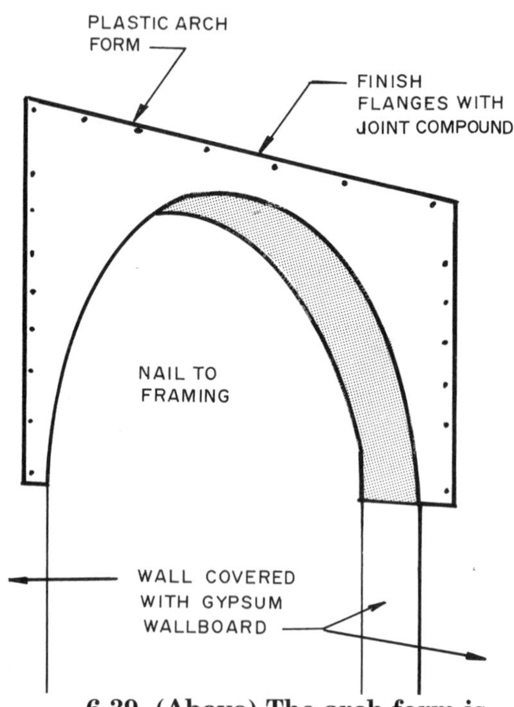

6-39 (Above) The arch form is nailed to the framing and the edges are finished with joint compound.

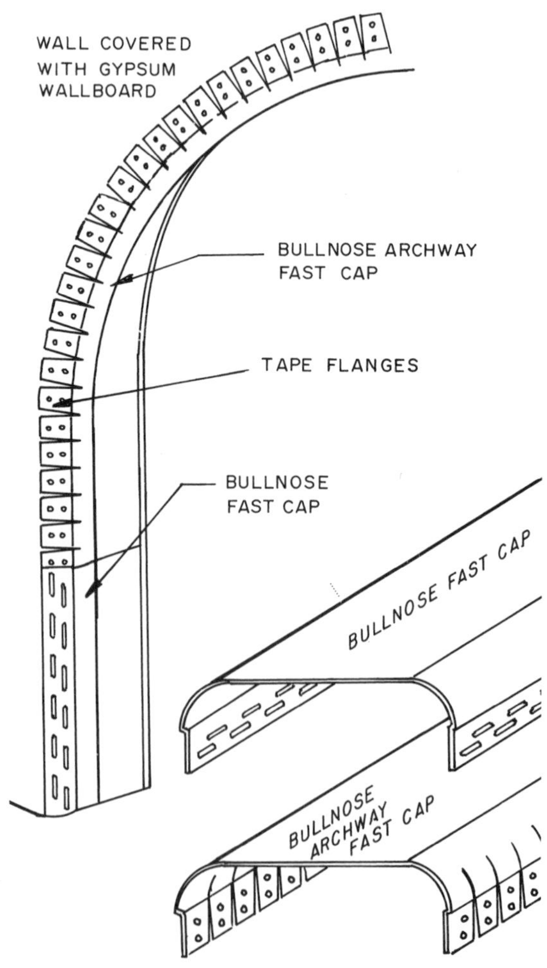

6-40 (Right) This vinyl bullnose cap quickly covers the arch opening. It is nailed to the framing and the flanges are finished with joint compound. (Courtesy Trim-Tex, Inc.)

Installing Predecorated Gypsum Panels

Predecorated gypsum panels have some form of finished surface applied during their manufacture. These are typically a vinyl or fabric covering, or a painted or other type of liquid coating applied to provide a smooth or textured surface.

Before installing the wall panels, finish the ceiling, tape, and sand it so all dust and tool work is complete. Some prefer to paint it so there is no danger of splattering the walls.

The easiest way for you to install predecorated panels is to place them in a vertical position and nail to the studs with colored nails supplied by the manufacturer. Use a plastic-headed hammer. The color helps the nails blend into the panel. The panels are typically 1/2 in. thick and the nails supplied are 1 3/8 in. long. Nail them 3/8 in. from the edge and 8 in. O.C. on the edges and in the field of the panel.

Since the panels are available in lengths of up to 10 ft. when applied vertically, no end joints occur. Cut the panels to length with a very sharp utility knife in the same manner as regular gypsum panels.

Since there can be some variation in the decorative surface you should line up a series of panels against the wall and rearrange them to get the appearance you like.

Joints are covered with a variety of moldings supplied by the manufacturer. Some examples are in 6-41. The snap-on panels have base strip that is nailed or screwed every 12 in. O.C. to the framing. The colored trim is pressed against it and snaps over the sides. These vinyl trim pieces are best cut with a fine-toothed hacksaw. The cuts can be smoothed with a fine-toothed file or sandpaper.

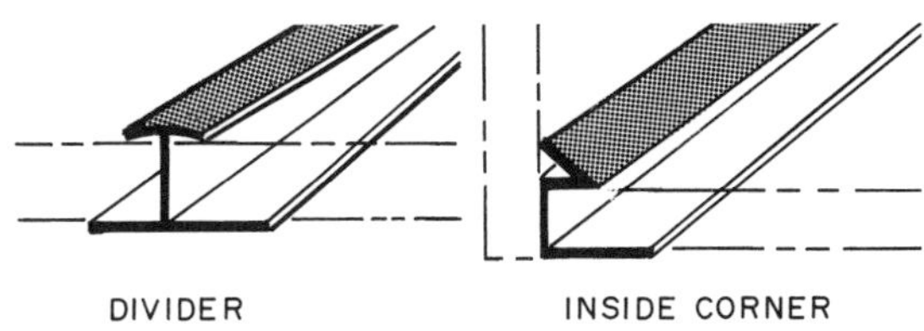

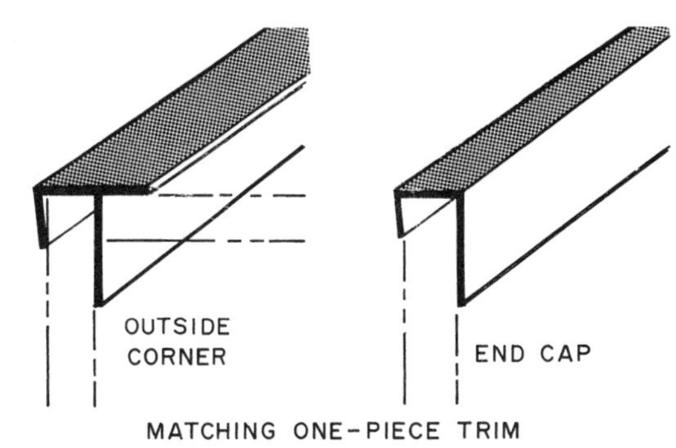

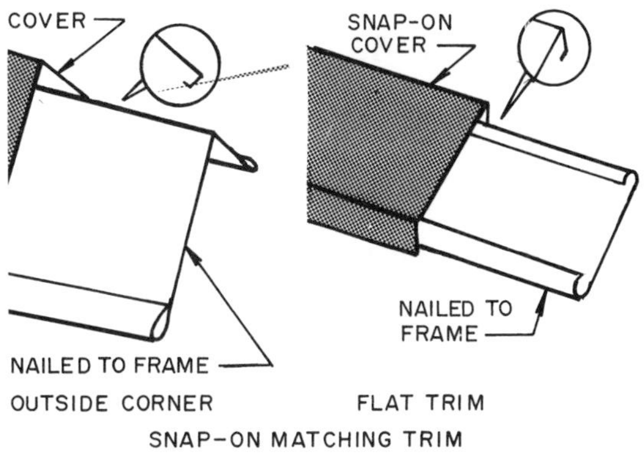

6-41 Examples of matching one-piece trim and snap-on matching trim used with predecorated drywall panels.

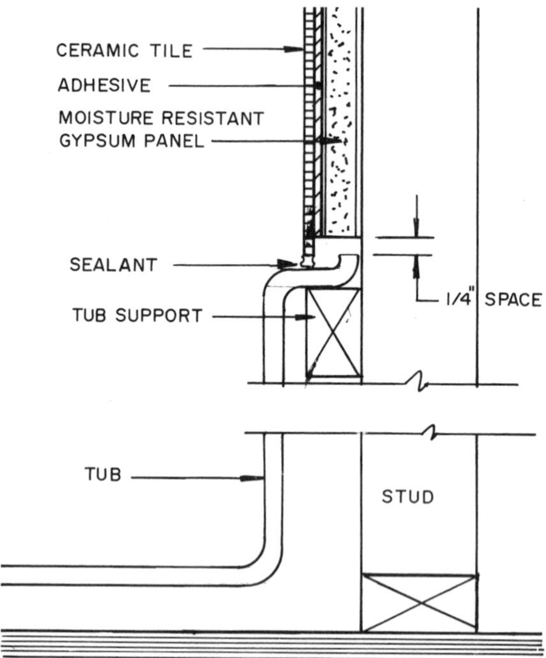

6-42 An installation detail for moisture-resistant gypsum wallboard as a base for ceramic tile around a bathtub. (Courtesy National Gypsum Company)

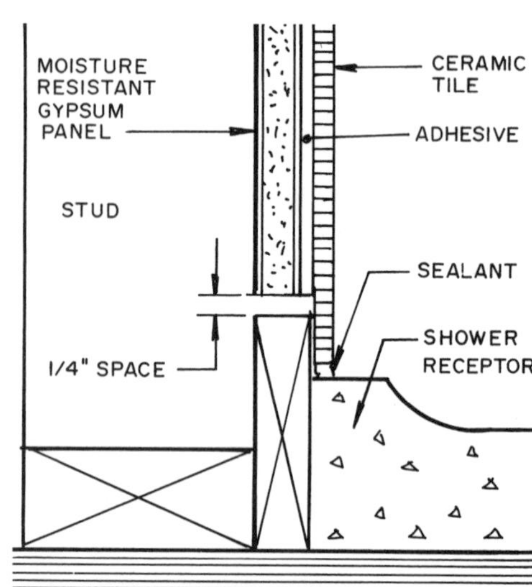

6-43 This shows the installation of moisture-resistant gypsum wallboard as a base for a shower with ceramic tile walls. (Courtesy National Gypsum Company)

Tile Wallcovering

Areas in high-moisture areas or walls to receive ceramic tile are covered with a moisture-resistant gypsum board. It should be applied horizontally with nails or screws spaced not over 8 in. O.C. and set flush with the face of the panel. All cut edges must be coated with a manufacturer-approved water-resistant adhesive. In baths and showers maintain a ¼ in. space between the lower paper-bound edge of the board and the lip of the tub or shower. Shower and tub installation details are in 6-42 and 6-43.

A bead of water-resistant adhesive is laid on the tub or shower lip, and on all corners and all openings such as where water pipes penetrate the wall. Nail and screw heads should be covered with water-resistant adhesive. Do not apply joint compound over joints or fasteners.

This series of steps is shown in 6-44.

Other products, such as cement board, are also used on a base for tile and other high-moisture installations.

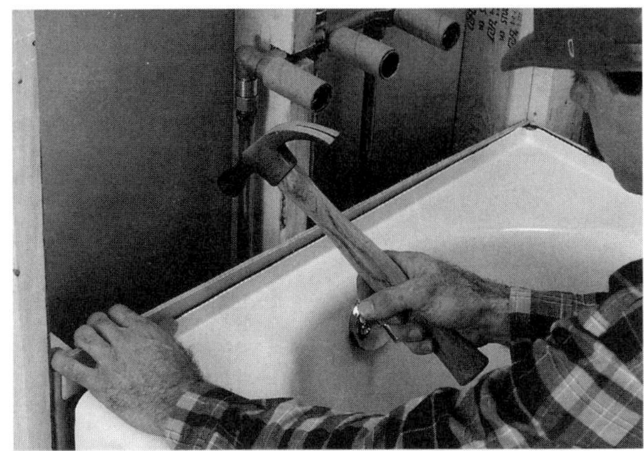

Shimming assures that the tub lip will be in the same plane as the installed moisture-resistant wallboard.

A quarter-inch shim is used to create necessary space between the wallboard and tub.

The moisture-resistant wallboard is applied to studs in the same way as gypsum wallboard.

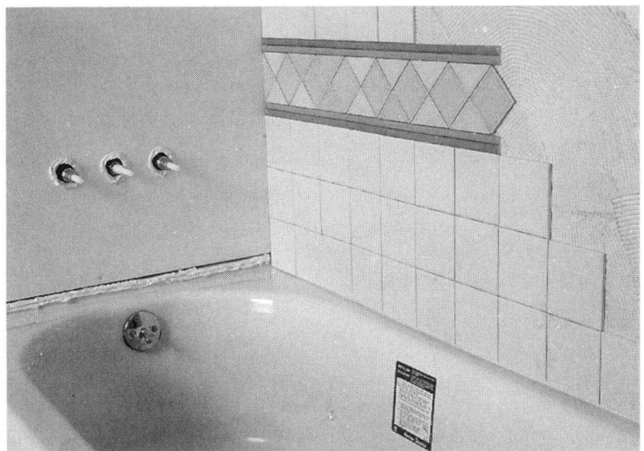

Water-resistant tile adhesive or elastomeric caulking compound is applied around cut-outs and tub lip.

6-44 (Above) Steps in installing moisture-resistant gypsum wallboard around a bathtub. (Courtesy National Gypsum Company)

Chapter 7

Installing Trim & Corner Beads

Trim and corner beads are metal or plastic strips used to finish or conceal the edges of gypsum wallboard. Proper selection and installation are critical to a professional job (*see* 7-1).

TRIM

Trim includes accessories used to cover the edges of gypsum wallboard where the edge on an opening or some other feature is exposed. The trim may be metal or plastic. The trim is placed over the gypsum panel and nails are driven through its flange, the gypsum panel, and into the stud. Nails are spaced 9 in. O.C. The flange is then finished with several coats of finishing compound. You can see some examples in 7-1.

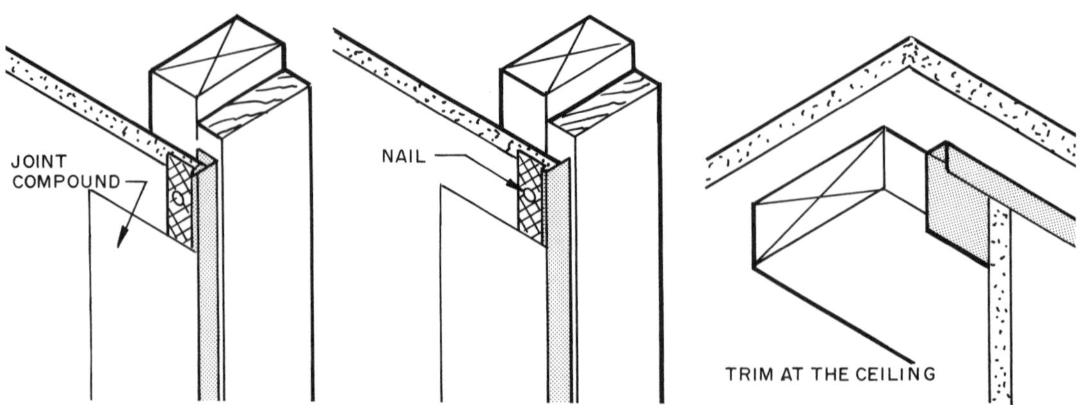

7-1 Trim can be used to cover the raw edges of gypsum board.

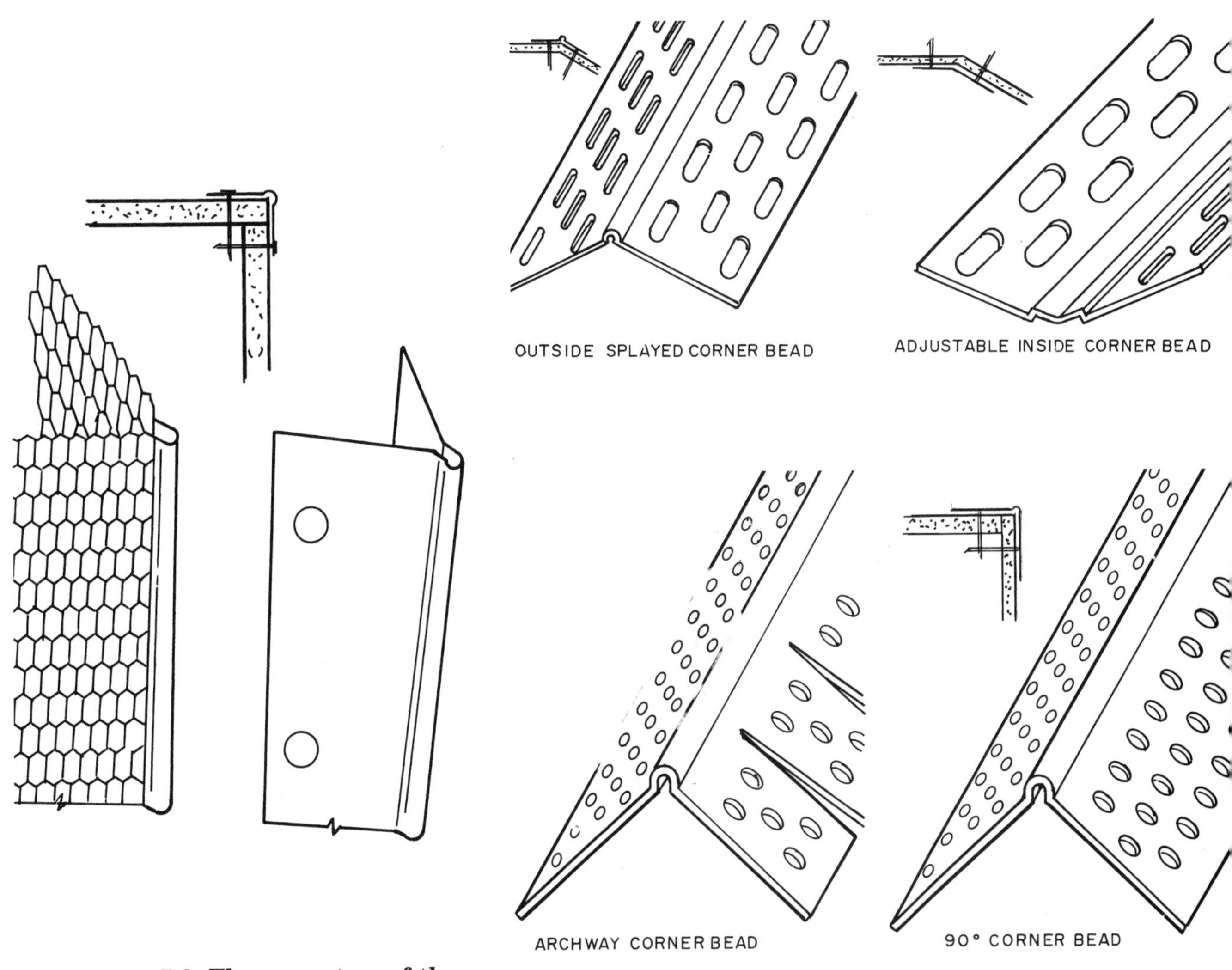

7-2 These are two of the many metal corner beads available. They are galvanized steel for 90-degree external corners.

7-3 Some of the vinyl corner beads manufactured. (Courtesy Trim-Tex, Inc.)

Corner Beads

Corner beads are used to reinforce and finish external corners on walls, soffits, pilasters, beams, and columns. Examples of those in common use are in 7-2, 7-3, and 7-4, on page 88. In 7-2 is a typical bead used on 90-degree corners.

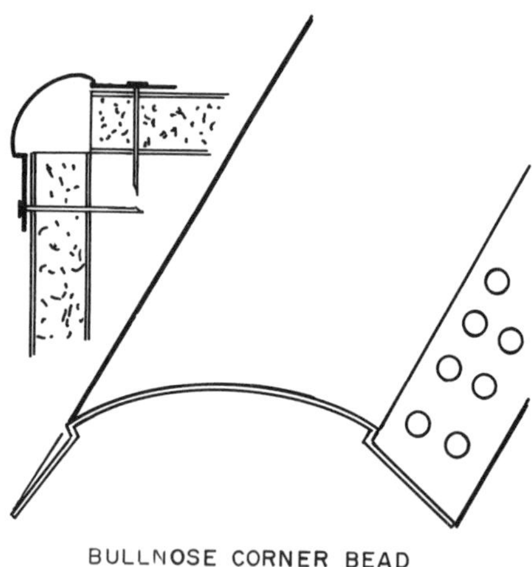

7-4 A vinyl bullnose corner bead is flexible and can be bent around a corner to form a rounded corner surface. (Courtesy Trim-Tex, Inc.)

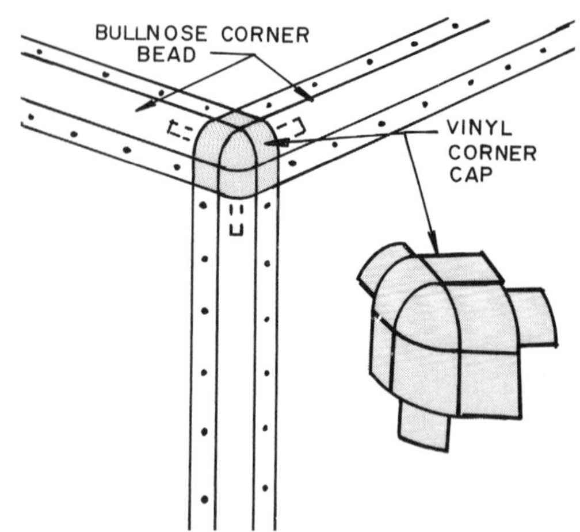

7-5 This corner cap is one of the various units used with vinyl bullnose corner beads. (Courtesy Trim-Tex, Inc.)

In 7-3, on the previous page, are vinyl beads used on arches, inside corners, splayed outside corners, and 90-degree corners. In 7-4 a vinyl bullnose bead is shown which gives a hard, smooth, rounded corner. There are a number of special units used with it to turn corners. One is shown in 7-5. Corner beads provide a hard, finished cover over the gypsum corner, which could easily be broken if struck without this protective covering.

You should use full-length strips of bead on each corner whenever possible. It is a waste of your time to piece several short pieces on a corner. The joints between the pieces are hard to get flat and you will have made a more difficult taping situation, wasting valuable time. Corner beads are typically available in 8- and 10-ft. lengths.

It is important that the gypsum board forming the corner is straight and smooth so the bead can fit up against it. The corner bead is placed against the gypsum wallboard and nailed through its flange, the wallboard, and into the stud. Nails are spaced 9 in. O.C. In some cases staples can be used. As you drive the nails, hold the bead firmly against the drywall corner panels. However, do not press so hard that the bead is forced out of its 90-degree angle. Drive the nails so they are below the rounded corner and dimple them just a little into the flange (*see* 7-6). The flanges must be below the rounded corners so that the joint compound can fill over them.

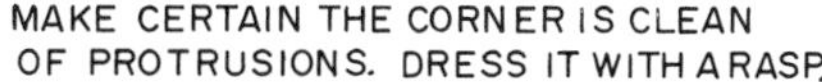

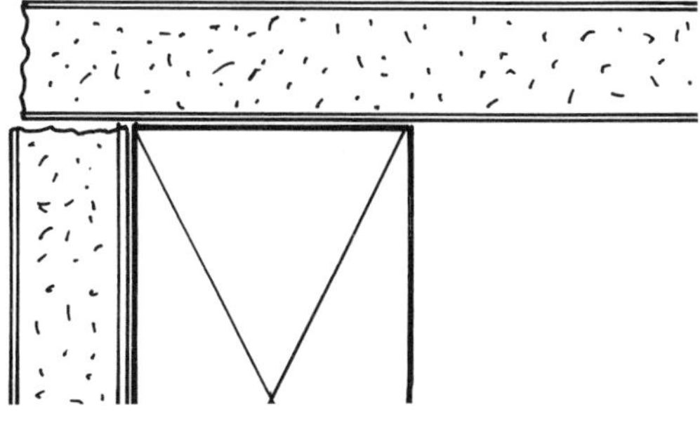

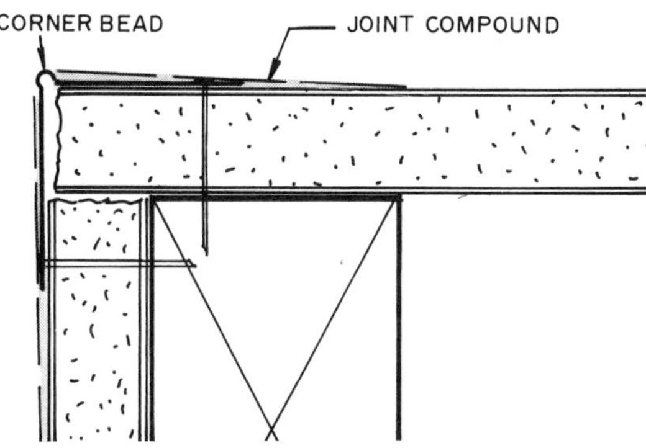

7-6 This corner bead has been installed over a clean-shaped corner and set so the joint compound can cover the nail and flange.

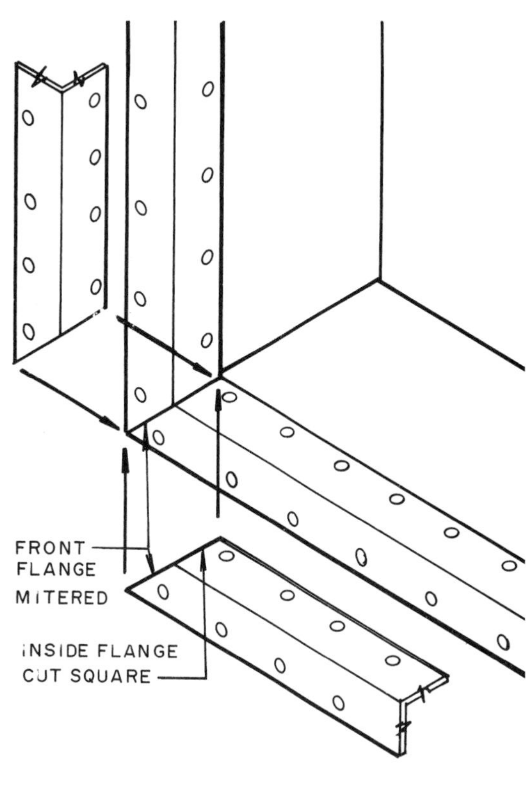

7-7 Corner beads installed around openings have the front part of the flange mitered and the part inside the opening cut square.

Some codes permit corner bead to be installed with a **clinch-on tool**. When the tool is hit with a mallet, it drives pins into the corner bead flange, which forms pins out of the metal and forces them into the gypsum. A picture of this tool is in Chapter 2.

If corner beads are installed around a wall opening, the front flange is mitered and the back flange is cut square to fit into the opening (*see* 7-7). Be certain all of the exposed edges of gypsum board are filed smooth. Protruding portions will make it impossible to set down the corner bead. Check to see that the opening has been framed square. Nail and finish in the normal manner.

If the intersecting surfaces do not form a 90-degree corner, metal corner bead cannot be used. A **flexible plastic bead** is used. It is installed like the material just discussed. See the outside splayed corner bead and the adjustable inside corner bead that are shown in 7-3, on page 87.

Arched openings require that a corner bead be applied. This gives a flexibility to bend around the arch. It is nailed in the usual manner. Plastic corner beads are available that will bend around the arch with no cutting required. One is shown in 7-3, on page 87. Vinyl arch forms and arch caps are shown in Chapter 6. When they are used they serve as the corner bead and the finished inside surface of the arch. Some types can be bonded to the drywall with a special high-tack spray adhesive. Be certain to firmly press each tab against the adhesive to get the maximum bond. Consult the manufacturer for specific recommendations.

Control Joints

When the size of the wall exceeds 30 ft. in length, or whenever the ceiling is longer than 50 ft. or has a total area of 2500 sq. ft or more, then a control joint is needed. (Information on these can be found in Chapter 6.)

Part III

Finishing

Chapter 8

Finishing Tools & Materials

After the drywall panels are securely in place it is time to begin the finishing process, which includes concealing the nails and screws and covering the joints between the panels. The materials used for this include joint compounds, joint reinforcing tape, and corner beads.

Joint Compounds

When you begin to purchase joint compound (often called mud) you will realize there is a large variety of types, each designed for specific purposes.

Drywall joint compound is available in premixed and dry forms. The dry form is a fine powder that is mixed with water. The proper amount of water is necessary to get the desired consistency. In general, it is more troublesome to mix and store than the premixed type. The premixed type comes ready to use in a strong plastic can or bucket which when properly closed will keep it in workable condition for a long time. For most people, premixed is the best type to buy (*see* 8-1).

8-1 This is a widely used ready-mixed all-purpose joint compound.

Basically, joint compounds are made up of water-soluble dispersible organic adhesives or synthetic resins. They gain strength and adhesion as they dry. As the water is lost there is some shrinkage. This is controlled by applying several thin layers of compound over the tape.

Joint compounds are subdivided into two additional types: drying and quick-setting (hardening) types. These provide a range of setting time ranging from 20 minutes to several hours.

The **quick-set** joint compounds cure rapidly and permit recoating with little time waiting for a cure. They have high strength and minimal cracking. However, they are difficult to sand and should be avoided by inexperienced workers. An exception is a powder type having a setting time of about 90 minutes. This gives an inexperienced person more time to make the application. It is available in a sandable version, so be certain to choose the one you want. Remember, it must be mixed with water to the required consistency. This can be an unwanted chore. It is especially useful, however, if you have to fill joints larger than 1/4 in. between panels. Fill them with this quick-set compound and let it harden before applying the tape compound and tape.

The **drying type** joint compounds are vinyl based and will not burn; this reinforces the fire-resistance rating of the installation. This type typically takes up to 24 hours' drying time between coats, and if possible you should allow even more time after the last coat before painting the wall. These joint compounds are of a consistency that makes them easy to apply and sand.

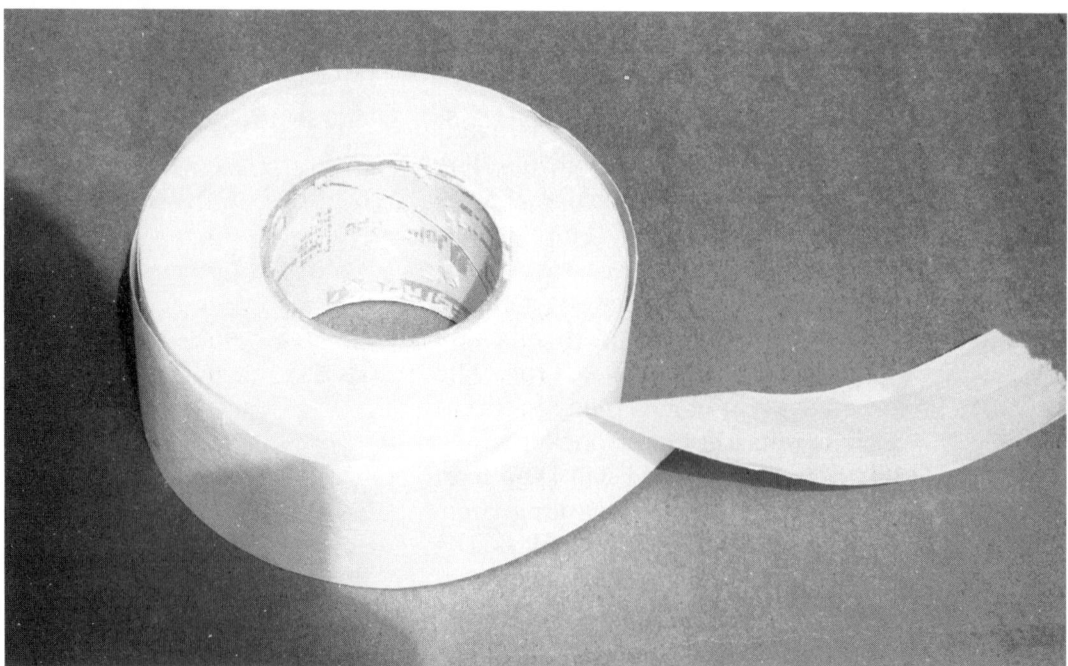

8-2 Paper joint tape reinforces the joint compound over a joint, producing a strong covering.

TYPES OF PREMIXED JOINT COMPOUNDS

Taping compounds are used to put the first coat over nails and screws, fill in the joints between panels, and bond the tape to the panel. Their adhesive properties provide a strong bond between the tape and gypsum wallboard. The taping compound is also used to laminate one panel to another in a multiple construction. It takes about 140 pounds to tape 1000 square feet of wallboard.

Topping compounds are used for the second and third coats over the taping compound and tape. While they do not contribute to the bonding of the tape, they do not shrink much and thus provide a firm crack-free finish. They are easy to apply and sand.

All-purpose joint compounds can be used for all three coats. They have adhesive properties to bond the tape in place, and there is very little shrinking or cracking after they have hardened. The inexperienced person would be wise to use premixed, all-purpose joint compound. It will give satisfactory results with the least problems.

Reinforcing Tape

Reinforcing tape is applied over the joints between panels and used to repair damaged areas. It is placed in the first layer of joint compound. This helps cover the joint and reinforces the compound, so it is less likely to crack. Tape is used on all joints between the edges and ends of panels and to reinforce inside corners.

PAPER TAPE

Paper tape is most commonly used. You will find that it is easy to handle and that it works into the joint compound with a few strokes of the taping knife. The tape has a slightly rough surface to increase the bond with the joint compound. Some types have small perforations to increase bonding strength. The tape has a crease run down the center, making it easy to fold it for use on inside corners.

Paper tape is available in 1 31/32 and 2 1/16 in. widths and is sold in 75-, 250-, and 500-ft. rolls (*see* 8-2). It takes about 370 lineal ft. to tape 1000 sq. ft. of drywall.

PREFINISHED CORNERS

Prefinished corner tape is used to finish inside and outside corners. After installation it does not require the several coats of drywall compound as does paper tape. It is ready to paint with no additional preparation. One such product, No-Coat Ultraflex, is a laminate consisting of a paper back ply, a copolymer in the center, and a paperboard front layer. It is 4 1/4 in. wide and has a molded center hinge to facilitate forming the corner.

FIBERGLASS TAPE

A strong fiberglass joint tape is available. It is made by weaving high-tensile-strength glass fibers into an open mesh. It has an adhesive backing, so you simply place it over the joint and press in place. Then the joint compound is placed over it. Fiberglass mesh is good for repairing small damaged areas with standard joint compound. If you plan to use it to tape long joints you must cover it with a quick-setting joint compound. If you plan to use drying tape joint compounds, paper tape will give a joint that is less likely to crack. For the inexperienced I would recommend using paper tape and drying type joint compound.

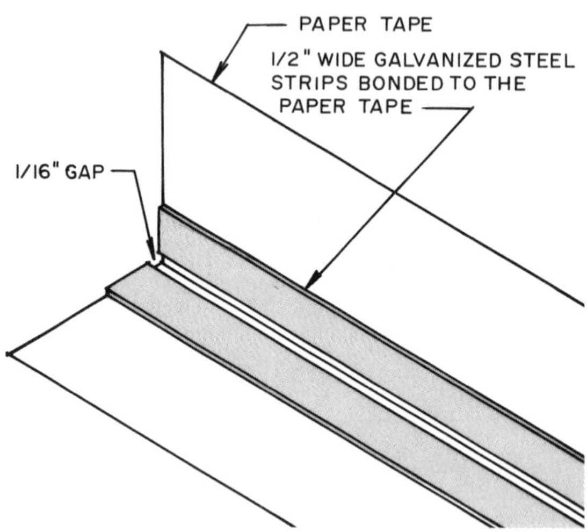

8-3 Typical flexible metal corner tape.

FLEXIBLE METAL CORNER TAPE

This is a combination of laminated paper joint tape and metal strips. It is recommended for use on inside corners or archways, drop ceilings, cathedral ceilings, kneewalls, stairways, or any inside or outside corner less or greater than 90 degrees. It is applied with the metal side to the face of the wallboard and is embedded into the joint compound (*see* 8-3).

Corner Beads

External corners are reinforced with metal or plastic corner beads (*see* 8-4). Since these corners are very likely to get bumped while the room is in use, the extra strength is needed. Paper tape will not give the corner needed for the long run. Some applications can be seen in Chapter 7. The flanges on the beads are nailed through the gypsum into the stud. Notice they are heavily perforated. This helps the joint compound to bond to them. The flexible metal tape in 8-3 is also used for corner beads.

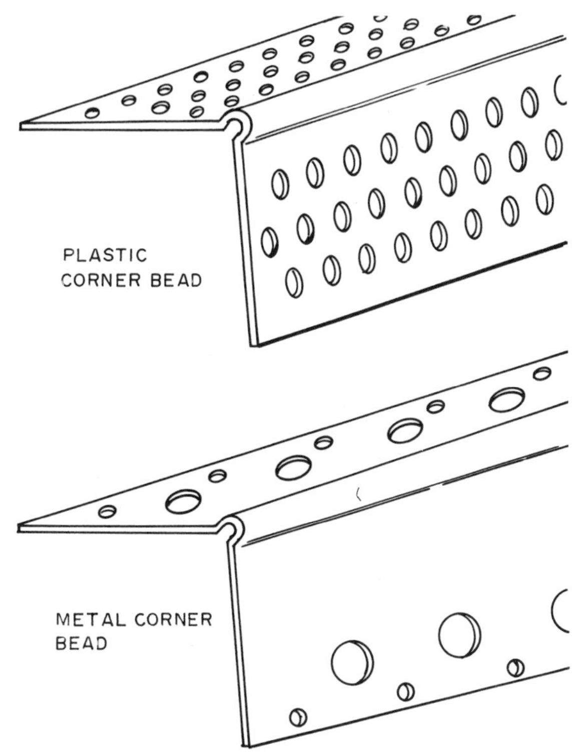

8-4 Typical plastic and metal corner beads.

Metal Trim

Metal trim is used to provide protection and neat finished edges to gypsum panels where they meet doors, windows, and intersect with panels made from other materials. (You can see some examples in Chapter 7.) Drywall manufacturers offer quite a variety of trim shapes for use on wood- and steel-framed buildings.

8-5 Joint taping knives are available with 4-, 5-, and 6-in. wide blades. (Courtesy Kraft Tool Company)

8-6 Finishing knives are available in widths from 6 in. to 14 in. (Courtesy Kraft Tool Company)

Finishing Tools

Possibly the most important finishing tool is a set of high-quality taping and finishing knives. The best have steel blades. Plastic-bladed knives are available. Experience with them is about the only way to see which you prefer.

You will need a 6 in. joint taping knife that is used to apply the filler coats of joint compound over the nail, screws, and joints (*see* 8-5) as well as 8-, 10-, and 12-in. finishing knives for spreading the finish coats over the tape coat (*see* 8-6).

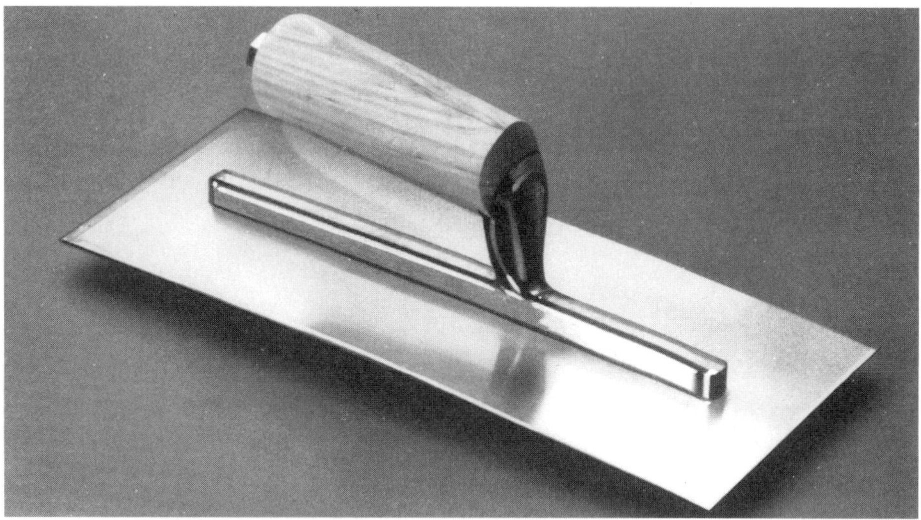

8-7 Drywall trowels have stainless steel blades ranging from 12 to 16 in. long. (Courtesy Kraft Tool Company)

8-8 These inside and outside corner finishing tools smooth both sides of the corner with one pass. (Courtesy Kraft Tool Company)

A 12-in. curved joint finishing trowel is used to finish the end butt joints, because they have a crown finish over the joint and this curved blade lets you lay it in properly (*see* 8-7).

Some drywall finishers like to use a corner joint finishing trowel (*see* 8-8). Using this trowel speeds up taping the corner because it can smooth both sides with only one stroke.

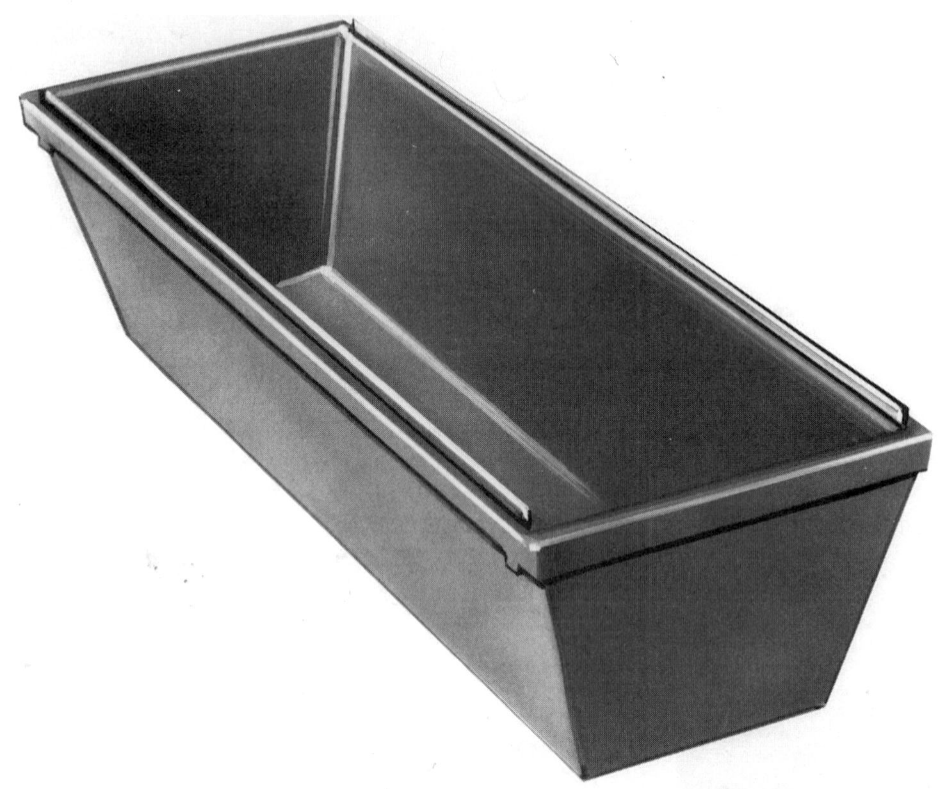

8-9 A mud pan is used to hold a supply of joint compound from which the taper gets the material to coat the joint. (Courtesy Goldblatt Tool Company)

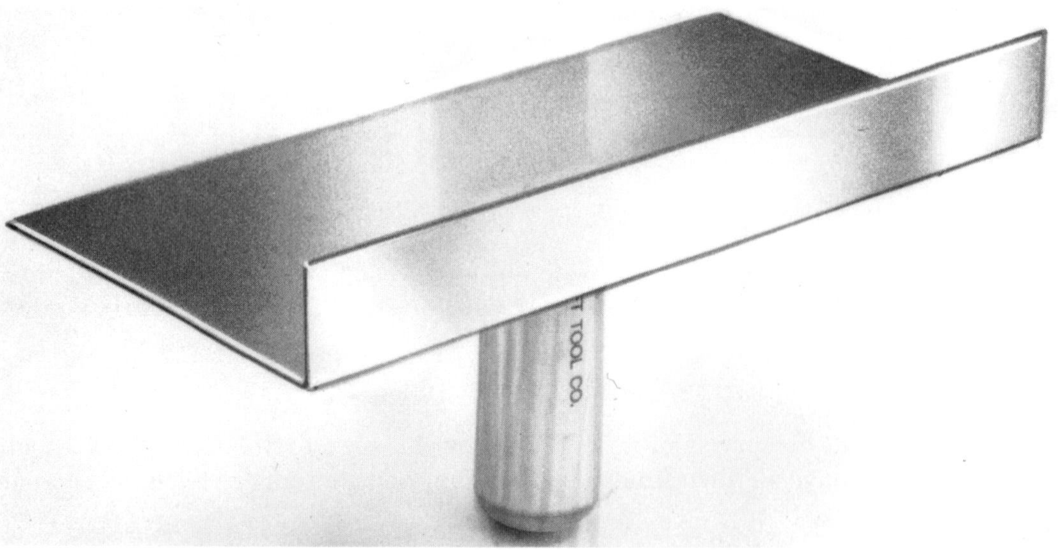

8-10 The drywall mud holder is held by the finisher and holds a small supply of joint compound for immediate use. (Courtesy Kraft Tool Company)

8-11 The wallscraper is a wide blade with a long handle. It is used to scrape excess compound from walls and ceilings. (Courtesy Kraft Tool Company)

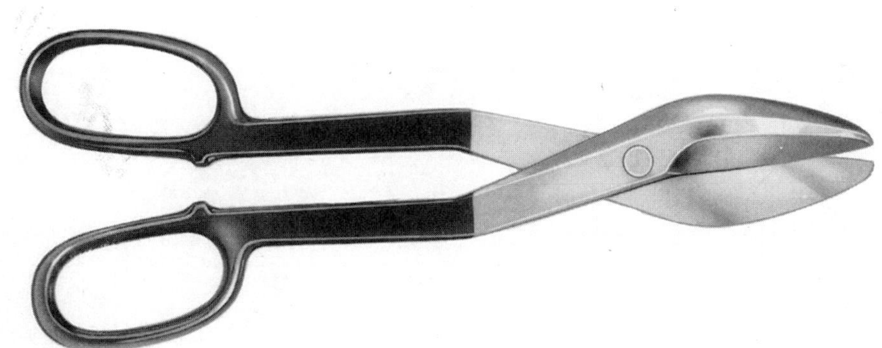

8-12 Tin snips are used to cut metal corner beads so they can be formed around a curved outside corner. (Courtesy Goldblatt Tool Company)

A mud pan is needed to hold the joint compound. The tape knife moves the compound from the pan to the wall (see 8-9).

The mud holder in 8-10 is carried by the taper. It stores a limited amount of compound for immediate use.

Excess compound on the walls and ceiling can be scraped away with the wallscraper in 8-11.

Some type of tin snips or aviation snips are needed to cut the metal and plastic beads and trim. Many finishers seem to prefer aviation snips (see 8-12).

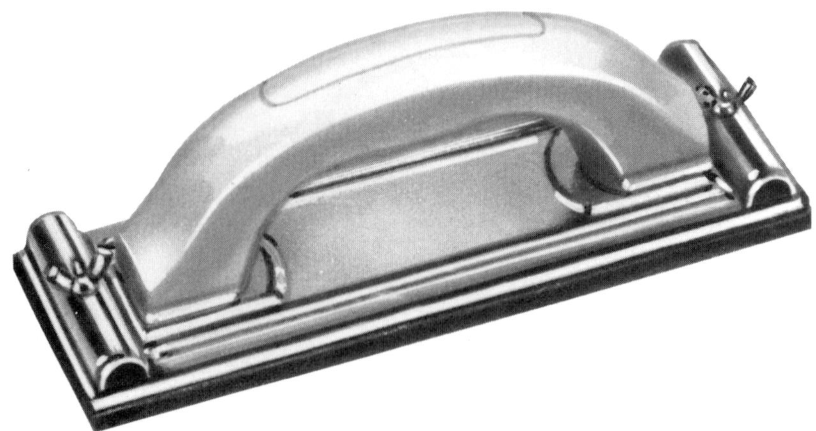

8-13 This hand sander has a comfortable handle, is made from lightweight aluminum, and has clamps that hold the sandpaper against the rubber bottom. (Courtesy Kraft Tool Company)

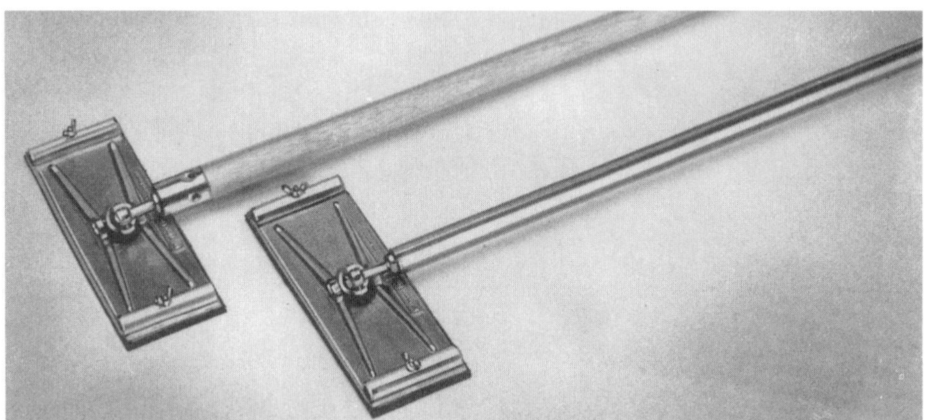

8-14 Pole sanders have aluminum bases with a rubber pad upon which the sandpaper is clamped. They have a long pole connected to the pad with a swivel. (Courtesy Kraft Tool Company)

Sanding Tools

Tools used for sanding include a hand sander, pole sander, sanding sponges, sanding screens, and carbide sandpaper.

The hand sander is about 3 in. x 9 in. It has clamps on each end to hold the sanding abrasive material (*see* 8-13).

A pole sander has a flat pad connected to a long pole, letting you reach the top of the wall and, in some cases, the ceiling from the floor (*see* 8-14).

A commercial sanding machine with a wet/dry vacuum greatly reduces the dust in the air (*see* 8-15).

8-15 This sanding tool is connected to a vacuum that pulls most of the gypsum dust out of the air. (Courtesy Hyde and Meeks Industries, Inc.)

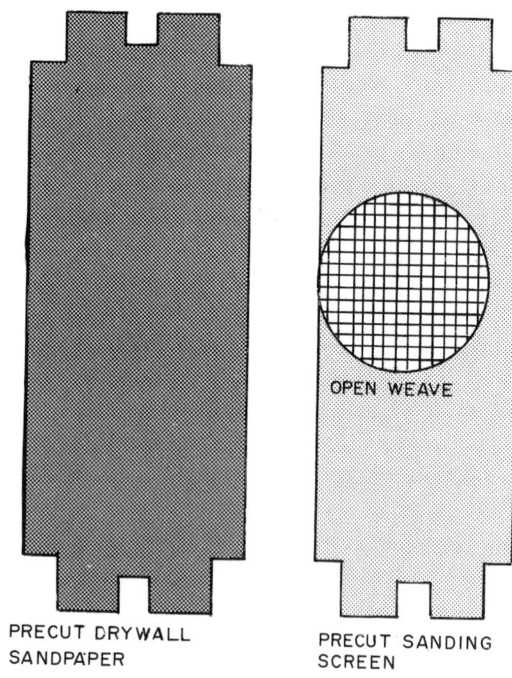

8-16 Drywall sandpaper and sanding screens are sold precut to fit the hand and pole sanders.

Sanding screens are carbide-grit-coated fiberglass mesh. Both sides are abrasive-coated and can be used until they wear out. The screen (mesh) has holes due to the mesh, which enable the dust to fall through and thus not clog the surface. Screens are available in degrees of coarseness from 120 to 200. The larger the grit number, the finer the abrasive. Sanding screens cost more than drywall sandpaper but last longer and cut faster (*see* 8-16).

Drywall sanding paper has a tough paper backing with a black carbide-grit surface. It is available in 80, 100, 120, 150 grit. The higher the grit number, the finer the abrasive. The fine abrasives are used for the final finish sanding. The coarser grits are used for the first sanding, to remove excess compound rapidly.

Sanding sponges are used if you decide to wet-sand the compound. They are a high-density polyurethane sponge that has a soft, nonabrasive surface. They are wetted and used to lightly blend in the feathered edges. They are not used on ridges, lumps, or other larger defects needing smoothing.

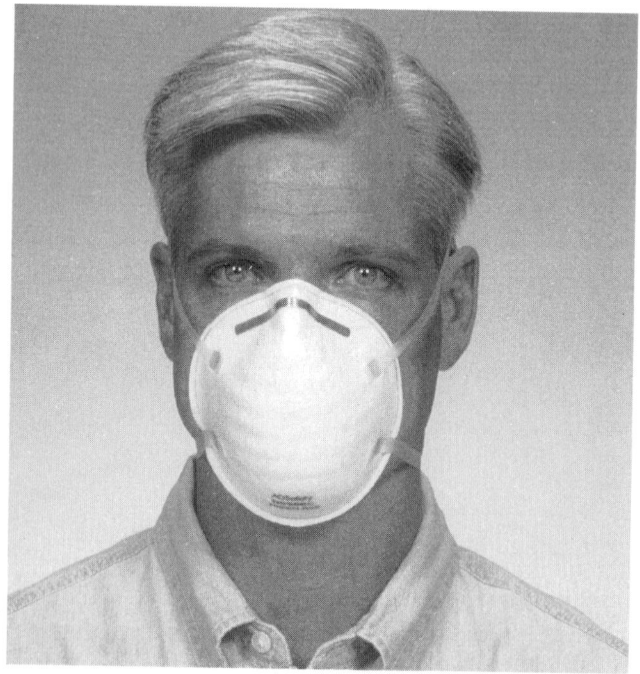

8-17 This is a low-cost, low-quality dust mask. If you use one replace it frequently. (Courtesy Aearo Company)

8-18 This is a higher-quality dust mask with a replaceable filter. Keep a supply of filter replacements. (Courtesy Willson Safety)

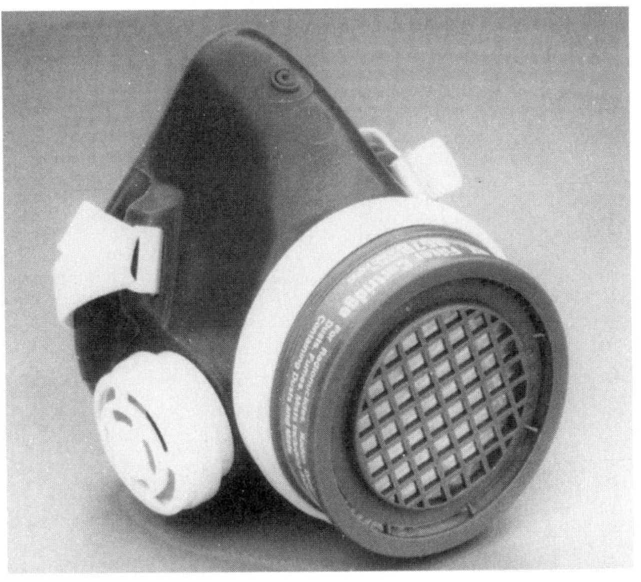

8-19 Another type of dust mask that is very effective in eliminating dust particles from your lungs. (Courtesy Aearo Company)

Dust Protection

A high-quality dust mask is essential. The thin throw-away types are inadequate. Your health is too important to risk lung contamination with an inadequate filter (*see* 8-17, 8-18, and 8-19).

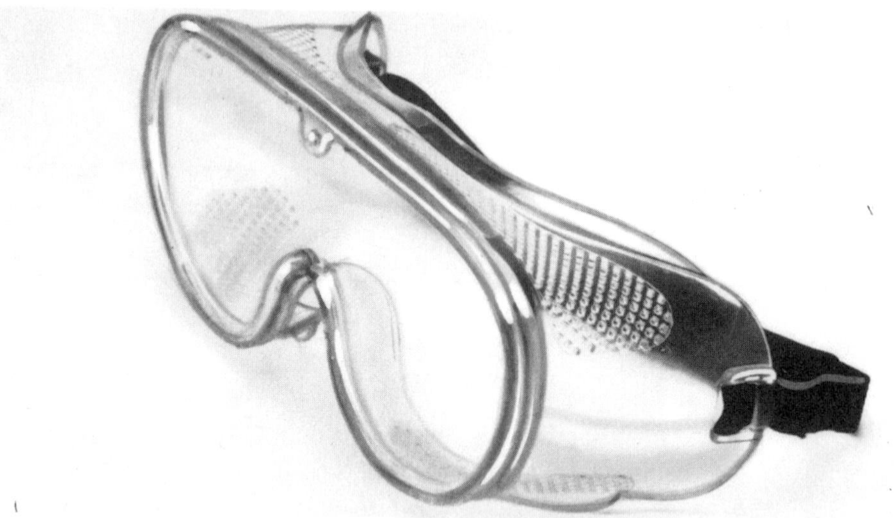

8-20 Tight-fitting goggles are needed to protect your eyes from sanding dust. (Courtesy Kraft Tool Company)

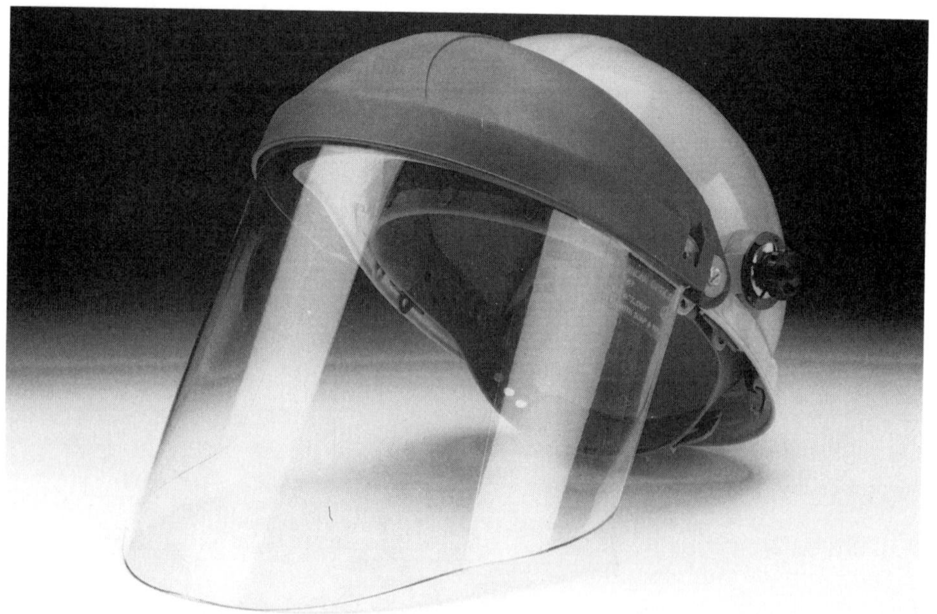

8-21 A full face mask worn with a hard hat will provide excellent protection when sanding overhead. (Courtesy Willson Safety)

Good-quality goggles are also necessary to keep your eyes from dust (*see* 8-20). Overhead sanding is a special problem when you must avoid dust in your face and hair. The full face mask with a hard hat as shown in 8-21 will provide excellent protection.

8-22 Plastic dust doors will keep the sanding dust within the room. This shows how the door can be opened to permit passage between rooms when necessary. (Courtesy Strom Closures)

Sanding also tends to let gypsum dust filter into adjoining rooms. Dust doors can be installed on all openings to contain the dust in the room being sanded. One type is shown in 8-22.

Chapter 9

Finding & Correcting Defects

Many problems that may affect the final quality of the finished wall can be present well before the drywall installers begin their work. Defects can be introduced as the carpenter frames the walls and ceilings. These problems need to be caught and corrected before the drywall process is begun. The general contractor should be informed about these so that the proper workmen can return to the site and make corrections. In addition to framing, the electrical, plumbing, and mechanical contractors need to do their job correctly. Following are some things to look for and possible corrections.

Panel Damage

Before installing gypsum drywall check to be certain that the material you have is in good condition. Improper handling and storage can render gypsum wallboard panels useless or at least in need of some remedial repair action. Following are things you should check.

DAMAGED EDGES

Improper handling may result in damage edges and broken corners to the gypsum drywall. This type of damage tears the paper and crushes the core. Before using these panels cut off the damaged section.

WATER DAMAGE

If the panels get wet, it is possible that the paper will come lose from the gypsum and that the gypsum core may even soften. Dry those panels that seem to still have the paper glue bond intact and a hard core. If greater damage has occurred, discard the panel.

MILDEW

Panels stored under moist conditions or that have accidently been wet will tend to have a growth of mildew. This can be prevented by storing panels in a dry area. If they have mildew separate them, carefully clean the paper with a mix of 1 cup of bleach and 3 cups of water. Do not scrub hard enough to damage the paper. Place flat with wood strips between each panel so air can circulate to dry the panel.

FRAMING PROBLEMS

Many of the problems that occur when installing drywall or that occur some time after the job is finished are due to framing defects.

BOWED STUDS

Before starting to install the drywall, check the studs and ceiling joists to be certain they are in the same plane. Run a chalkline down the wall or ceiling joists. This quickly shows if something is out of line. If a stud is bowed it can be straightened by cutting into the concave side of the bow and driving a wedge into the cut (*see* 9-1). This wedging will correct small bows. Generally, the best solution is to replace the stud.

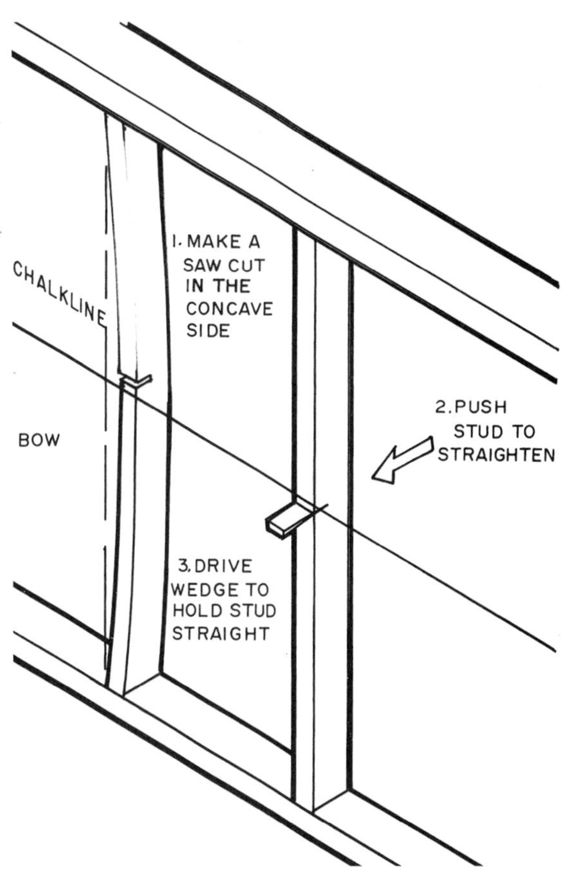

9-1 Run a chalkline to check for bowed studs. Straighten those slightly bowed by driving a wood wedge in a saw cut made in the concave side of the bow.

STUDS OUT OF ALIGNMENT

This often occurs when the stud is not placed flush on the bottom or top plate (*see* Chapter 5 for nailing problems). When gypsum wallboard is nailed to this, nails will puncture through the panel or the panel will fracture due to the hammer blow. If the misalignment is small (1/8 in.) remove problem fasteners and only nail at a place where the panel touches the stud.

THE FRAME PROTRUDES BEYOND THE STUDS

As shown in Chapter 5, parts of the framing such as fire stops between studs or bridging between floor joists occasionally extend beyond the stud. This holds the gypsum panel out from the wall. The wallboard will not fit tight and nails will generally tear through the paper and even fracture the gypsum core. These defects must be made flush with the studs or joists before installation starts.

TWISTED FRAMING MEMBERS

Any time a framing member, as a stud, is not nailed square, some part of it will protrude beyond the line of the wall (*see* Chapter 5). Also the same thing can happen with warped stock. These should be straightened before installing the drywall. Warped members should be replaced. If the warping (due to improperly dried lumber) occurs after the wall is finished, do not bother to make repairs until the house has gone through one heating season. When you think they have stabilized, remove the problem fasteners and replace with screws. Drive them carefully so you do not crush the core.

DEFECTS DUE TO FASTENERS

Possibly the most common defect in a drywall installation is improper nailing. It is well worth your time to slow down just a little and get each fastener in straight and with the proper degree of tightness. These are the major cause of nail-pops.

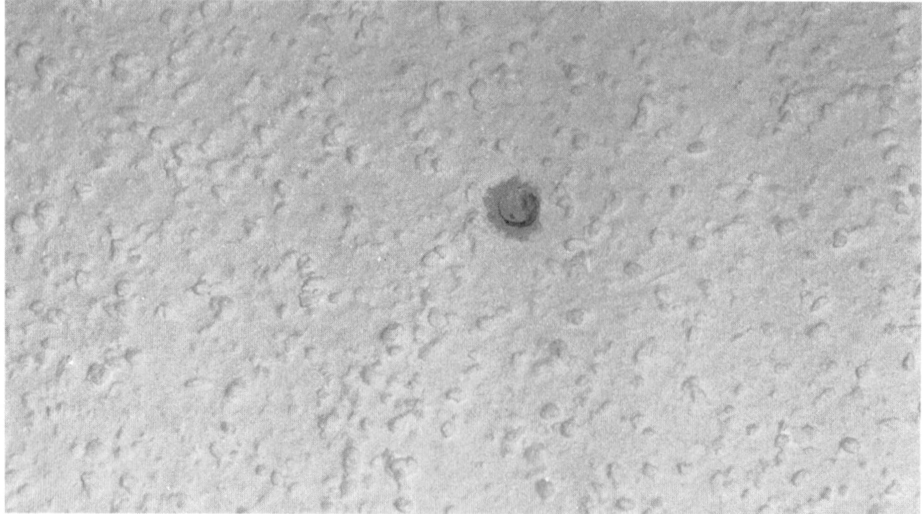

9-2 Nail-pops produce an unsightly spot on the panel. They are usually due to improper installation.

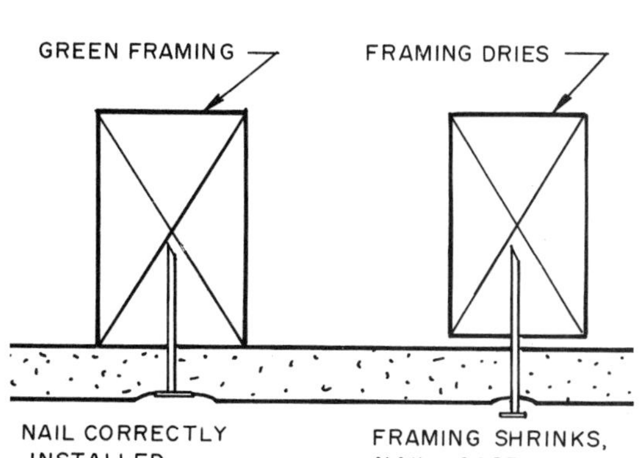

9-3 (Above) Green studs shrink as they dry, producing a loose panel that can cause the nail to pop through the gypsum coating.

9-4 (Right) This electrically driven automatic screw delivery tool will rapidly drive screws and produce the proper dimple for covering the screw. (Courtesy Grabber Construction Products)

NAIL-POPS

Nail-pop refers to when the head of a nail pops through the face of the joint compound, creating a defect (*see* 9-2). These are caused by many of the problems just mentioned: stress, improperly driven nails, and loose panels. The major cause of pops is lumber shrinkage. Pops occurring several months after the walls have been completed are usually due to lumber shrinkage (*see* 9-3). One way to correct this defect is to place the blade of an old finishing knife over the nail and hit it with a hammer to try to set it flush. Do not set it so hard it breaks the gypsum core. It is usually best to drive another nail or screw about 1 in. from the defective one. Screws will give you the best repair and reduce possible future nail-pops. The tool shown in 9-4 quickly drives screws and produces the proper dimple, simplifying the recoating of the nail pop and the new screw. After removing any loose compound or paper, recoat both nail heads.

DEPRESSED NAILS

Nails that are dimpled too deeply or driven when framing defects have not been corrected typically break the paper on the panel. This is sometimes caused when too few nails are used and the weight of the panel tends to pull them through the surface. Remove the depressed nails if this can be done without breaking the gypsum core. Then renail the entire panel. Consider double-nailing as an extra precaution. (*See* Chapter 5 for more on nailing problems.)

RUPTURING THE FACE PAPER

There are any number of reasons that the face paper may be broken. Carelessly driven nails, too deep dimpling, or improper framing are common causes. Sometimes the panel is not held tight to the framing and a hammer blow will break the paper. Often when the face paper is ruptured, the core is also broken. This gives the panel almost no support.

Remove the faulty nails and then renail. Be sure to keep the wallboard tight to the framing and drive the nail straight. Be careful to set the head in a very shallow dimple.

POUNDING

Sometimes when the second side of a wall is being nailed, the pounding can jar and loosen the nails on the other side. If you hold the panel tight when nailing this is less likely to happen. After both sides have been nailed, go over those loose carefully to reset and dimple them. If screws or adhesive are used, the panels are less likely to come loose. You may want to double-nail close to a loose nail in a single-nail application.

LOOSE SCREWS

Since the screwgun can have the proper torque set, it is not likely that loose screws occur. However, if the gun is not set properly or the wallboard is not held firmly against the wall, this will occur. Recheck for loose screws and reset them with a screwgun that has been properly adjusted.

LOOSE PANELS

Loose panels are caused when the fasteners are driven and the panels are not held tight against the framing. Before giving the nail or screw its final setting, press the panel firmly against the framing.

BULGES AROUND THE FASTENERS

Bulges can occur around a fastener if it is driven too deep, the wrong tool is used, or the facing paper and core are damaged by a loosely installed panel.

When joint cement is placed over this damaged area it tends to swell, creating an unwanted bulge. If possible, remove the improperly driven fastener, drive one or more screws on each side, and clean out the damaged core and loose paper. Then coat with joint compound.

IMPROPER PANEL FITS

If a panel is a bit too long and you try to force it between two panels or a panel and framing, it will tend to bow (*see* 9-5). It will not have firm contact with the framing. It is not possible to properly nail this panel, and nail-pops or a crushed panel core are certain to occur. Always cut the panel a bit shorter than the space to be covered. Panels that have already been installed—but are too long—must be removed and new ones set in place.

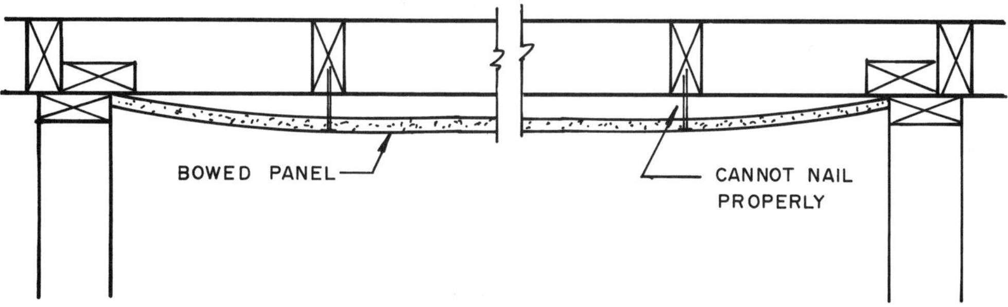

9-5 Gypsum panels that are too long will tend to bow, producing nail-pops. (Courtesy United States Gypsum Corporation)

SAGGING PANELS

Panels can begin to sag some months after installation due to the excessive weight of insulation or a textured ceiling or excessive humidity or wetting from some other cause. Using panels that are too thin or not designed for use on the ceiling will eventually lead to sag.

To correct remove the panel, replace with the proper panel thickness and double-nail. Consider using high-strength gypsum ceiling panels designed to resist sag. The ceiling can be furred down and completely recovered. In any case the weight causing the sag must be handled in some way to prevent a recurrence.

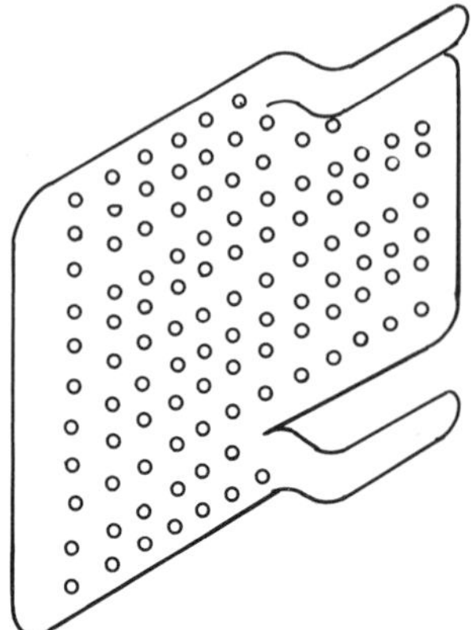

9-6 (Left) A metal clip used to hold repair patches in holes in gypsum drywall.

9-7 (Below) A typical procedure for installing a repair patch using metal support clips.

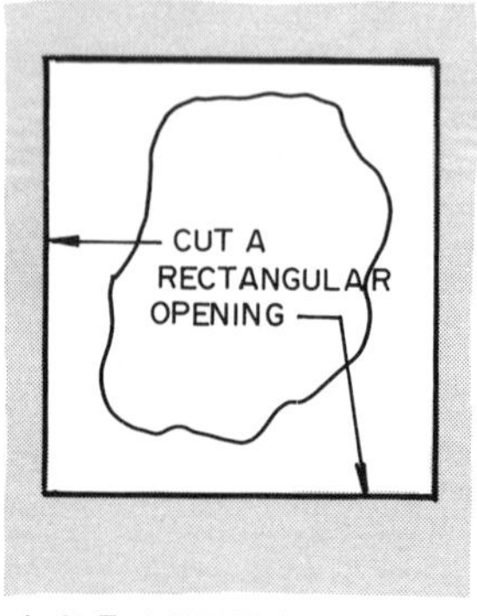

1. CUT A RECTANGULAR OPENING AROUND THE HOLE.

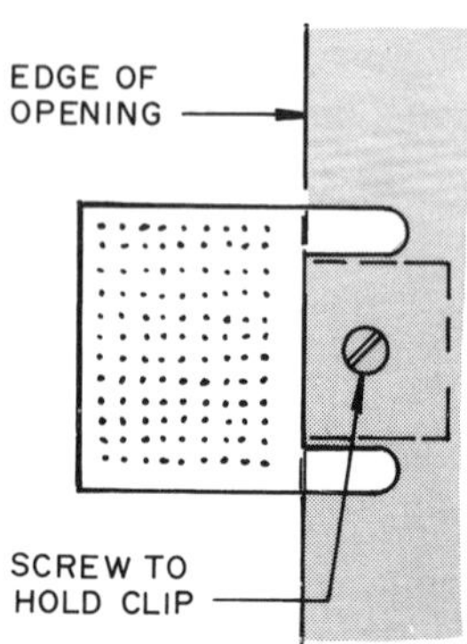

2. SLIP THE CLIP OVER THE EDGE OF THE OPENING AND SECURE WITH SCREWS.

Joint Problems

The visible defects on a finished panel occur at the taped joints or the heads of fasteners. Proper installation over adequate framing will reduce these defects to a minimum. Following are some typical examples.

RUPTURED PANELS

Occasionally during construction and often after the building is occupied, the gypsum wallboard will receive a blow that fractures the surface, causing a hole. There are a number of ways these can be repaired. Possibly the easiest way for the homeowner to repair a ruptured spot is to buy a repair kit at the local building supply store.

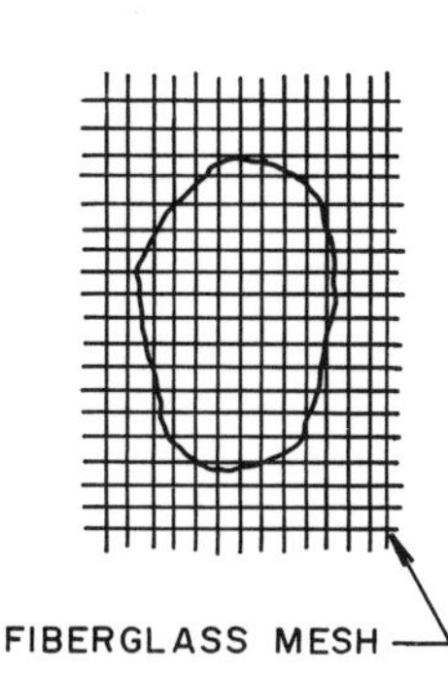

1. PRESS THE ADHESIVE SIDE OF THE FIBERGLASS PATCH TO THE WALL.

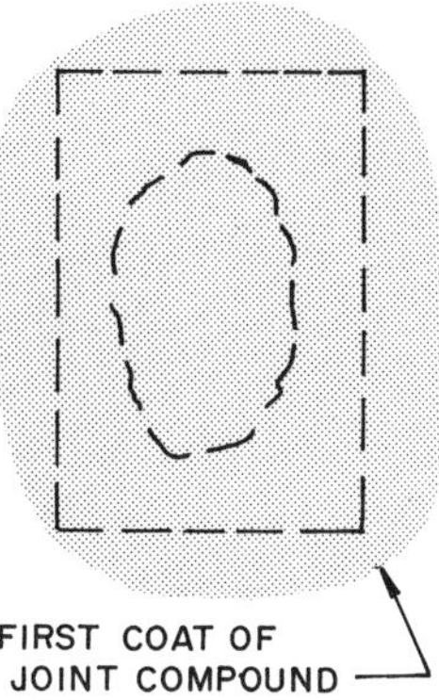

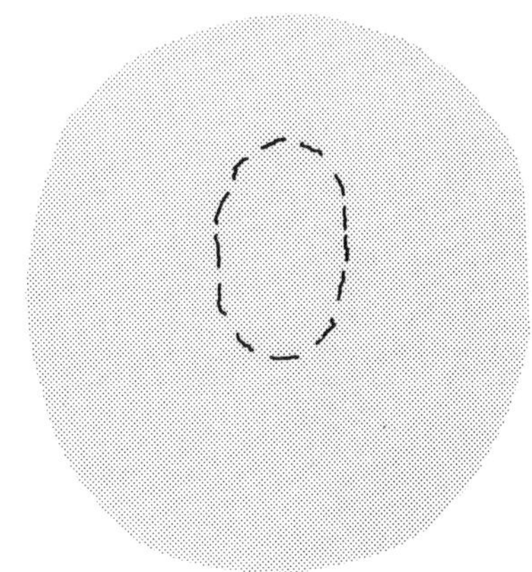

3. APPLY 2 OR 3 THIN FINISH COATS FEATHERING EACH OUT WIDER. WHEN DRY SAND TO A SMOOTH FINISH.

9-8 Small holes can be repaired using an adhesive-backed fiberglass patch that is covered with joint compound in the normal manner.

One variety of repair kit uses metal clips secured to the edges of the opening after cutting them straight and clean. Cut a square or rectangular opening, install the clips. Cut a gypsum wallboard patch to fit the opening. Screw through the patch into the clip and finish the joints in a normal manner (*see* 9-6 and 9-7).

Another product uses a fiberglass tape patch with an adhesive back. Remove any loose core material and face paper from the patch. Press the adhesive back side of the tape over the hole. Apply a coat of joint compound over the entire patch. When dry, sand and apply 2 or 3 thin finishing coats in the normal manner. After the final coat, lightly sand to a smooth surface (*see* 9-8).

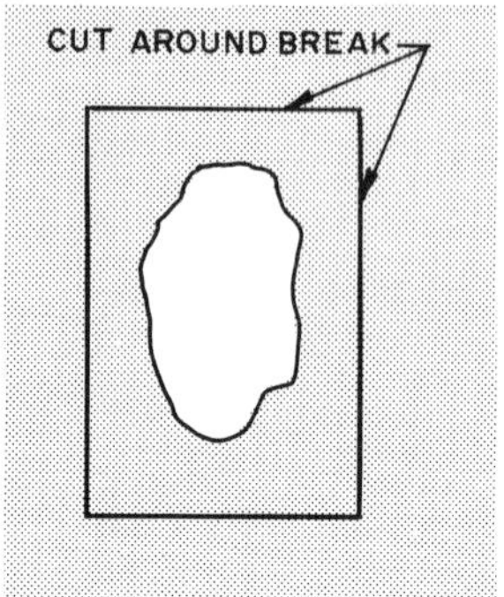

1. MARK THE OUTLINE OF THE PATCH AND CUT ON A 45° ANGLE.

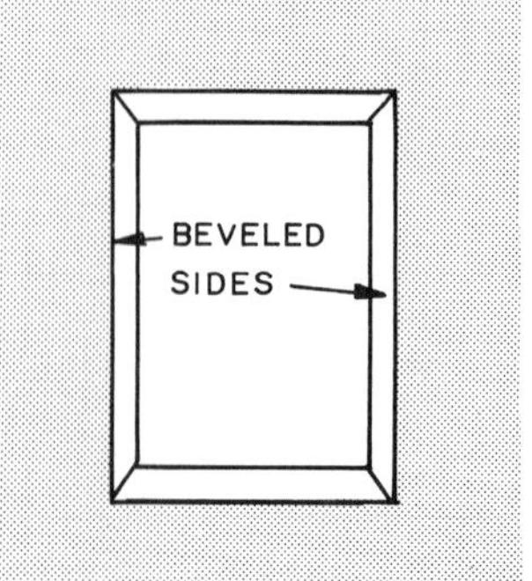

2. THIS PRODUCES THIS OPENING WITH BEVELED SIDES. SMOOTH THE FACE OF THE BEVEL.

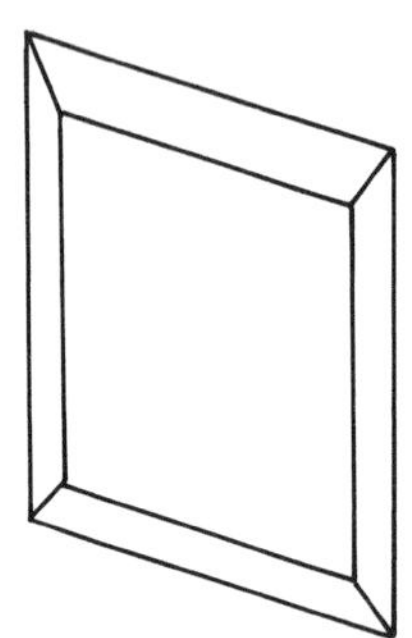

3. THE PATCH IS CUT WITH 45° BEVELED SIDES. IT MUST EXACTLY FIT THE OPENING.

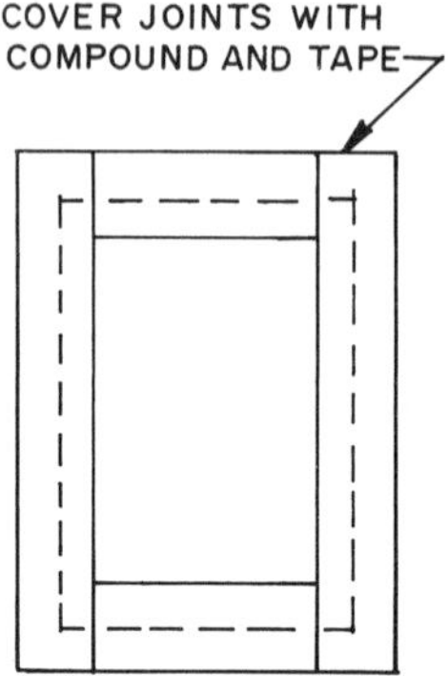

4. PUT JOINT COMPOUND ON THE BEVELED SIDES OF THE OPENING AND SET THE PATCH IN PLACE. COVER THE JOINTS WITH COMPOUND AND TAPE.

9-9 This patch requires that you bevel the edges of the hole and the edges of the patch.

Another repair procedure is shown in 9-9. Mark a rectangular section around the damage and cut on this line on a 45-degree angle. Smooth the edges of these cuts on the sides of the opening. Then cut a patch from a piece of scrap. The patch has 45-degree bevels facing the back paper. It must be cut and smoothed to fit exactly in the wall opening. Apply joint compound to the beveled sides of the wall opening and set the patch in place. Then tape the joint edges in the normal manner.

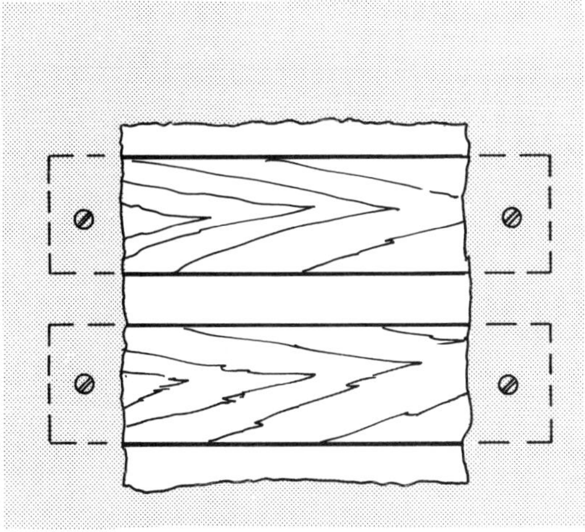

1. SMOOTH THE EDGES OF THE OPENING. PLACE AS MANY WOOD STRIPS INSIDE THE OPENING AS NEEDED TO BACK UP THE GYPSUM PATCH. SECURE THE STRIPS WITH SCREWS.

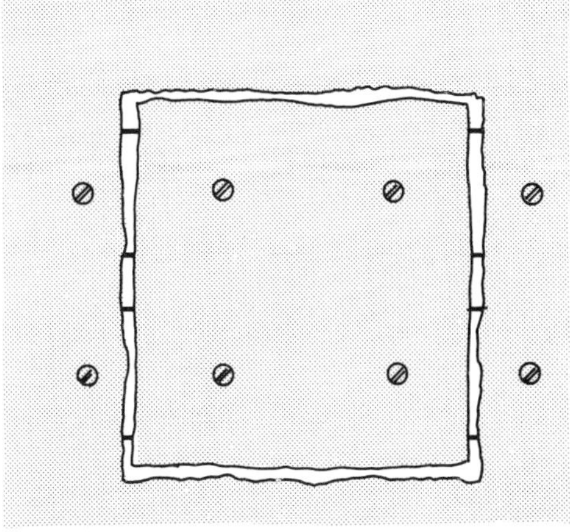

2. PLACE A GYPSUM BOARD PATCH INSIDE THE OPENING AND SCREW IT TO THE WOOD STRIPS.

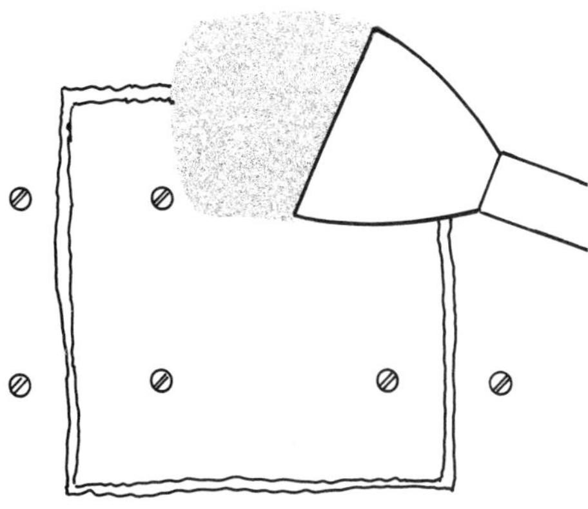

3. FILL THE GAP BETEEN THE PATCH AND THE SIDES OF THE OPENING.

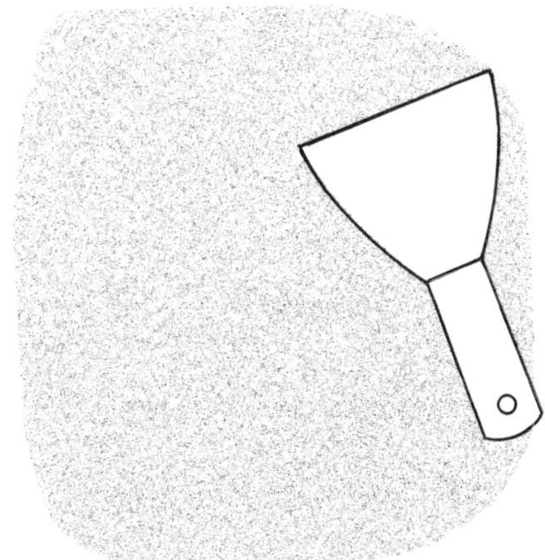

4. COVER THE JOINT WITH COMPOUND AND TAPE. COVER THE SCEWS AS YOU FEATHER THE COMPOUND.

9-10 Wood backup strips can be used to support a gypsum repair patch. Finish the joints in the normal manner.

A repair of a fairly large hole can be made by installing wood backup strips, as shown in 9-10. Install the wood strips with screws. Then cut a patch close to the shape of the opening. Fasten it to the wood strips with screws. Fill the gaps between the patch and wallboard with joint compound and then cover the joint with tape and compound.

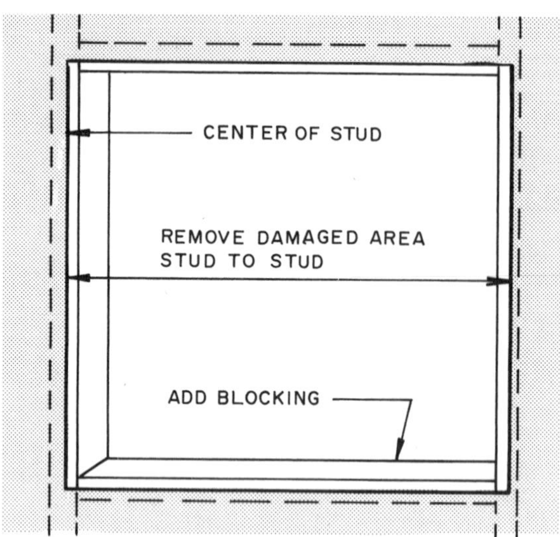

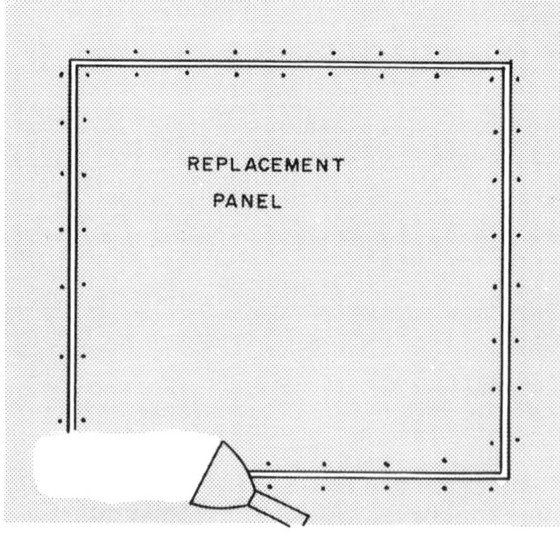

9-11 Large damaged sections can be removed from one stud to the other and a new gypsum panel inserted. The horizontal edges should have blocking or metal clips.

9-12 Very small punctures can be filled with spackling compound.

A very large damaged area or a wall area where a window was removed during remodeling requires a drywall patch that runs from stud to stud, as you can see in 9-11. Be certain to install horizontal blocking on the unsupported edges or use the metal clips mentioned earlier in this chapter. After the patch has been nailed or screwed in place, fill the gap between it and the wallboard. Then finish the joint in the normal manner.

Very small holes, such as 1/4 to 1/2 in., can be filled using spackling compound. It is available in hardware stores in tubes and squeezes out like toothpaste. Press some compound into the hole and let it dry. If it has shrunk while drying, reapply some compound. When it is dry and flush or slightly above the surface of the panel, sand smooth. It is now ready for you to paint over it (*see* 9-12).

BLISTERS IN THE TAPE

After the tape has been installed and the joint compound has dried, blisters may occur. These are caused by using a too thin coat of joint cement under the tape, not pressing the tape firmly into the compound or by pressing the tape too hard against the undercoat—which squeezes out too much compound.

To repair a blistered area, slit each blister with a knife, fill it with joint compound, and press the tape down with the finishing knife.

EDGE CRACKING

Sometimes long, narrow cracks will appear along the edges of the tape. Many things can cause this to happen. It could be caused by drying at too high a temperature (which causes rapid drying), using the wrong joint compound or one that has been diluted too much, leaving too much joint compound under the tape, or wet or cold conditions at the time of application that has resulted in reduced bonding between the tape and paper on the panel.

To correct this defect cut away any poorly bonded sections of tape. Cover these hairline cracks with a 2- or 3-pound cut shellac and cut a groove into any wide cracks and coat with shellac. Once the shellac has dried, recoat with joint compound and a new layer of tape.

CRACKS IN THE CENTER OF THE JOINT

These occur less frequently than the other joint defects that have been discussed. Cracking at the center of the joint is usually caused by stress built up from excess structural deflection or racking of the wall. Excess heat or moisture in the room can also cause cracking.

To correct this defect you must remove the cause of heat, moisture, or racking and after making these changes retape the joint. Remove any tape that may have lost its bond to the panel. Sometimes control joints can be installed, allowing for some panel movement, especially if it is caused by moisture or excessively high temperatures. (*See* the use of control joints in Chapter 6.)

CORNER CRACKING

Sometimes the internal corners run a crack toward the ceiling. This can be prevented by placing very little joint compound at the actual intersection of the panels. Sometimes the tape is accidently split with the finishing tool and the joint compound over this will surely crack. To correct, retape and refinish the joint. Consider using the floating interior-angle corner described in Chapter 6 (page 67) or a vinyl inside corner, as shown in Chapter 7.

CROWNING

Crowning refers to the development of an excessively high arcing of the joint compound over the joint. This produces a bulge or ridge that ruins the flat appearance of the wall.

To correct a crowning problem, sand down the bulge or ridge that has formed. Then re-coat the area of the joint with joint compound. Feather it out wider than it was originally.

STARVED JOINTS

If a joint is recoated before the previous coat has had sufficient time to harden or if not enough joint compound was used in the first place, the joint may have a hollow concave surface due to shrinkage. Recoat the joint and allow sufficient drying time between coats. Use a low-shrinkage compound.

RIDGING

Ridging is a continuous ridge running the length of the joint usually down the center. It is caused when panels are butted too tight, placing them under stress, and causing the butting panels to bend out slightly along the joint.

To correct, let the wall react for several months and at least through a hot season. Then sand down the ridge and fill the concave areas with joint compound. Let it thoroughly dry before applying a final thin float coat over the entire area.

SEALING AROUND PIPES

The open space between the drywall and pipes must be sealed. It is a major source of energy loss. If the pipes will not show, as under a sink, and the openings are not large, fill them with caulking. If they are too large for this you can patch around them with tape (*see* 9-13).

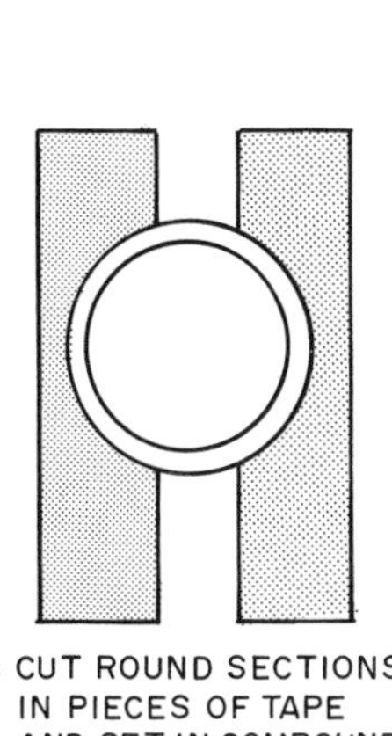

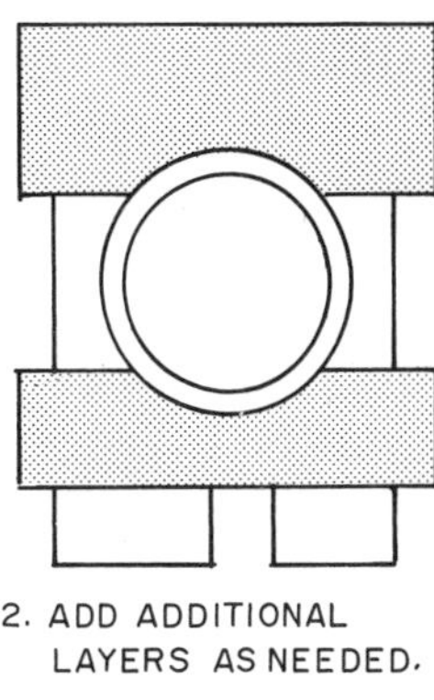

9-13 You can seal around pipes by cutting and fitting the tape to the pipes and finishing with joint compound.

Paint Problems

Often after the finished panel is painted, various irregularities in the appearance of the surface are noticed. Following are the most common.

VARIATIONS IN PAINT APPEARANCE

Due to differences in the surface of the panel paper and the dried, sanded joint compound the paint on these areas may vary from a sheen on the compound to a flat on the paper. This occurs over each joint and fastener. The difference is caused by the difference in suction in the two surfaces. When light hits the walls and ceilings, the difference can be quite pronounced.

To prevent this, seal the entire surface with a latex or solvent sealer or a coat of alkyd flat wall paint. Drywall manufacturers have a product designed especially to coat and seal the joint compound for painting. It provides a better base for paint than conventional sealers. These are applied by roller, brush, or spraying.

VARIATIONS WHEN USING HIGH-GLOSS PAINTS

Again, the difference in suction in the gypsum panel paper and the joint compound produces a higher gloss on the areas covered with compound. To prevent this, apply a skim coat of joint compound over the entire surface.

DARKENING OF THE JOINTS

Sometimes the joints may tend to darken over time. This is usually caused when the paint is applied over a joint compound that has not been permitted to dry completely.

To reduce this occurrence, prime the joints with a latex- or solvent-based sealer or a white alkyd flat wall paint. Drywall manufacturers have a product designed especially to coat and seal the joint compound for painting. It provides a better base for paint than conventional sealers.

Chapter 10

Taping Joints, Finishing Trim & Corner Beads

After the drywall panels are installed and everything has been rechecked to be certain it is ready for finishing, the taping can begin. The panel with its paper cover is strong. Poorly taped joints tend to be the major place where a job may fail. It is very important that the joints be properly taped to resist cracking and to provide for the required fire protection expected from the finished wall.

Before you begin taping, be certain that all fasteners are properly set, all openings—such as for electrical boxes—are properly cut, and the corner bead is installed properly. Make certain that the area in which you are working is ventilated and provision has been made to maintain the proper temperature (45 degrees F to 70 degrees F—approx. 7 degrees C to 21 degrees C).

Make certain trestles or scaffolding needed for cathedral ceilings or other high surfaces are available (*see* 10-1). These must be quality units meeting federal OSHA safety requirements.

10-1 High-quality scaffolding is among the things you will need when finishing high walls and ceilings.

Make a Plan

Drywall finishers, through experience, develop a plan for the sequence of steps they follow. Various individuals and a full-time finisher will no doubt follow a different plan from the homeowners doing their own work. Some prefer to complete the ceiling before beginning the walls. Following is a six-step sequence that serves well for many people. It assumes the use of paper tape and three coats of joint compound.

1. Put the first coat over all fasteners and minor nicks on all walls of the room.

2. Put the first coat and tape on all horizontal and vertical joints.

3. Install corner tapes and when dry apply the second coat.

4. Put the first coat on trim and corner beads. When dry, apply the second coat.

5. Apply the second coat on the fasteners, horizontal, and vertical joints.

6. Apply the third coat on fasteners, joints, corners, and beads.

Some Things to Consider

1. Feather joints by running the knife on one side and then the other, and finish by stroking down the center.

2. When feathering, start at one end of the joint and do not lift the knife until you get to the other end.

3. After you have worked over the compound on a joint three or four times, it begins to get sticky and should not be worked any more.

4. Make certain the compound in your mud pan is stirred occasionally so that the consistency is constant.

5. If the compound has dry chunks of compound, discard it.

6. Keep the inside of your pan, the lid on the compound bucket, and the tools used to move it to the pan, free of dried lumps.

7. If there are ridges on the dried joint, remove them by scraping with a clean drywall knife before applying the next coat.

8. Do not put compound on more joints than you know that you can finish before it starts to harden.

9. Before applying a coat of joint compound be certain the wall is free of sanding dust. Joint compound will not stick over sanding dust.

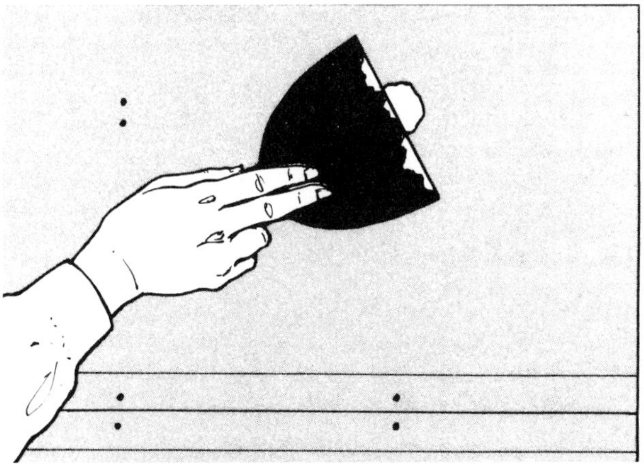

10-2 (Left) The heads of fasteners are given the first coat of compound with a 4-in. taping knife. (Courtesy National Gypsum Company)

10-3 (Below) The heads of fasteners are coated as a strip.

As you tape a job, you will be faced with tapered edge joints, square nontapered joints, inside and outside corner joints, as well as control joints. In addition you will have to conceal fasteners and sometimes you will need to repair damage that has been done to the panel.

Covering Fasteners

Fastener heads are covered by passing a 5- or 6-in. taping knife loaded with joint compound over the head. Keep the blade almost flush with the panel (*see* 10-2). Then raise the knife to about a 45-degree angle and scrape off excess compound. You only want to fill the dimple. Some finishers will pass the trowel down a row of fasteners, covering several with one stroke (*see* 10-3). After this first coat is dry, repeat the operation until the dimple is flush with the surface.

Finishing Around Openings

Electrical outlets, light boxes, and other openings need to be finished so that when the installation is complete the compound flows smoothly behind the cover plate or light base. Hopefully the drywall opening was accurately located and cut to fit closely. In this case fill the slight opening with compound and lightly feather it away as shown in 10-4. This provides the needed fire rating of the wall and seals the crack, reducing air infiltration. If the crack is so large that the compound falls out, you will have to place tape over the crack and finish as you would a joint.

10-4 The space around this outlet has been properly sealed. The extra compound that has hardened around the edges will be cut away.

Taping Tapered Joints

The first decision is whether to use paper of fiberglass mesh tape. Paper tape is stronger and can be used with a wide variety of joint compounds. Fiberglass mesh tape is easier to install but must be covered with a setting-type joint compound. The mesh tape is not strong enough to use on square butted end joints.

USING PAPER TAPE

The steps to finish a tapered joint are shown in 10-5. Begin by laying down a coat of joint compound in the tapered area (*see* 10-5A). Use a 5- or 6-in. tapering knife and spread the compound in a rather even layer about 1/4 in. thick. Do not work too far ahead of the actual taping or the compound may start to set. Now unroll a section of tape and press it lightly into the compound. The tape should be long enough so that it covers the entire length of the joint. It should go all the way to the corner (*see* 10-5B).

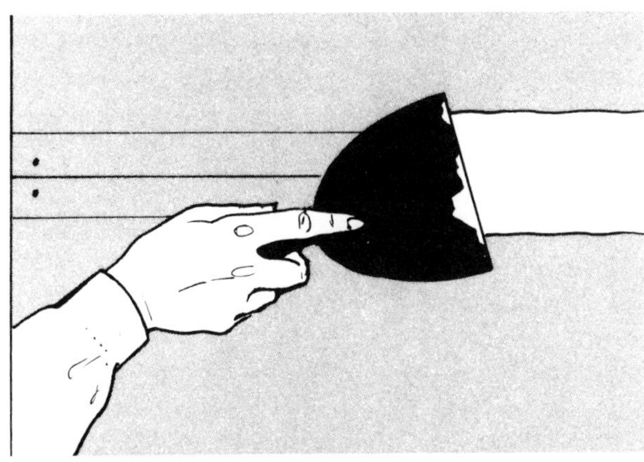

10-5A Lay the first coat of joint compound in the recessed area produced by the tapered panel edger.

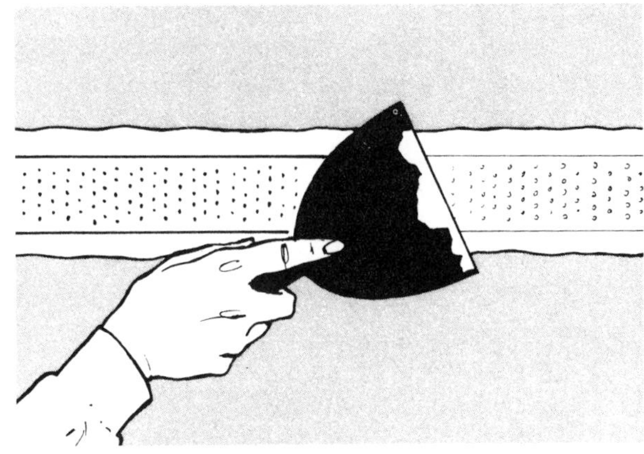

10-5B Press the paper tape into the first coat and smooth it out with a trowel, removing excess compound and thinning the compound under the tape.

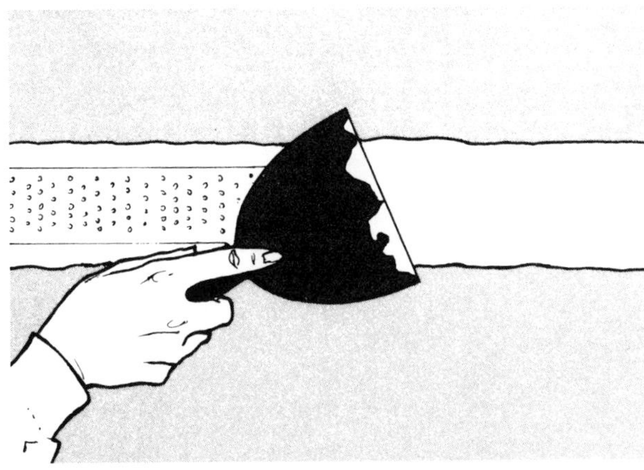

10-5C After the first coat has dried lay the second coat over it feathering it, about 4 in. on each side of the joints.

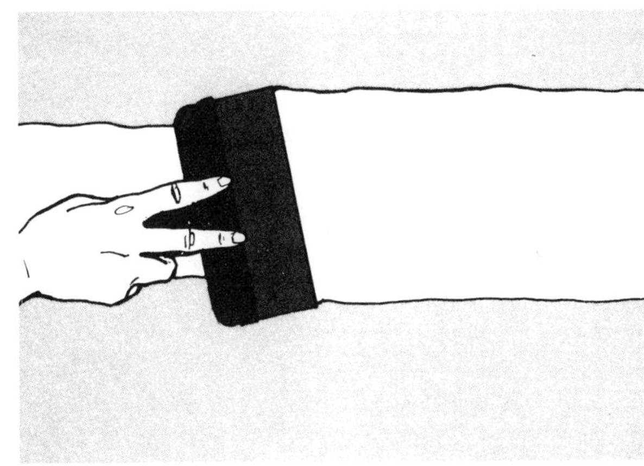

10-5D After the second coat has dried apply the third coat, feathering it 7 or 8 in. on each side of the joint.

10-5 (Above) Four steps typically used to apply joint compound and tape to gypsum wallboard joints. (Courtesy National Gypsum Company)

Now, keeping the tape tight pull the taping knife along the tape, pressing it into the compound. The knife will be on a low angle (*see* 10-5B). This pushes out some of the joint compound from below the tape, leaving a layer about 1/8 in. thick in the cement and 1/32 in. on the edges to bond the tape to the wallboard. As you do this, excess compound will squeeze out at the edges and have to be removed. The finished first coat will have the tape embedded and the compound feathered out on each side.

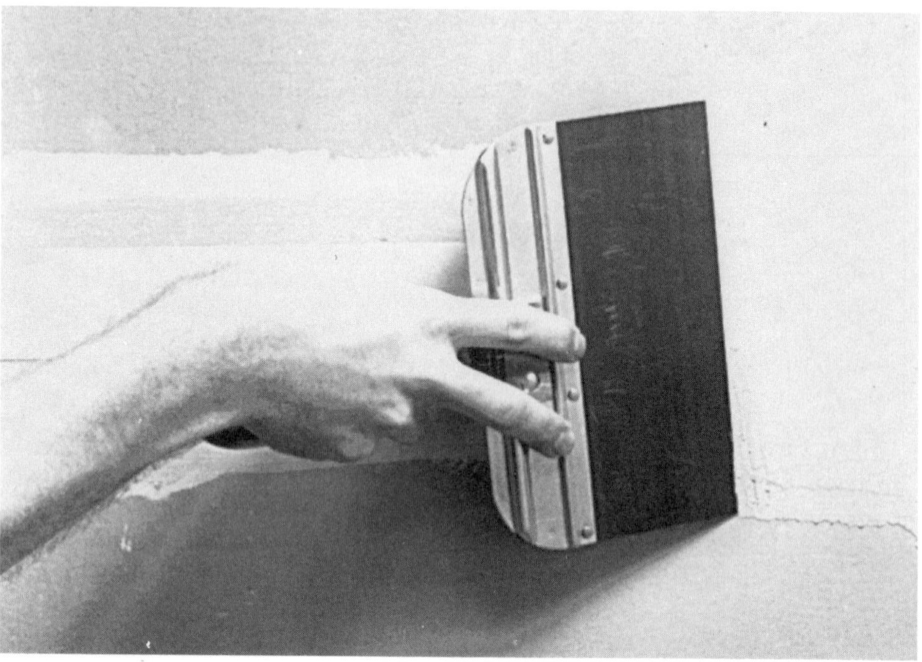

10-6 The final finishing of the second coat of joint compound is best done with a 12- to 14-in. finishing knife. (Courtesy National Gypsum Company)

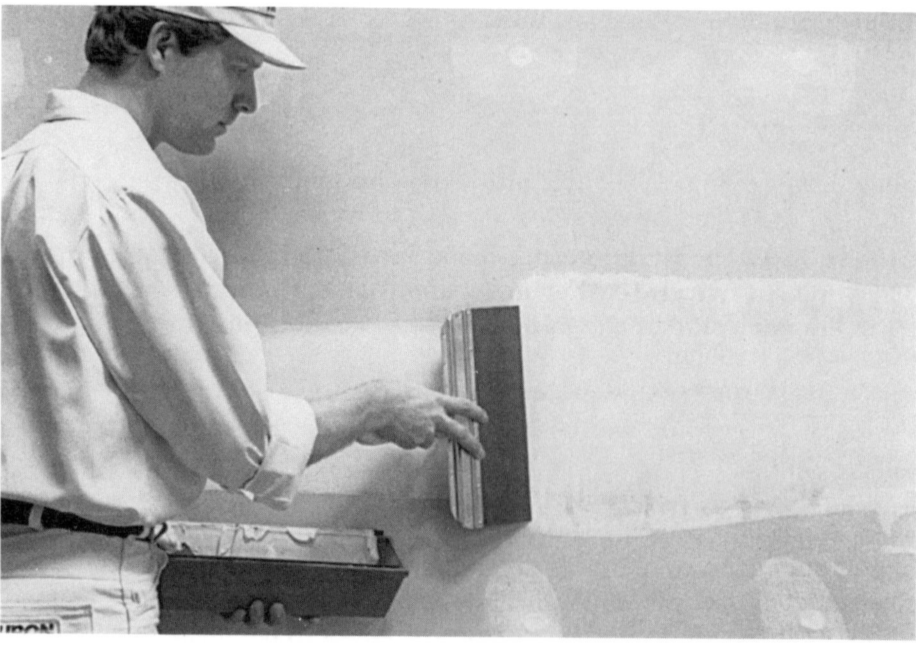

10-7 The third (finish) coat is feathered several inches beyond the second coat with a finishing knife. (Courtesy United States Gypsum Corporation)

If the paper tape wrinkles, it means you may have not kept it pulled tight as you pressed it in the compound or you put down too thick a layer. You may have to remove it and reapply.

Sometimes you will cover a very long joint with two pieces of tape. Be certain they overlap at the center and work each from the center toward the corner.

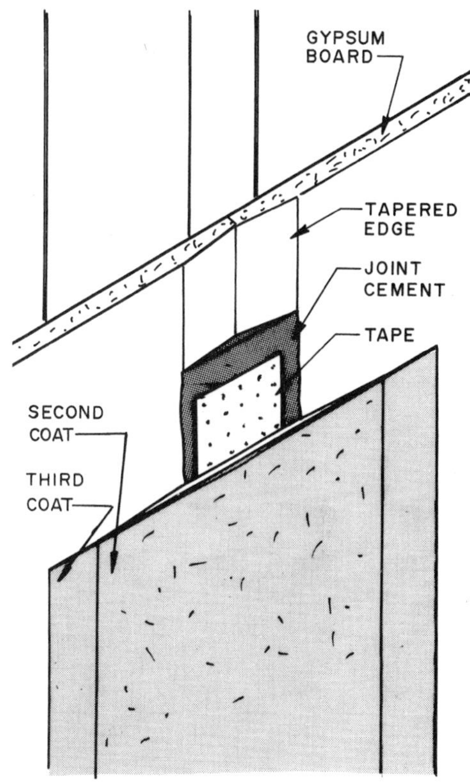

10-8 A finished joint.

Second Coat

The second coat (*see* 10-5C, on page 127) adds additional compound to the tapered joint and helps fill the recess. Before you apply it, check the joint for smoothness. Remove any lumps or ridges. Usually the sharp edge of the taping knife will cut these off, leaving a relatively smooth surface. The second coat is applied after the first coat has dried. The drying will vary with the relative humidity, temperature, and the time lapsed. This can range for all-purpose compounds from around 10 hours for zero-percent relative humidity and 70 degrees F (21 degrees C) to 3 days (72 hrs.) if the relative humidity is 90 percent at 70 degrees F. The second coat widens out the feathered area and is smoothed to blend into the panel as much as possible. It can be an all-purpose joint compound or a taping compound.

Apply the compound with a 6 in. taping knife and work the coating down with a 12-in. or 14-in. beveled trowel or finishing knife (*see* 10-6).

Third (Finish) Coat

The third coat (*see* 10-5D, on page 127) is usually just a very light skim coat. If you have done a good job of smoothly applying the first two coats, you will only need to do a little light sanding to prepare for this final coat. Usually a 100-grit or 120-grip sandpaper is used. Be certain to remove all gypsum dust from any sanding before applying the third coat. Feather the edges of the third coat about 2 in. wider so they flow into the paper on the panel (*see* 10-7). You can feel them with your hand or turn a light on them to see if there is any small edge left. Do not sand the paper surface because this will roughen it. If you do damage the paper it will be necessary to float a very thin coat of joint compound over it.

This third coat will be just a little wider than the second coat and is usually thinner. Remember to coat the fasteners with the same materials. The layers of a finished joint are shown in 10-8.

10-9 Notice that this vertical square butt end joint is about twice as wide as the horizontal joints above and below it.

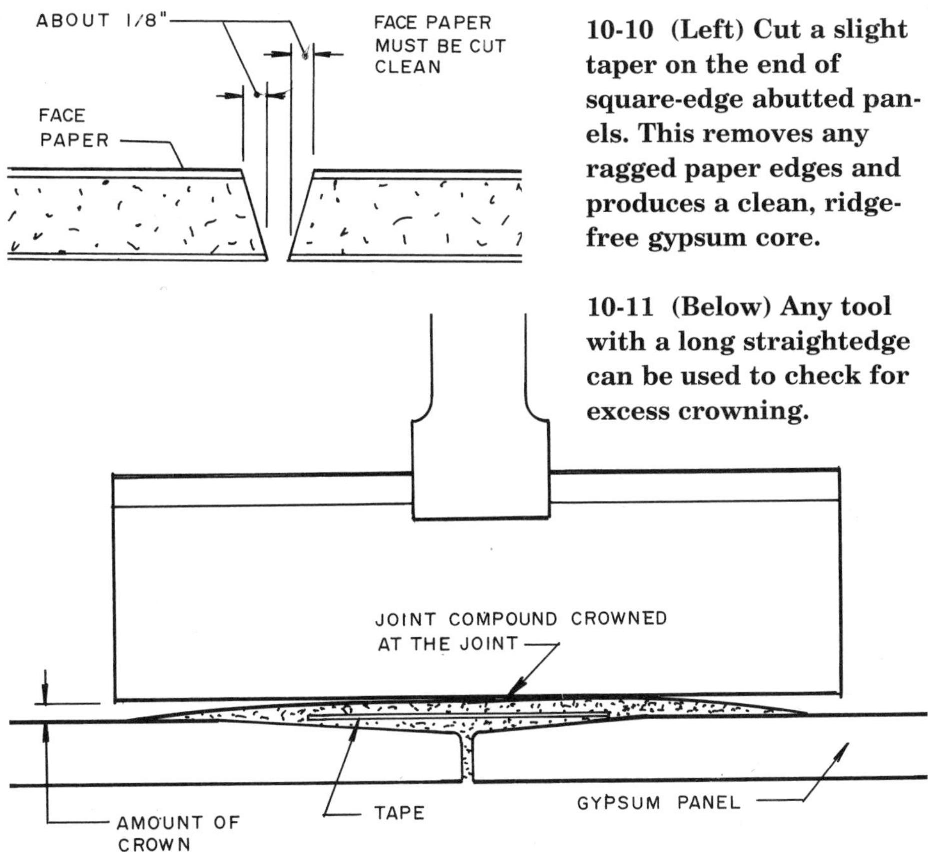

10-10 (Left) Cut a slight taper on the end of square-edge abutted panels. This removes any ragged paper edges and produces a clean, ridge-free gypsum core.

10-11 (Below) Any tool with a long straightedge can be used to check for excess crowning.

Taping Abutted End Joints

Abutted end joints have no tapered area to receive joint compound or tape, so a wide-feathered joint area is need, (*see* 10-9). They are difficult to tape and it is hard to keep the crowned appearance—created by building the finish on top of the panel—from being noticed.

Before you secure butted ends to the framing, bevel them slightly on a 45-degree angle. This cuts away only raw paper edge. Be certain the ends are close but not touching (*see* 10-10).

Begin by applying the compound over the surface of the joint and embed the tape as described for tapered joints. Press the tape tightly against the panel, yet leave enough compound to bond it to the panel. After it dries apply the second and third coats as described for a taper joint. To reduce the appearance of a crown, feather each layer about about twice as wide as a taper edge joint. One such application is shown in 10-9. Typically the tape and compound on a finished abutted end joint will be 1/8 in. to 3/16 in. thick and 18 in. to 24 in. wide.

You can check the joint with a straightedge to see just how much of a crown exists (*see* 10-11). If it is excessive, apply additional coats of compound and widen the feathered area.

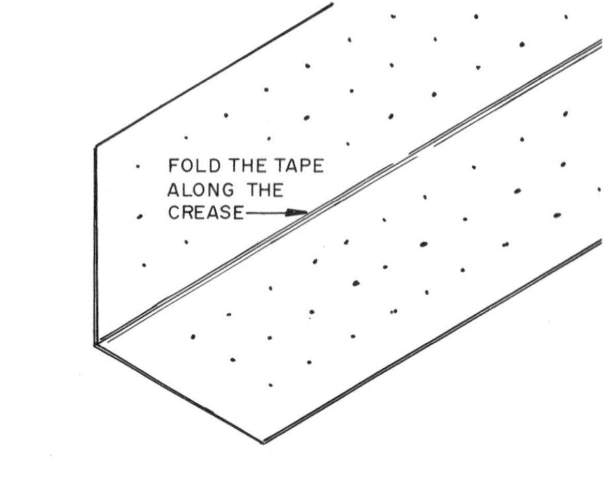

10-12 (Left) The paper tape has a crease in the center which helps you fold it for use on inside corners.

10-13 (Left and Below) An inside corner—seen from above—has each side feathered without striking the other side or damaging the paper in the corner.

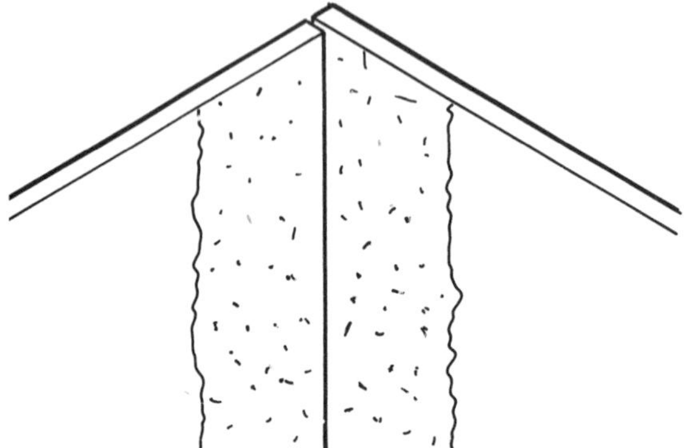

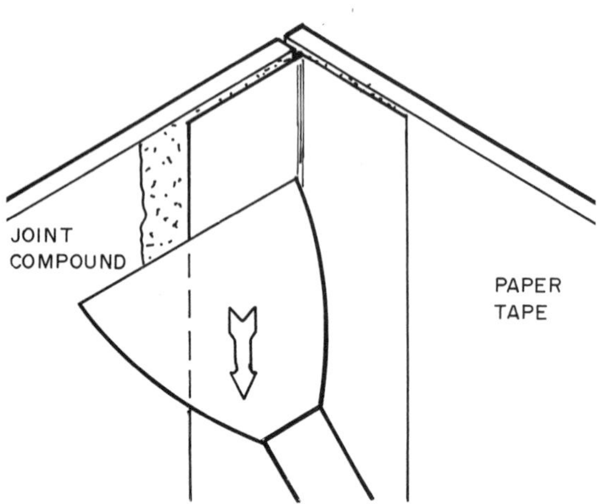

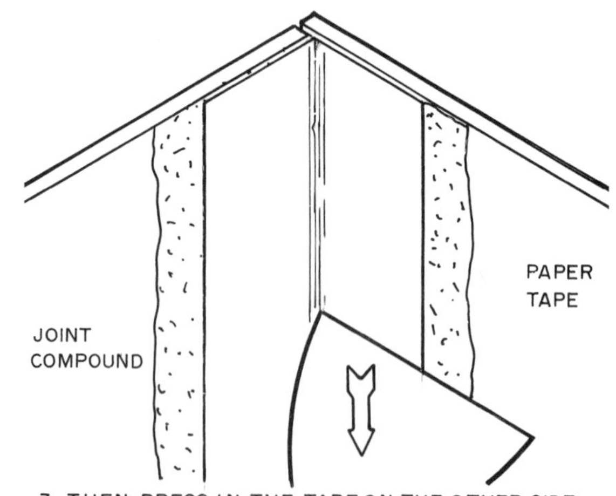

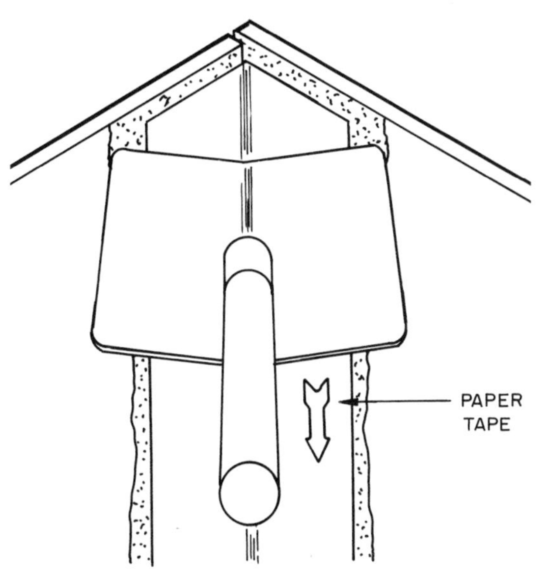

10-14 This corner trowel can be used to apply compound. Smooth it on both sides of the insider corner.

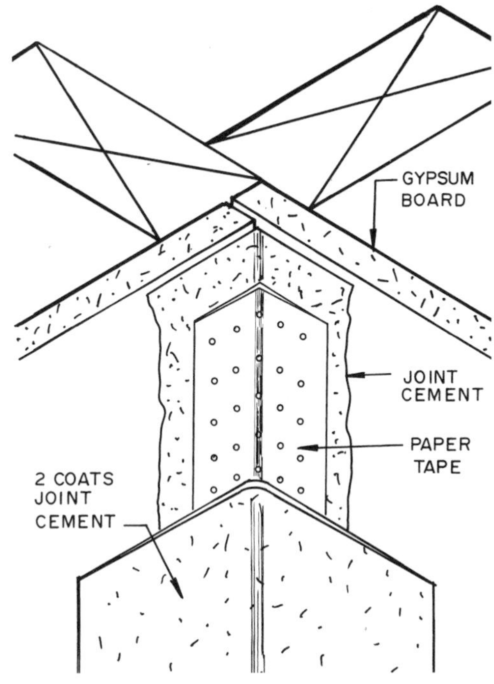

10-15 A finished inside corner joint.

Taping Inside Corners

Inside corners should be taped with paper tape or plastic inside corner beads (*see* Chapter 7). Fiberglass mesh will not fold to form a permanent corner. The trick to an inside corner is to get both sides covered with compound without messing up one of the sides of the tape.

Begin by laying joint compound on both sides of the inside corner. Usually a 4-in. layer around 1/8 in. thick will be used. Fold the paper tape (*see* 10-12) along the crease in the center. Starting at the ceiling, press the tape into the compound. Keep the tape tight as you move down the wall. Then go back and embed the tape in the compound as discussed earlier (*see* 10-13).

When doing the joint between the ceiling and a wall, some finishers prefer working from the center to each end wall. Again, try to use one piece of tape.

The second and third coats are applied as discussed earlier (on page 129). Work carefully so that you do not cut through the tape or disturb the compound on the other side. Available is a special corner trowel that is used to dress both sides of a 90-degree corner (*see* 10-14).

Some drywall finishers prefer to apply the second coat to one side, let it dry, and then apply it to the other side. The same could be done with the third coat. This reduces the chance of smearing one side as you tool the other. A finished inside corner is shown in 10-15.

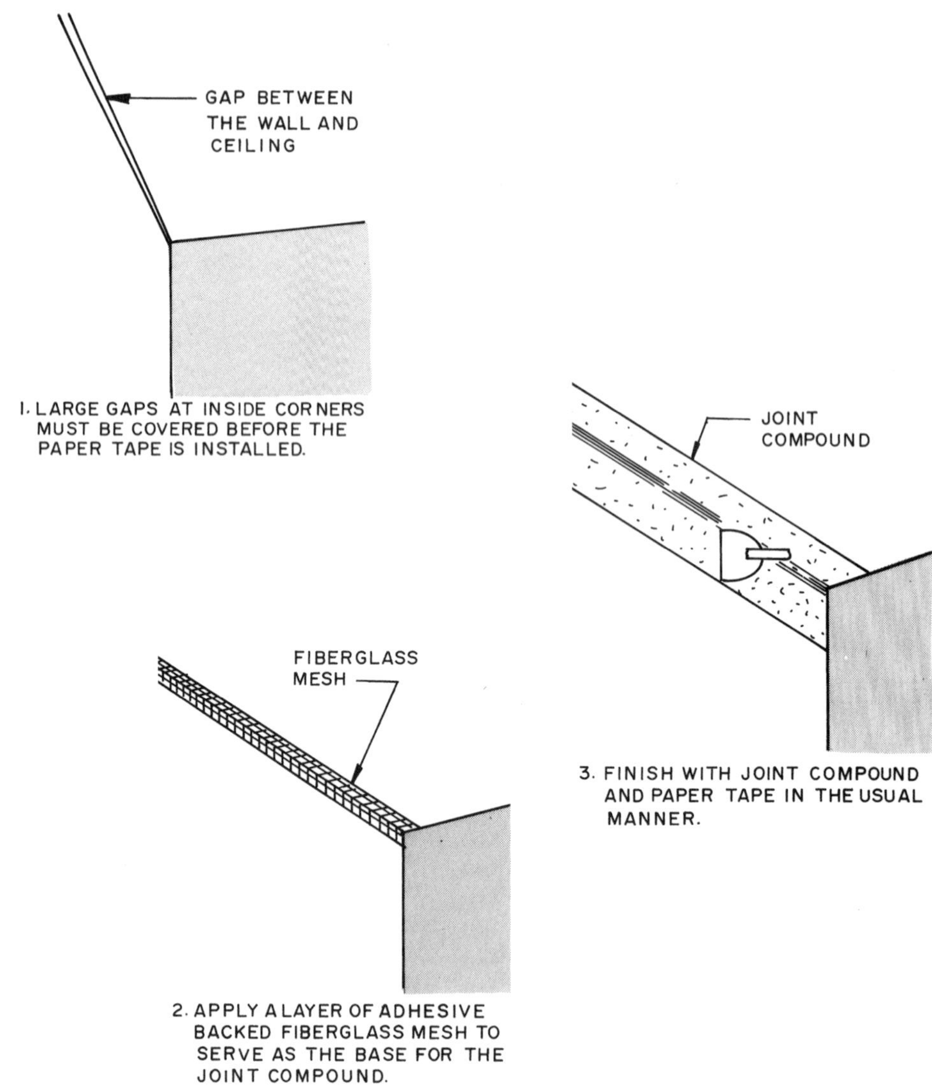

10-16 Rooms out of square require extra work to cover over any gaps at the ceiling.

Sometimes you will find that the wall or ceiling panel was hung leaving a pretty wide gap in the corner. This can occur especially when the walls of the room are not square (*see* 10-16). If the gap is small (on the order of 1/4 in.) It can be filled with joint compound. If it is between 1/4 in. and 1/2 in. it can be covered with several layers of adhesive-backed fiberglass mesh. When the filled area has hardened, finish the joint with paper tape in the usual manner.

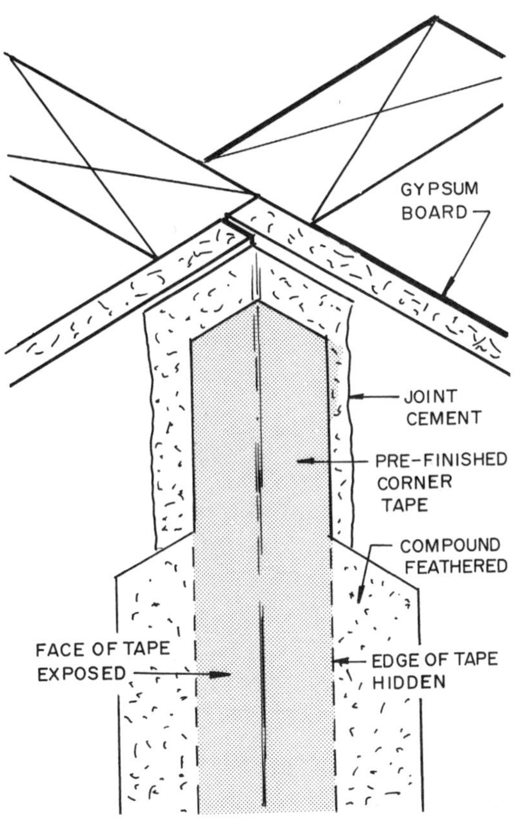

10-17 Prefinished corner tape is installed in the same way as paper tape; however, the edge is hidden by feathering the drywall compound. No compound is placed over the tape.

If the joint is 3/4 in. or wider you might consider cutting a strip of drywall and nailing it in place. This is difficult, because nails will often fracture narrow strips. If you can get a strip in place, cover it with joint compound, forcing it in the cracks on each side. Then finish the corner in the normal manner.

Installing Prefinished Drywall Corners

Prefinished drywall corner tape is a laminate consisting of a paper back ply, a copolymer center, and a paperboard front layer.

The corners are installed in the same manner as paper tape. The gypsum wallboard is given a coat of drywall compound and the tape is troweled in place. Immediately the compound on the edges is feathered to cover the edge of the tape (*see* 10-17). The face of the tape does not need to be finished with compound—it is ready to paint as soon as the compound hardens. This speeds up the finishing by removing the need to apply compound over the tape—and the application requires only a minimum of sanding. Since only one application of compound is required, this eliminates the time-consuming wait for the multiple layers of compound to dry between the steps of application.

10-18 Clean, sharp corners are an indication of a quality job.

Finishing Beads & Trim

Beads and trim are filled by applying joint compound over the flange. A 6-in. taping knife is a good size to use. Run the compound into the openings on the flange for its entire length. Then hold the knife at a 45-degree angle and smooth the compound by letting one side of the blade slide along the metal corner of the bead and the other side along the surface of the panel. Use enough compound to get it to flow about 4 in. out on the panel. After it dries, additional coats can be applied until the coating extends about 6 in. from the corner. The object is to produce clean, sharp corners (*see* 10-18). This second coat may be a topping compound or an all-purpose compound. A third coat is troweled and sanded as described earlier (*see* 10-19).

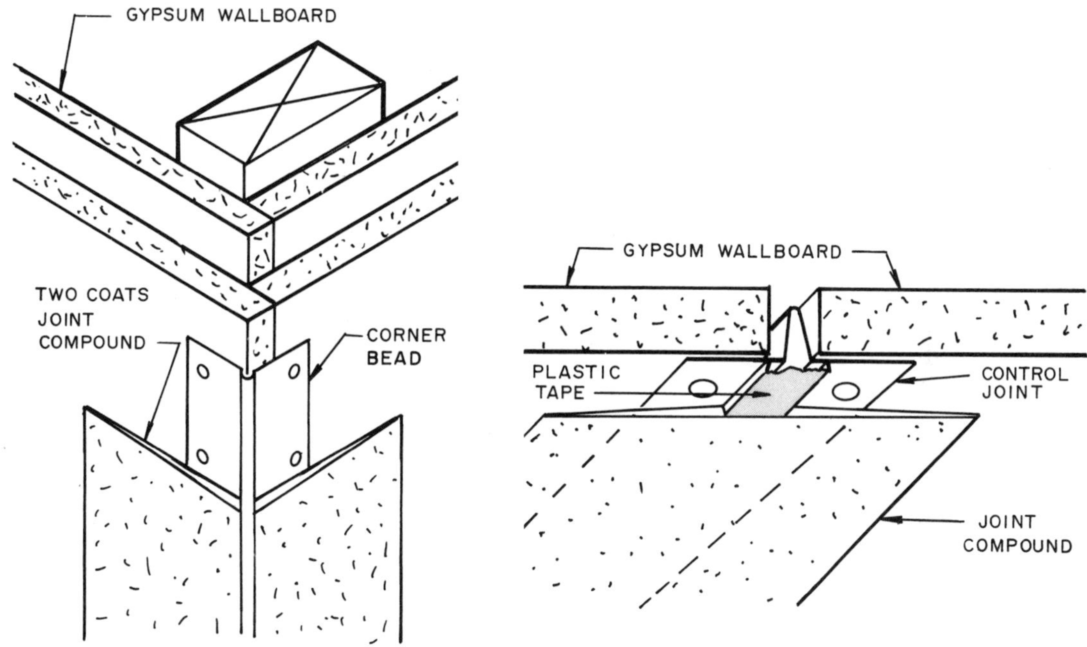

10-19 A finished exterior corner.

10-20 A finished control joint.

Occasionally you will have to tape corners that are not on a 90-degree angle. Use plastic adjustable bead or a paper tape that has metal strips along each edge.

The sharp, clean, finished corner beads that are evident in 10-18 are an example of quality work.

Finishing Control Joints

Control joints have flanges that are fastened to the sides of panels spaced 1/2 in. apart. Apply joint compound to the flanges and feather it out about 4 in.; then apply two more coats as described for other trim and beads. These two coats will completely cover the joint because the opening of the V-shape is covered with a tape. After the final coat of compound, remove the plastic tape that reveals the inside of the control joint (*see* 10-20).

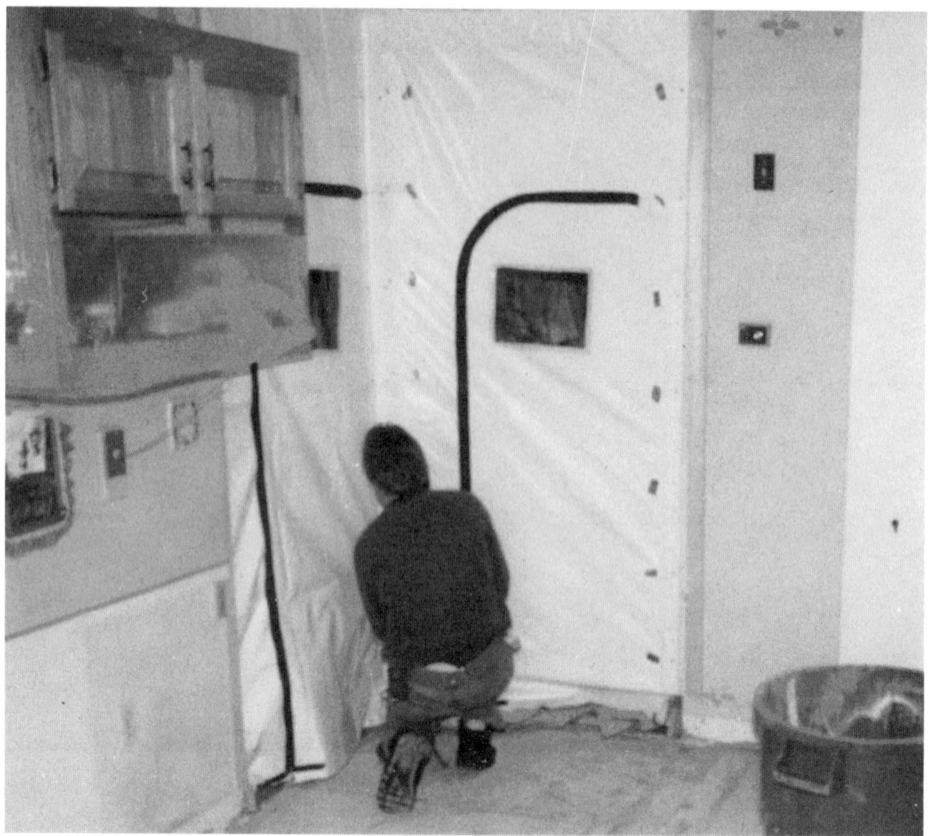

10-21 This type of dust door effectively seals off the door to an adjoining room. (Courtesy Brophy Design, Inc.)

Sanding

Sanding produces a lot of very fine gypsum particles. They flow everywhere and are hazardous to your health. You must wear a dust mask that really filters the particles. The typical low-cost discardable mask must be replaced frequently and is considered by many as inadequate. What you need is a mask that has a heavy replaceable filter pad that does not let the particles in around the edges (*see* Chapter 8). In some places a hard hat is required. It does provide protection for your head but is often bulky. You do need some type of hat to keep your hair protected from dust. Sanding the ceiling causes more difficulty from dust than sanding the walls.

Several manufacturers have pole-type dusters connected to a wet/dry-type vacuum that greatly reduces the dust in the air (*see* Chapter 8).

In new construction it does not matter a great deal if the dust filters into adjoining rooms. A room addition or remodeling presents a case where you need to keep the dust within the room. You can do this by sealing the doors or arched openings with sheet plastic. The edges should be tightly taped to the wall or trim. Several manufacturers make "dust doors," designed for quick installation and providing a good seal. Some can be opened to allow a worker to pass through (*see* 10-21).

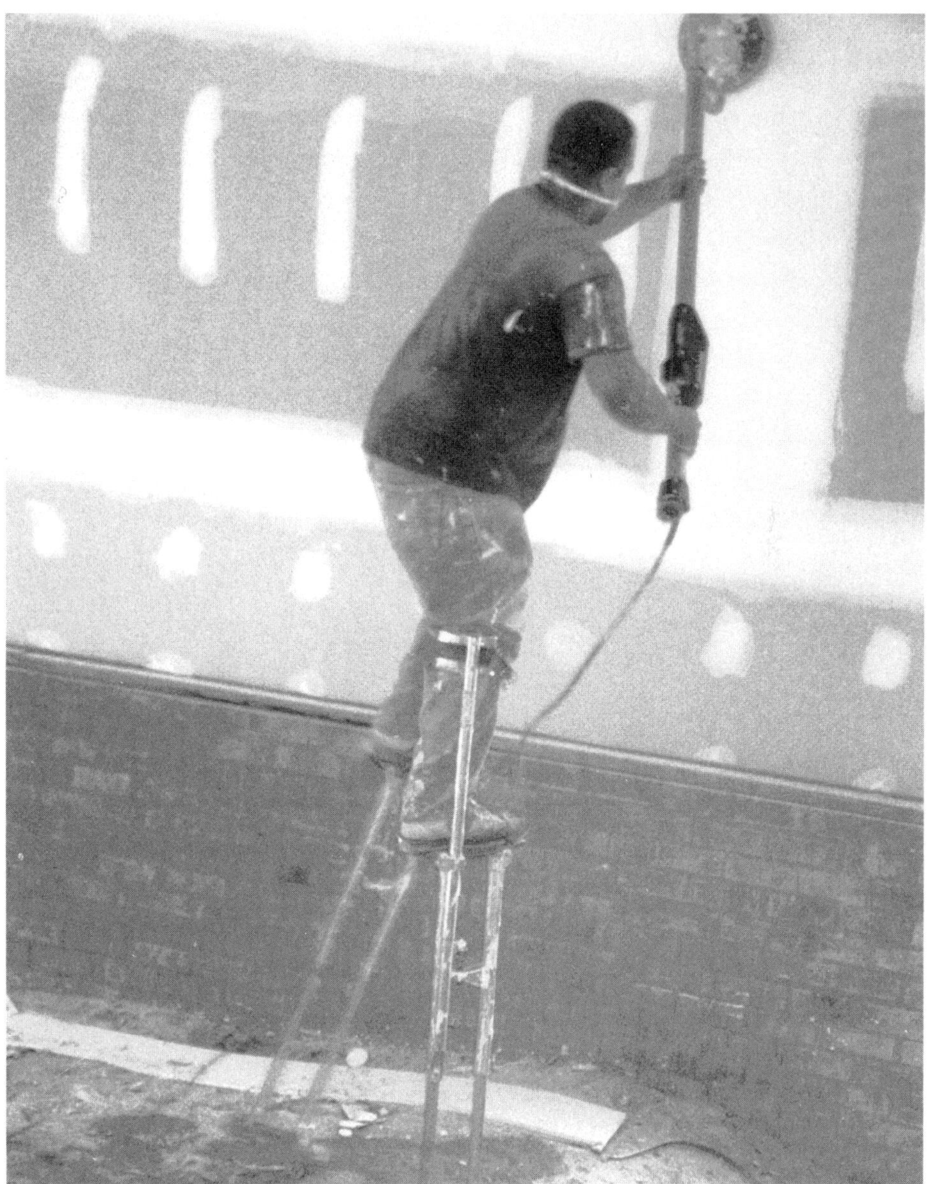

10-22 An experienced finisher can use a power sander to speed up the work.

SANDING STEPS

Some finishers use power sanders, but they cut fast, can damage the paper, and are difficult for inexperienced people to use (*see* 10-22). They will probably cause more damage than good if you are inexperienced. If used, work very carefully. It only takes a few seconds to cut through to the tape. Then it is necessary to re-coat the surface with a joint compound.

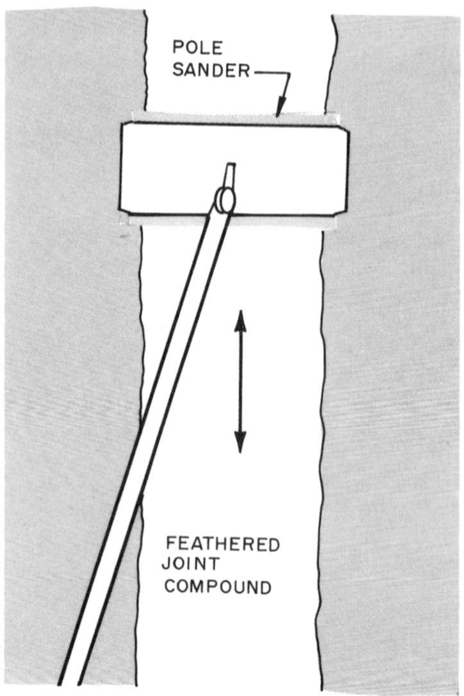

10-23 A pole sander permits you to sand the walls and ceiling while standing on the floor.

More typically you will begin by using a **pole sander** rather than a power sander to remove any excess buildup on the fasteners and joints. Be attentive and very careful as you proceed. Crowned surfaces are especially a problem. Then finish with some type of hand sander.

POLE SANDING

The pole sander is used for the first sanding and, if used properly, will leave very little finish sanding to be done (*see* 10-23). The grit of the sanding screen to be used varies with how good a taping job you did. Either a 100- or 120-grit screen is good. You may want to finish up with a 150-grit screen.

Sand the compound over the fasteners in the direction in which you applied the compound (*see* 10-24). Keep a good lookout for fasteners that were not properly secured. You may find that you have to make repairs and then re-coat some areas. Apply enough pressure on the pad to make it cut, but do not press too hard. Gentle is the touch.

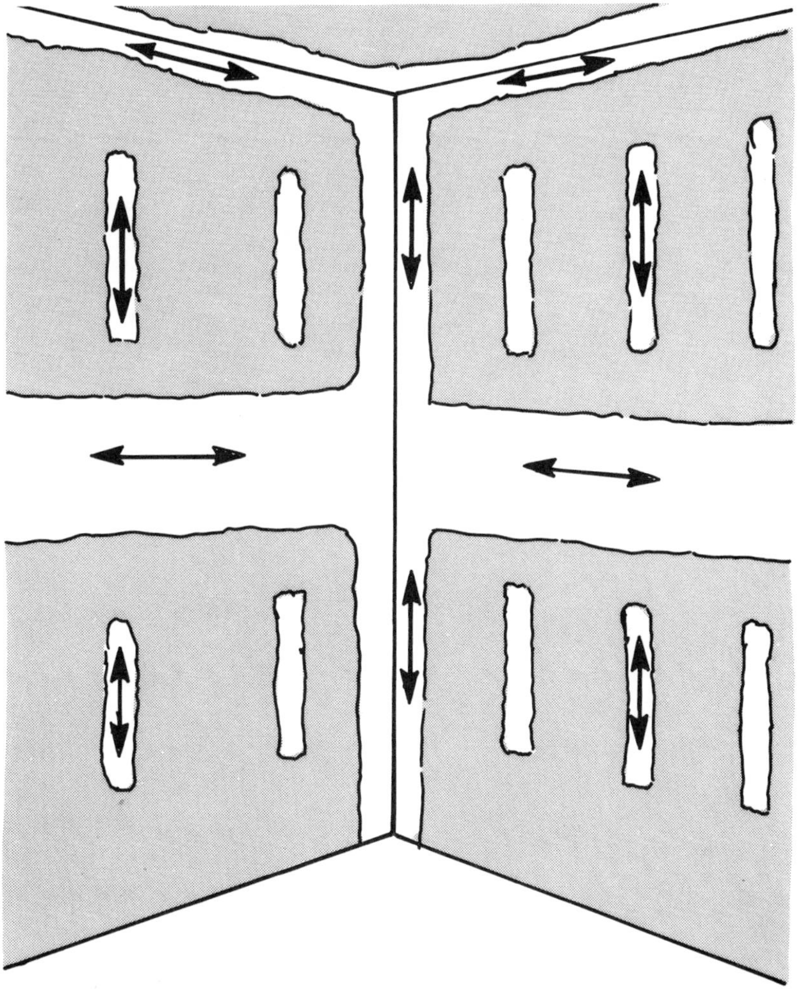

10-24 Sand the compound in the direction of the joint or row of fasteners.

If there is a large chunk of compound, cut it off with a finishing knife. Most small ridges can be sanded down. Inside corners require special care because the compound layer is rather thin. In general, work the area near the inside edge of the corner with a hand sander or a folded piece of sanding paper.

If you see defects—such as a long, deep scratch caused by a lump of compound—re-coat the area rather than trying to sand it out. Any seams that are underfilled need to be recoated. Excessive crowns may need to be re-coated and feathered wider. Then re-sand when dry. The sanding process reveals these defects. They should be corrected as soon as you notice them so that they can dry and be re-sanded as soon as possible.

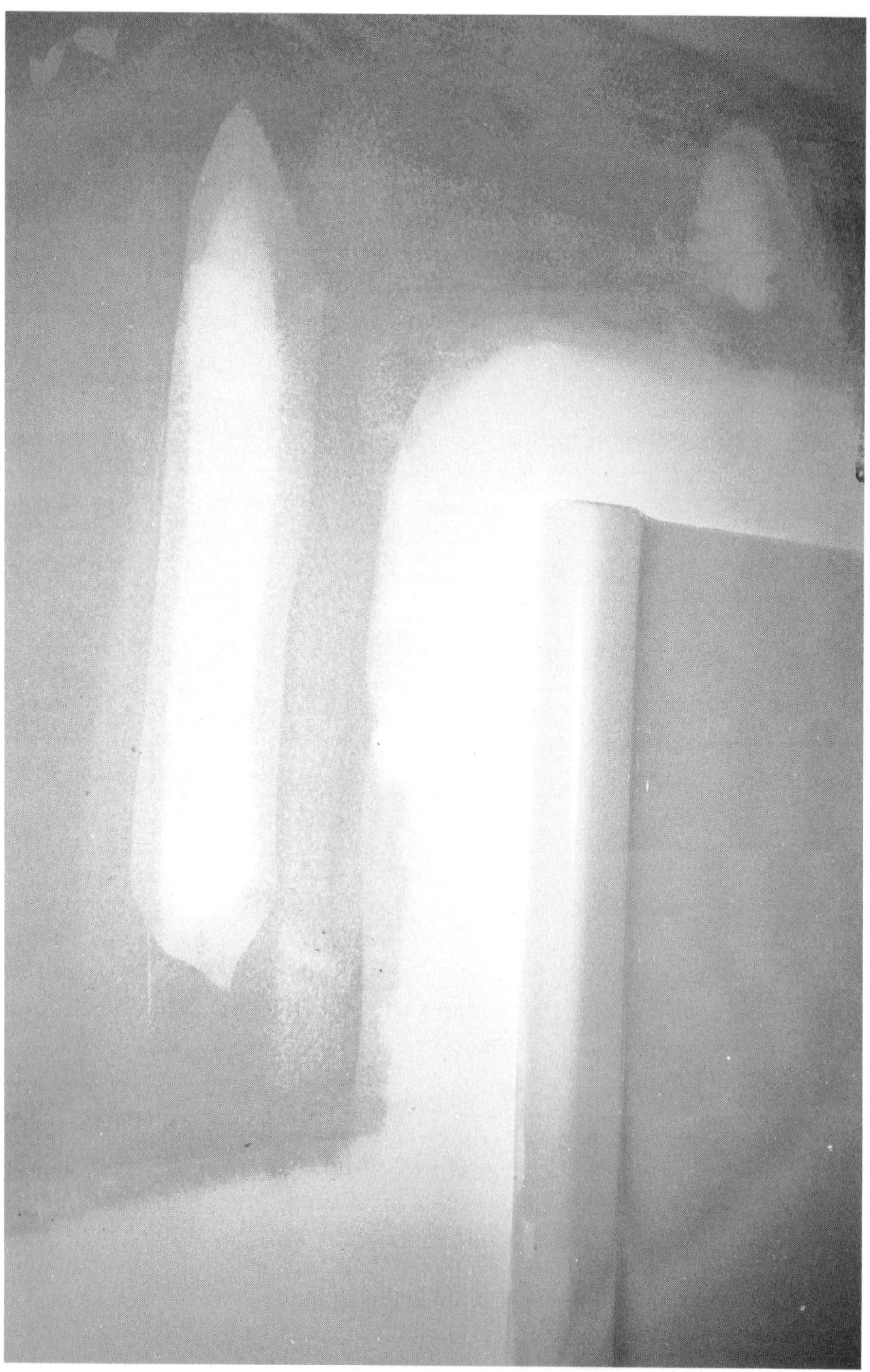

10-25 The moisture-resistant wallboard abutting the edge of this fiberglass shower has been carefully taped, finished, and sanded without damaging the shower.

When you are sanding around things already installed, such as bathtubs and showers, be especially careful you do not scratch their surface. Some units, e.g., a fiberglass shower (*see* 10-25), can be easily damaged. You may want to carefully hand-sand these with a folded piece of sanding paper.

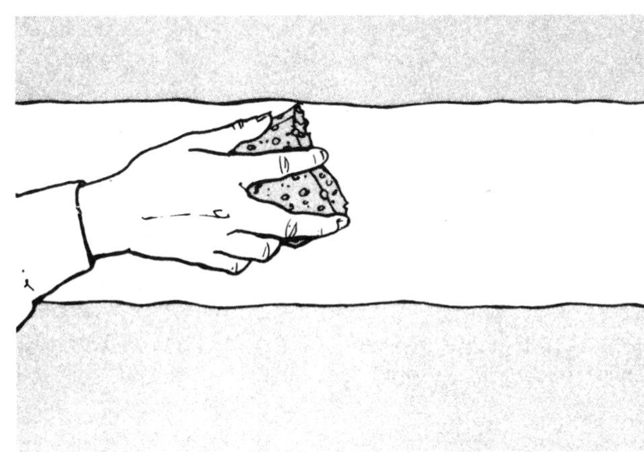

10-26 Hand sanding is done in the direction of the joint or row of fasteners. It is a very light sanding producing the final finished surface.

Hand Sanding

After the pole sanding is finished, hopefully all defects have been corrected. This is the final touch-up of the surface and requires close inspection. Good lighting helps reveal areas needing special care. A portable light on a stand is very helpful.

Usually the hand sanding is done with 150-grit or finer sanding paper. Carefully, gently sand over all fasteners, joints, and corners. Visually keep a lookout for defects (*see* 10-26). Run your hand over the surface to try to feel for areas needing additional sanding. Areas in which the hand sander will not fit easily can be sanded with folded pieces of sanding paper. Sand in the direction of the joint or the row of fasteners.

Wet Sanding

An alternate sanding method is wet sanding. It involves blending in the edges of the joint compound by stroking them with a wet sponge. This technique requires a certain level of experience. Aside from this mention, wet sanding will not be covered in this book.

When You Are Finished

Cleanup can be a big job. After taping, the lumps of compound that fall on the floor should be scraped up and removed. The gypsum dust is best removed with a commercial wet/dry vacuum. Remember, the dust filters everywhere—around windows, under doors, into electrical boxes. A thorough cleanup is necessary so that painting or wallpapering can begin.

Chapter 11

Texturing & Decorating Drywall

Textured gypsum surfaces provide a wide variety of decorative treatments and also can help to cover any minor imperfections that might still be present in the wallboard surface. It is recommended that textured surface not be used in areas with high humidity.

Also, remember that texture compound adds weight to the drywall. Since the compound is wet and heavy it could cause a ceiling to sag. To avoid this, always use 1/2-in. drywall on the ceiling with joists spaced not over 16 in. O.C. If 5/8-in. drywall is used, the joists can be spaced 24 in.

Another possibility is using **high-strength gypsum ceiling panels**. They resist sagging and warping. Check the manufacturer's installation instructions to verify the thickness recommended. Texture application requires the air and drywall to be at least 55 degrees F (13 degrees C) and kept above that temperature as it cures. The room should also have some ventilation.

Texture Finishing Materials

Texturing can be done with standard joint compound, all-purpose joint compound, topping compound, or a premixed texturing compound.

Textures may be applied by hand or with special spray equipment. Manufacturers have available a wide range of texture materials for both hand and spray application. Some are in powder form and are mixed with water, while others are premixed. The aggregate materials in the mix, such as silica sand, produce textures from very fine to heavy and coarse. Some materials can have a tint added, whereas others can be nearly white. Such whitish materials must be painted if a colored surface is desired.

You can add small amounts of water to the texturing compound if you want a thinner application. Likewise, small amounts of aggregate can also be added if you would like to change the texture. If you choose to do either of these alterations in the misture, measure the amounts added carefully so that each batch has the same fluidity and texture.

11-1 Texture can be produced by using many objects commonly available in the home.

HAND-TEXTURING TOOLS

The hand tools used to create textured patterns are many and varied. Most often they are some type of brush, sponge, roller, or trowel. You will find many of these in your home (*see* 11-1).

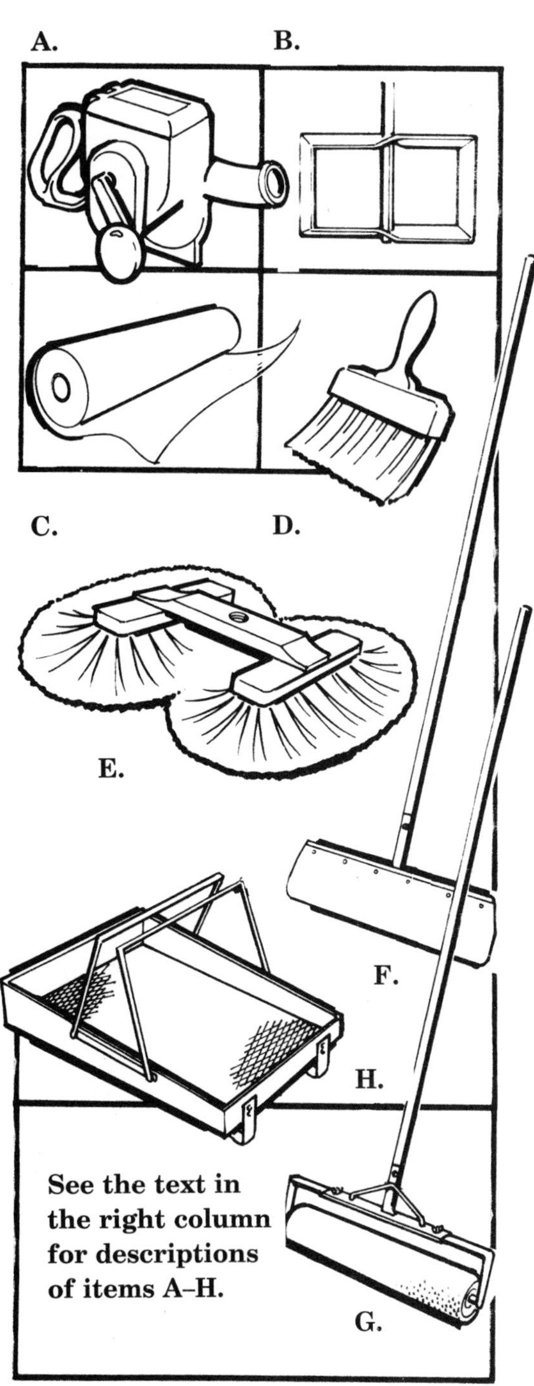

11-2 Equipment used for hand-texturing walls and ceilings. (Courtesy United States Gypsum Corporation)

The common available hand-texturing tools used by drywall finishers are shown in 11-2.

A. The glitter gun is for embedding glitter in wet textured ceilings. The hand-crank model shown is most economical but it is not as efficient as the air-powered type (not shown).

B. Mixing paddles are available in various styles. Paddles are used with aheavy-duty 1/2-in. electric drill for thorough, time-saving mixing of joint compounds and texturing products.

C. Polyvinyl roll material is used to protect doors, windows, and other things in the room.

D. The stucco brush is used for creating a variety of textures from stipple to swirl. Other variations can be achieved with thicker application and deeper texturing.

E. Texture brushes are available in many sizes and styles; tandem-mounted brushes cover a large area to speed the job.

F. A wipe-down blade has a hardened steel blade and a long handle to speed the cleaning of walls and floors after the application of joint compound or texture materials. The blade has rounded corners to prevent gouging.

G. The standard paint roller is adapted to the particular type of finish required. Several varieties of roller sleeve are available including short-nap, long-nap, and carpet types in professional widths.

H. The roller pan is for use with the rollers. Some models can hold up to a 25-pound supply of mixed texture material.

11-3 These special rollers can produce a variety of textures when rolled over a freshly textured surface. (Courtesy Kraft Tool Company)

Rollers and various pads with long handles are available; they let you texture the ceiling as you stand on the floor. When you use small brushes and sponges you will need a ladder or scaffolding. There are also available a series of rollers with textured surfaces that can enable you to roll on a uniform, repetitive texture. They fit on a standard 9-in. paint roller (*see* 11-3).

The compound hopper and spray nozzle.

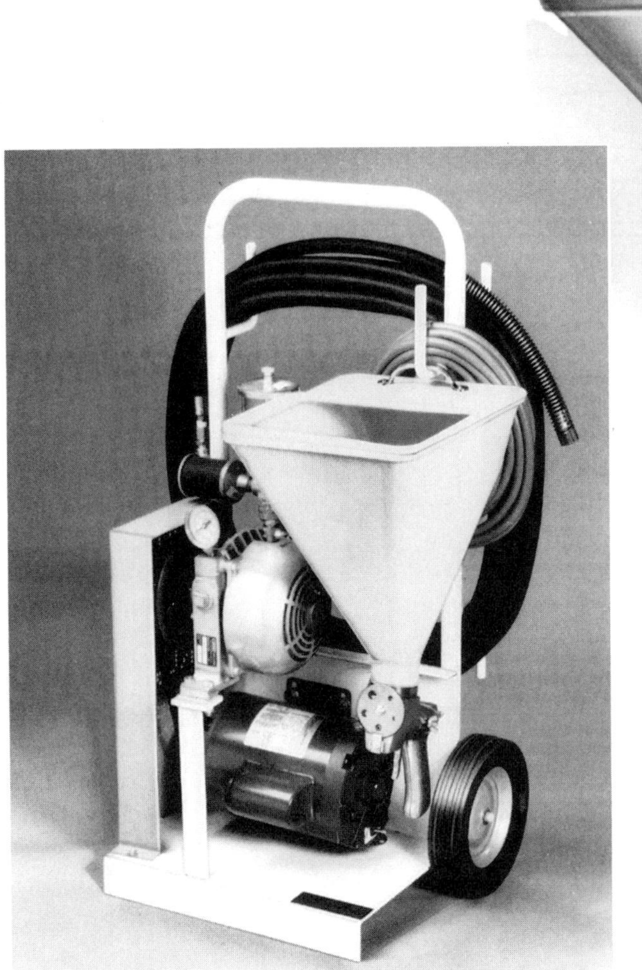

11-4 A spray-texture machine with compound hopper. The hopper holds the texture compound that is sprayed by compressed air through a nozzle at the bottom of the hopper. (Courtesy Kraft Tool Company)

SPRAY-TEXTURING EQUIPMENT

A spray-texturing machine is shown in 11-4. The texture compound is fed to a spray nozzle from a hopper. Compressed air is introduced at the nozzle—where the compound is atomized and sprayed on the wall or ceiling.

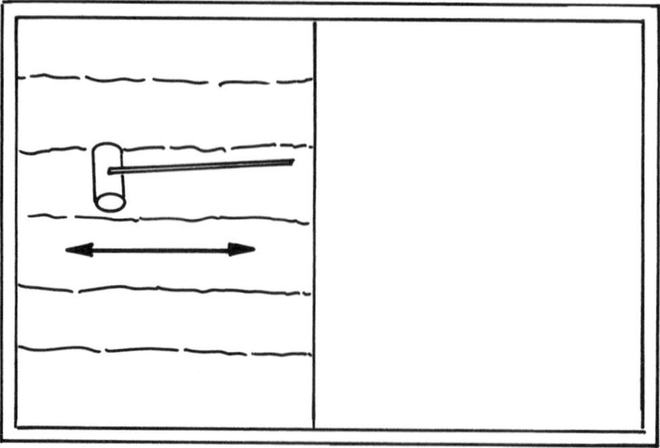

1. Roll the texture compound over part of the ceiling parallel with one wall.

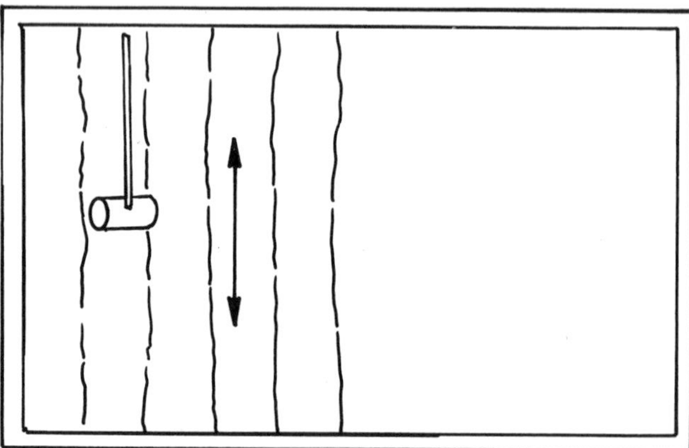

2. Roll a second layer of texture compound over the first layer and perpendicular to it.

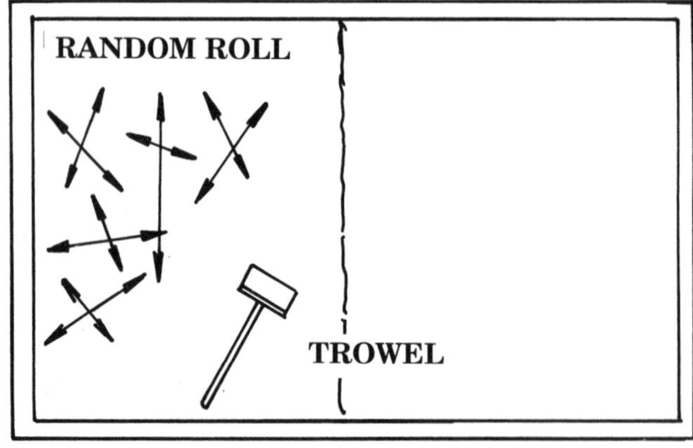

3. Move the roller in random directions to smooth and produce the desired finish, or lightly trowel the surface.

11-5 When rolling on texture compound, be sure to follow a predetermined plan.

Preparation for Texturing

Before doing anything, finish the joints and cover the heads of fasteners the same as you would if you were going to paint the wall. Do a good job. Texture will hide small defects, but most defects will show even when textured. Some finishers only apply two coats of compound. This is satisfactory if a good job is done and the material is feathered out sufficiently.

Now you should cover the surface with a primer coating (available from the drywall manufacturer) or at least a coat of alkyd paint or a latex-based primer. When you do this you will have sealed the surface at the joints so it has the same degree of absorption as the paper. This greatly reduces the chance that fasteners and taped joints will show through.

Manual Application of the Texture Compound

Texture compound is manually applied with a trowel or roller.

ROLLER TEXTURE APPLICATION

The easiest way to apply the compound is with a roller on a long handle. Put the compound in a roller pan. It will hold about 25 pounds of compound. Roll the roller in the compound, being careful not to load it up too much. Apply compound to the ceiling much like you paint with rollers.

It is necessary that you establish a regular plan for applying the texture compound. This will produce uniform results in every room you finish.

One plan is to begin in a corner along a wall. Be very careful to keep the compound off the wall. To do this you can tape (masking tape) a piece of paper or plastic on the wall so that it touches the ceiling. Generally the large ceiling area will be textured by breaking it up into smaller areas such as 6 x 6 ft. or 8 x 8 ft. If you work rapidly, much larger areas can be covered and, perhaps, all of a small room. Roll the first layer parallel with one wall. Keep the coating thin. Then roll a second coat over the first coat perpendicular to the first coat (*see* 11-5). After the second coat you may want to roll over the surface with the roller (do not add more compound) just to smooth and touch it up. This is done by rolling at random angles as you see a need for touching up the finish. Now repeat this for another area. Let it overlap slightly with the first area, and clear this up with the final smoothing roll.

If the compound begins to dry and you wish to touch up an area, do it with the roller. Coat it with a very thin coating. A brush will damage the texture, leaving a visible defect. Usually you will have to thin the prepared texture compound so it will flow off the roller. If you get it too thin, it is going to run down the roller handle and across your arms as well as drop off the ceiling.

If you prefer, you can lightly trowel the applied rolled texture compound to get a slightly different look.

Some Hand-Texturing Examples

The texture patterns are limited only by your imagination. Following are some of the conventional types.

ROLLER PATTERNS

In 11-6 is a texture produced by a long-napped paint roller. The degree of coarseness is produced by the texture of the roller sleeve. Try it out on some scrap before doing the ceiling. The fabric sleeve can be removed and other types bought and installed.

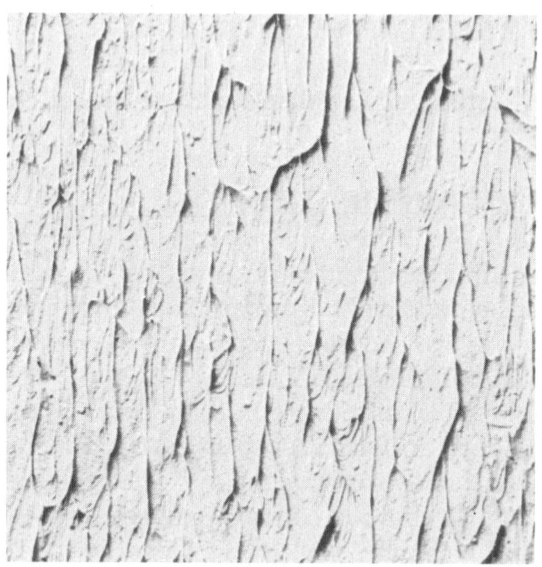

11-6 This texture was produced with a long-napped roller. (Courtesy United States Gypsum Corporation)

STIPPLED PATTERN

A very fine stippled finish (*see* 11-7) can be produced by a texture brush like those shown in 11-8. Brushes with coarser bristles will produce a slightly different texture. Remember, first experiment on some scrap stock.

To stipple a surface with joint compound, use a mud pan and a brush of your choice. While any brush will do, special brushes are available. Place the brush in the compound and then press to the surface. Each impression should touch or blend with the one beside it. Most prefer to work on an area such as 6 x 6 or 8 x 8 feet. Finish it and move on down the ceiling. Usually you will want to go over the area lightly with a finishing knife to even it up. Do this before the compound begins to harden.

11-7 A stippled texture created with a round texture brush. (Courtesy United States Gypsum Corporation)

11-8 These texture brushes will create a stippled surface. The pattern will vary because the smaller brushes have stiffer bristles. (Courtesy Kraft Tool Company)

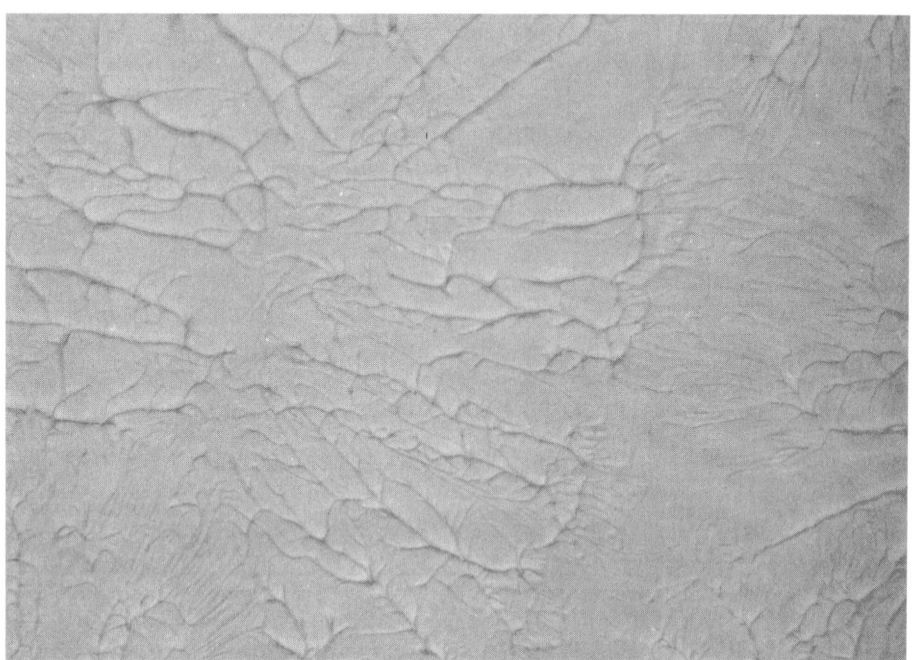

11-9 This is typical of textures that can be made by pressing a sponge coated with compound against the drywall.

11-10 Swirl patterns can be produced with a brush rotated in the layer of joint compound rolled on the surface.

SPONGE PATTERNS

By placing a rather open-surfaced sponge in joint compound and pressing it to the surface, you will get a texture something like that in 11-9. The shape of the image can be regulated by cutting the sponge to some shape, such as a circle or ellipse. As you press it to the surface, overlap each impression and vary the sponge's angle.

SWIRL PATTERNS

Begin by rolling on a layer of joint compound. Then place your brush on this surface and twist to produce a texture like the one shown in 11-10. The swirls can be made at random angles to each other or be lined up in carefully placed rows.

TROWELED PATTERNS

Troweled textures are heavier and more pronounced than those made with a brush or sponge. In 11-11 a texture is shown that has been laid down with a hand trowel. The size of the blade will influence the overall pattern. This is a heavy texture.

To apply a troweled texture you will need a trowel or taping knife. A 10- or 12-in. taping knife is frequently used. The larger tools will cover more area faster but require more strength to move across the surface.

1. Begin by placing the texture compound on the blade of the trowel. It should extend across the width of the blade.

2. Place the edge of the blade about 1/2 to 1 in. above the surface of the panel. Make a sweep across the surface, laying out about a 1/16- to 1/8-in. thick layer.

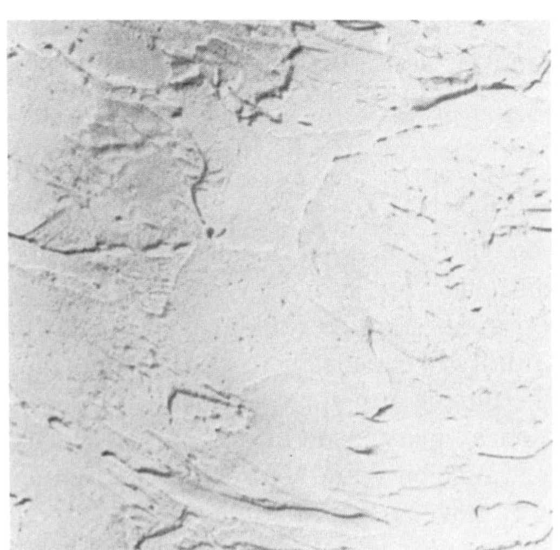

11-11 After the texture compound has been applied to the surface, it can be smoothed and the texture varied with a trowel. (Courtesy United States Gypsum Corporation)

3. Now go back over the area with the trowel and even the compound. You can var the angle of the trowel to produce the look you want. Do not overtrowel, becaus doing so will cause a tearing of the compound.

4. Repeat this on an area next to the first effort and blend them together. Continu with area after area until the ceiling is covered. This produces a fairly smooth thi coat of texture compound.

You can produce a more dramatic appearance by using a procedure often referre to as "skip-texture." The surface produced is much rougher than that produce with the ordinary trowel method. However, the degree of roughness can be regulated by the movement and pressure placed on the trowel.

To apply a skip-texture use a large trowel:

1. Put a heavy coating of texture compound on the trowel. It should cover th entire length of the blade.

2. Place the edge of the blade just above the surface of the drywall panel and the move the blade across the surface. This action will deposit a layer of compound o the surface.

3. As you draw the blade across the surface, lower the angle. With experience yo will find out how much pressure to use. In general a light pressure is best. This wi apply the compound in irregularly shaped deposits—some parts of the drywall getting no coating. This is the result you should try to achieve.

4. Now draw the trowel back across these deposits—carefully smoothing them an getting a fairly consistent height (*see* 11-12). This will leave some flattened hig spots and some areas with no compound—producing the particular rough textur you desire.

5. Continue across the ceiling, working each trowel load of compound as you go Carefully work the areas as they abut each other so that you are able to achieve smooth transition.

GLITTER

Glitter is a shiny material that comes in the form of fine granules. After the textur compound has been applied, glitter is sprayed on it with a glitter gun (*see* 11-13 While you can manually broadcast it toward the surface, this tends to gives a ver uneven coating. The glitter gun sprays the material in an even pattern—much lik the device used to spray grass seed and granular fertilizer over a lawn. The application of the glitter must be done before the texturing compound hardens. Glitte can also be applied to a wet painted surface.

1. First, sweep an irregular layer of texture compound over the ceiling.

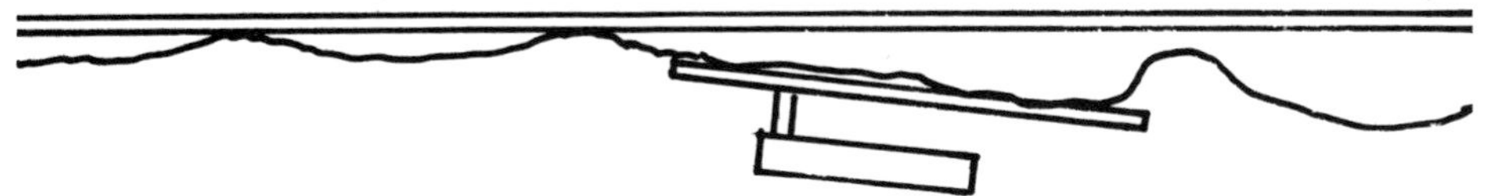

2. Then trowel flat the high spots, leaving low spots and areas with no compound untouched.

11-12 After the texture compound is applied roughly to the surface, a trowel is run over it leveling some of the high places and leaving low places untouched.

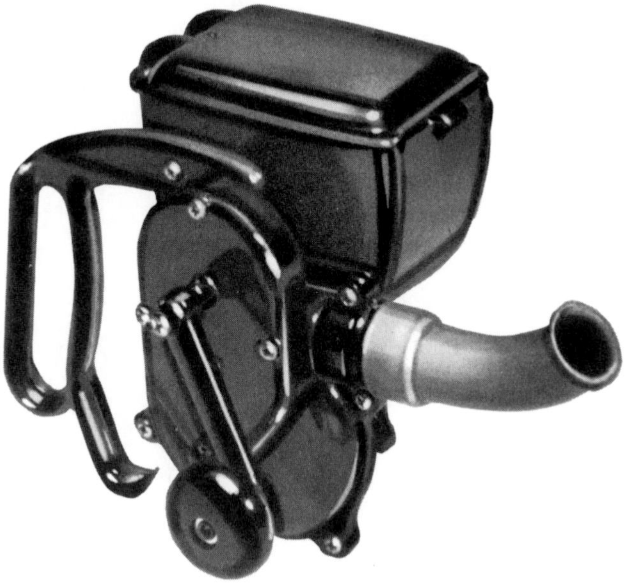

11-13 A glitter gun is used to apply glitter to ceilings and walls. (Courtesy Kraft Tool Company)

Perfect Spray Ceiling Texture—Coarse

Perfect Spray Ceiling Texture—Medium

Perfect Spray Ceiling Texture—Fine

Perfect Spray II Ceiling Texture

Perfect Spray EM Orange Peel

Perfect Spray EM Spatter Finish

11-14 Some of the texture patterns available to those using spray equipment. (Courtesy National Gypsum Company)

11-15 A spray shield is used to protect surfaces from overspray while texturing. (Courtesy Kraft Tool Company)

Spray Textures

Several of the many spray texture finishes are in 11-14. Spray-texturing requires spray equipment and some experience. Since it tends to overspray, your doors, windows and trim (if installed) should be covered. Drywall finishers use a spray shield (*see* 11-15) to keep overspray off walls, window frames, and floors. It is placed over the surface to be protected as the drywall in that area is textured. You can also use masking tape and plastic sheets, but this is time-consuming. If some gets on the wall use a finishing knife to scrape it off. After the surface has hardened, a light sanding will smooth it up.

An acoustic spray-applied texture gives a sound-absorbing, sound-rated decorative finish to gypsum panels, concrete, and some types of plaster ceilings. This treatment can help meet code regulations for sound transmission control.

The spray equipment consists of an air compressor, a hand-held hopper (*refer to* 11-4) containing the texture compound, and a hose with a nozzle, from which the compound is atomized and applied to the gypsum wallboard (*see* 11-16).

11-16 The hand-held hopper on the spray equipment applies the texture compound to the ceiling.

Texture Paints

Texture paints are a heavy latex interior paint that has a texturing additive. It is a little thinner than joint compound. However, it is thicker than regular latex paint. When applied to the surface with a roller or sponge it gives a light, stippled finish. Read the manufacturer's instructions before proceeding with the application.

Preparation for Painting

After the drywall has been taped and sanded, it is generally painted. However, it can be textured or covered with wallpaper, vinyl wallcovering, fabric, or some other material.

PREPARING THE SURFACE FOR PAINTING

Assuming that the taping and sanding was satisfactorily completed and all minor defects have been repaired, the wall is ready to paint. It should be clean and have no materials, such as adhesives or oil, that will keep the paint from bonding. Use a vacuum or at least clean rags or brushes to remove sanding dust.

APPLY THE PRIME OR SEALER COAT

The first coat is the **prime coat**. It should be the one recommended by the manufacturer of the finish paint you plan to use. It will have fillers and pigments that equalize the absorption properties of the finished wall, and it provides a base upon which the finish coat can bond.

Sometimes the taped joints and fasteners "photograph" (i.e., show) through even the final coat of paint. The primer or sealer will help reduce this.

The wall may be coated with a **sealer** instead of a primer. It contains a resin and is better suited for equalizing the porosity of the surface than most primers. Photographing can occur even with a sealer.

Also on the market is a primer-sealer. It provides good results and is often used.

One way to totally eliminate photographing is to skim-coat the drywall. This involves covering the entire wall with a thin coat of joint compound after the joints have had their three coats. This is time-consuming and expensive, so is not done except on the jobs requiring the highest quality. After skim-coating, the wall must be sanded and sealer-primer must still be applied.

Skim coating can be done with all-purpose joint compound or a special covering compound. Keep the consistency about the same as when taping joints. Apply with a wide trowel, joint knife, or long nap roller. The coating should be very thin. Then wipe down the surface with a broad finishing knife to get the final deposits as thin and smooth as possible.

Preparing Drywall for Wallcovering Materials

It is a common practice to apply regular wallpaper, fabric-backed wallpaper, and paper-vinyl-backed fabric wallcovering materials over the finished drywall surface. The surface should be taped and finished as described earlier in this chapter. While some heavy fabric coverings will hide small surface blemishes, many regular papers will not.

Since these wallcoverings are applied wet, it is necessary to seal the wall surface so the moisture will not soften the joint compound. After three coats of joint compound are applied and sanded smooth, apply a coat of white flat latex wall paint. After this is dry, apply a primer–sizer coat to prepare the surface to accept the adhesive-backed wallcovering.

Chapter 12

Other Useful Applications

Gypsum panels are used for many applications besides finishing interior walls and ceilings. The following examples illustrate some that are useful for residential and light commercial construction.

Steel Studs & Joists

Steel studs have been used extensively in commercial construction for many years. More recently they are being used for residential exterior wall and interior partition framing.

The metal stud wall will be installed by others—as is the case with wood stud walls. The metal studs are cut to length so that they are a little shorter than the floor to ceiling length as shown in 12-1. The wall is assembled by securing the metal track to the floor. Then, using a plumb line, the ceiling track is located and secured to the ceiling. The studs are usually joined to the tracks with sheet-metal screws (*see* 12-2).

Your job as finisher is to apply the gypsum wallboard to this metal framework. A typical metal stud partition and wall are shown in 12-3.

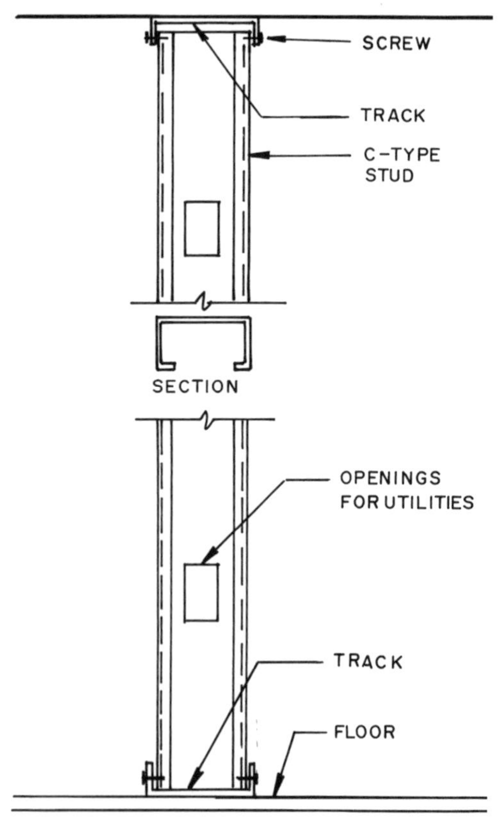

12-1 A typical C-type steel stud installation.

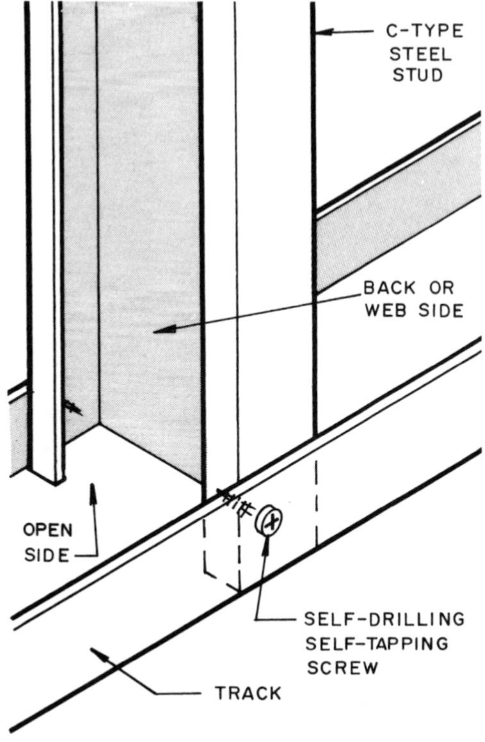

12-2 (Left) Steel studs are usually secured to the top and bottom tracks with self-drilling self-tracking screws.

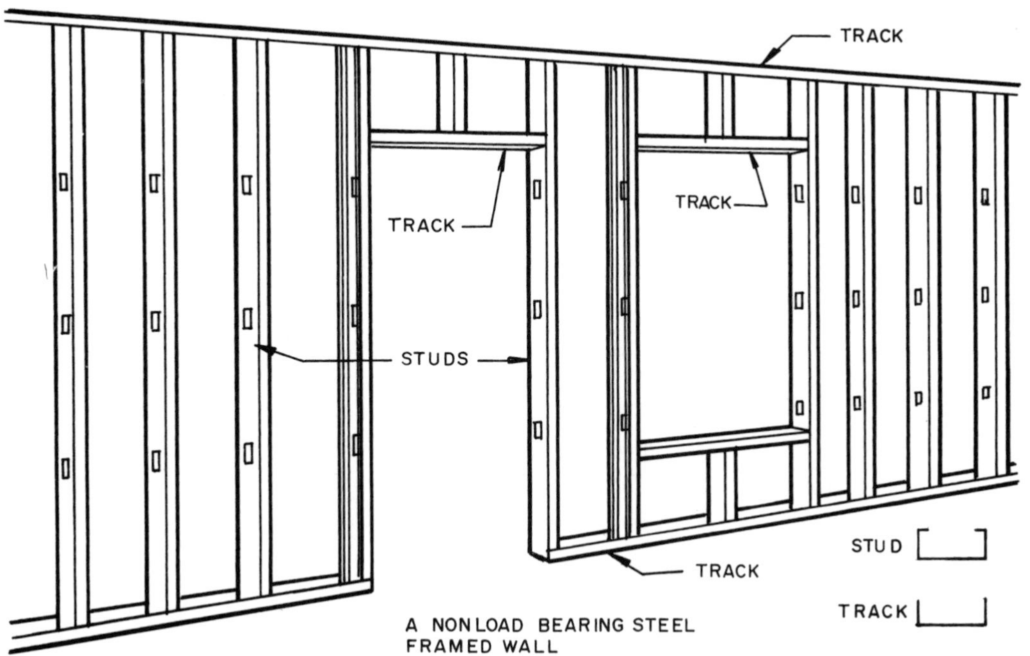

12-3 This is a typical steel-framed, nonload-bearing wall that has been framed with C-type studs and tracks.

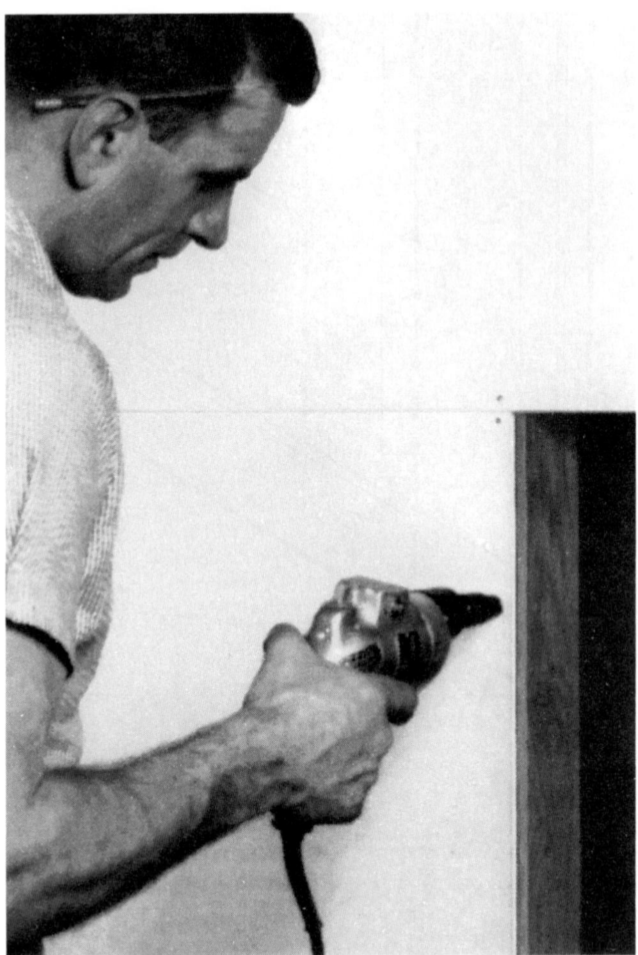

12-4 When driving screws, be certain to install them perpendicular to the face of the gypsum wallboard. (Courtesy National Gypsum Company)

Before hanging the drywall check the walls to be certain they are straight and plumb as discussed for wood-framed walls. Make certain the open sides on the studs all face the same direction (*refer to* 12-5). Check the building inspection record on the job to be certain that the electrical work, plumbing, and other trades have completed their work and they have passed inspection before you start to work.

Gypsum drywall is installed on metal studs with self-drilling self-tapping steel screws. The tips are designed to drill through the steel stud and the threads provide great holding power. Type-S bugle-head screws are used. (These are shown in Chapter 3.) Panels 1/2 in. thick require a 1-in.-long screw. They are driven with an electric screwgun (*see* 12-4). (Screwguns are described in Chapters 2 and 5.)

The screwgun can be adjusted to drive the screw to the proper depth. With experience you will know what setting to use. If you are not certain, drive a few screws into scrap pieces of stud. The screw head should be recessed slightly below the surface of the panel but not break the paper or the core. It is especially important to drive the screws straight. When the screw is set the correct depth, the screwgun head will automatically stop and the clutch releases the screw.

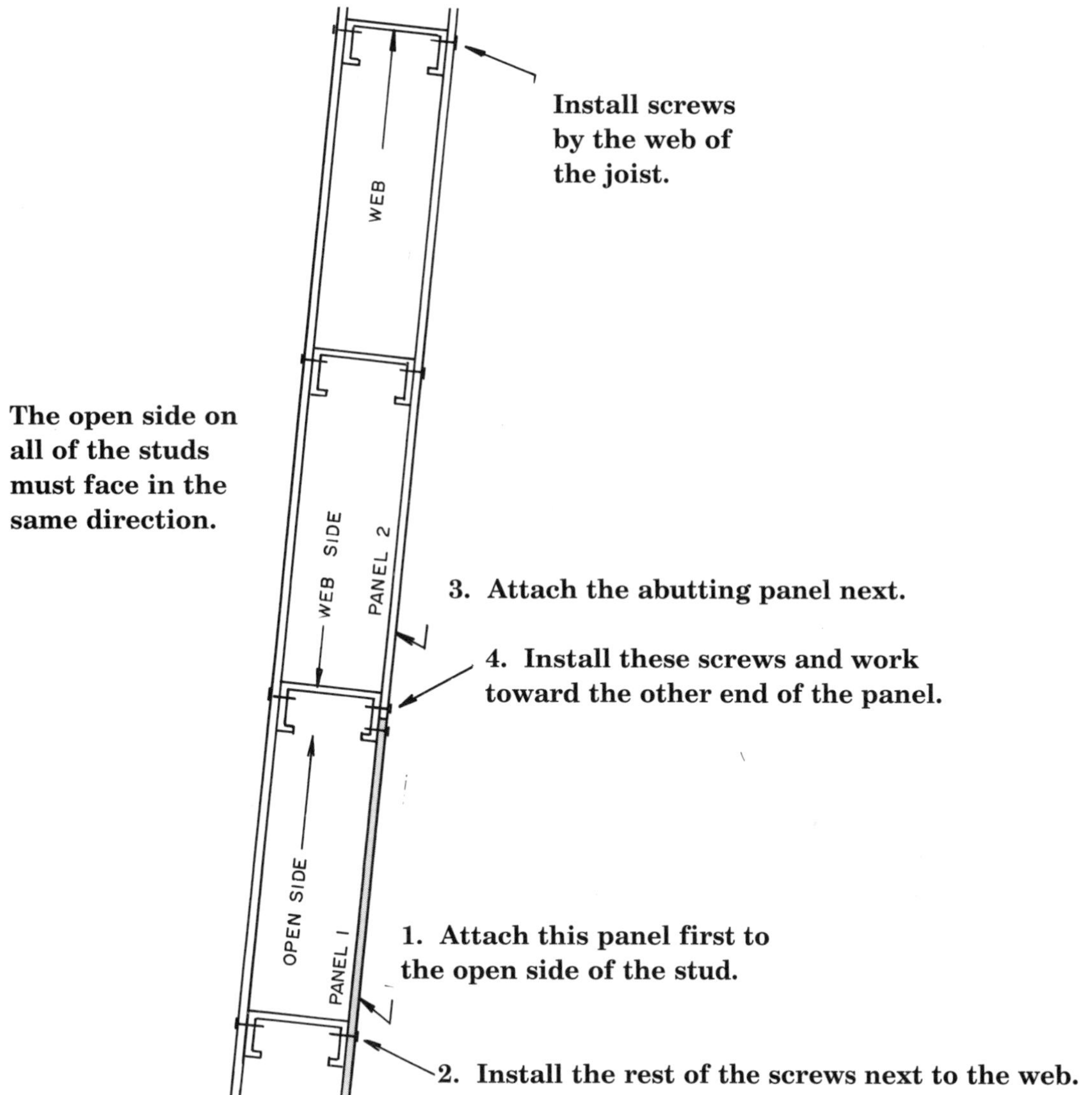

12-5 Always join abutting panels by securing the panel on the open side of the stud first. After that panel is secure, install the abutting panel.

Single-layer gypsum wallboard can be applied horizontally or vertically as described for wood stud application. All edges and ends of the panels should be located in the center of the metal stud. Begin securing the panel by starting with the lead edge or end attached to the open side of the stud. Fasten the entire edge to this open edge and finish installing the panel. Then abut the next panel to it and set the screw close to the stud web (the solid side). Set all screws next to the web—except as described earlier for an end joint. If you join the solid side before the open side, the screw will tend to bend the open end out so that the panels will not abut squarely (*see* 12-5).

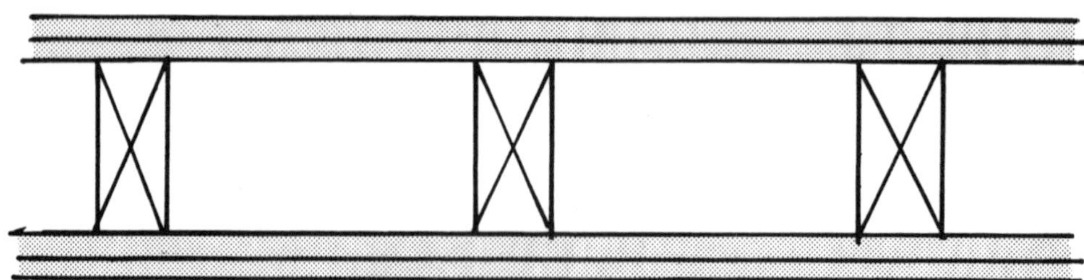

DOUBLE-LAYER APPLICATION

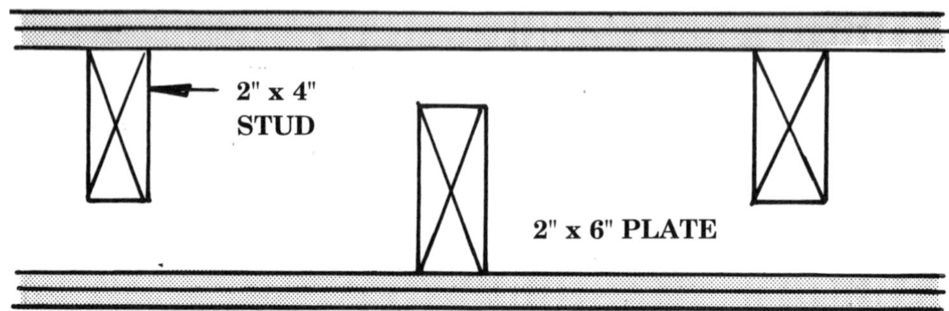

DOUBLE LAYER WITH STAGGERED STUDS

12-7 Two ways used to reduce sound transmission. Either wood or metal studs can be used.

Screws in single-layer applications are spaced 16 in. O.C. when the steel studs are spaced 16 in. O.C. Ceilings are secured to steel joists with screws spaced 12 in. O.C. when the joists are spaced 16 in. O.C.

Sound Isolation

Gypsum wallboard contributes a great deal to the reduction of sound through a wall, floor, or ceiling. If it is combined with various other materials and is properly installed, it is quite effective.

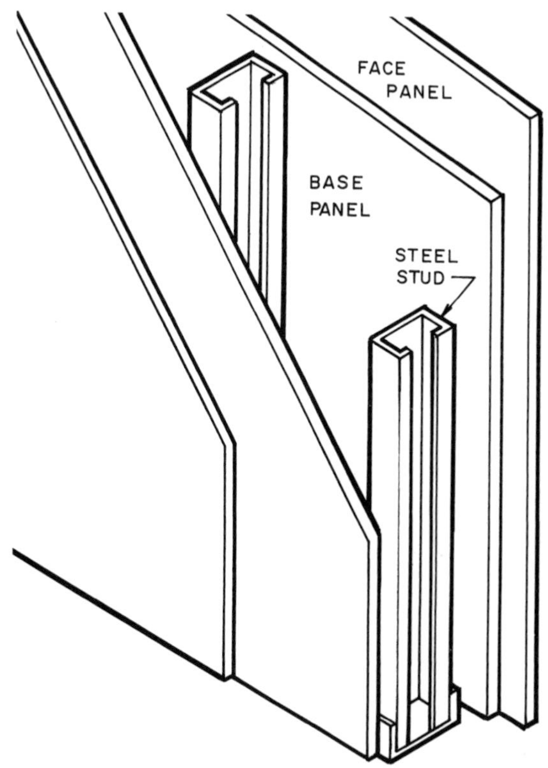

12-7 Double-panel application reduces the amount of sound transmission and increases the fire rating of the partition.

DOUBLE-LAYER INSTALLATION

The easiest way to achieve reduction of sound transmission is to apply a double layer of wallboard to both sides of the wall. The effectiveness can be increased by staggering the studs (*see* 12-6).

Double-layer screw application to steel studs also greatly increases the fire rating. The first layer is applied with the long side of the panel parallel to the studs. The second layer is screw-applied with the long edge parallel to the studs (*see* 12-7). The joints in the second layer must be staggered from those in the base layer and those in the panels on the other side of the wall. The first layer has screws spaced 24 in. O.C. If the second layer is to be adhesively attached, space the screws in the first layer 8 in. O.C. at joint edges 16 in. O.C. in the field.

If the second layer is 1/2 in. thick and the studs are 16 in. O.C., fasten to the studs with 1 5/8 in. type-S screws 16 in. O.C.

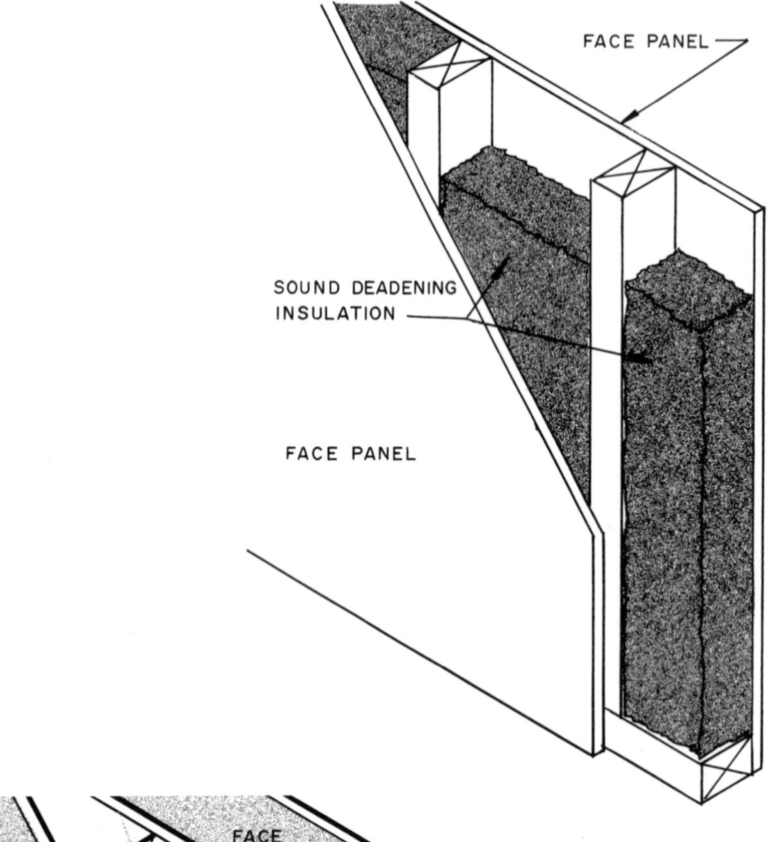

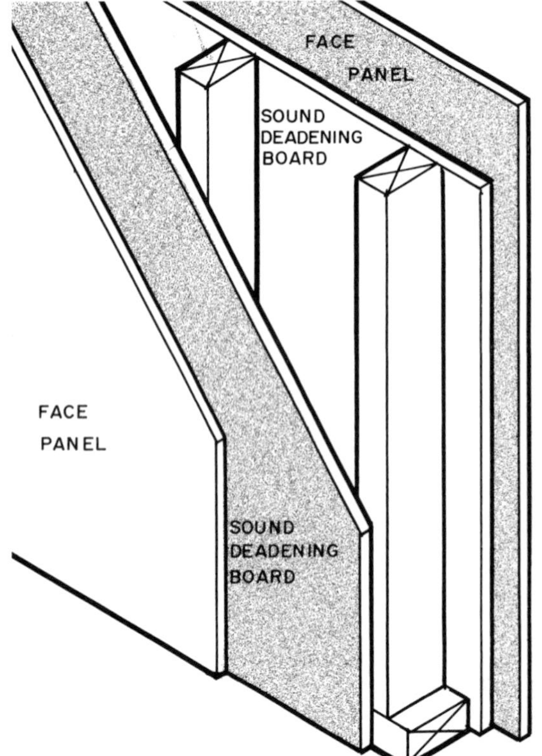

12-8 (Above) Sound transmission through walls can be reduced by installing sound-deadening insulation blankets in the wall cavity.

12-9 (Left) Sound-deadening board installed below the gypsum wallboard helps reduce sound transmission through the wall.

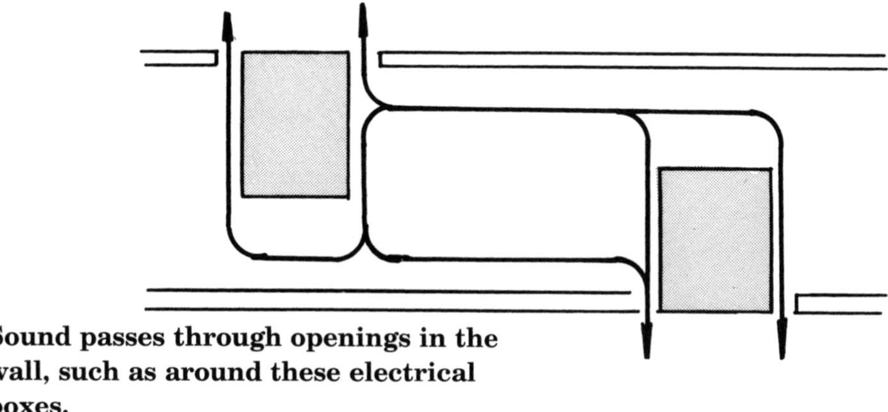

Sound passes through openings in the wall, such as around these electrical boxes.

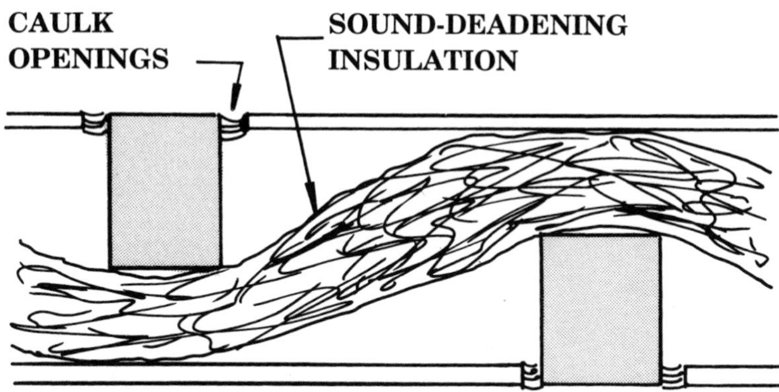

Block all openings to reduce the passage of sound.

12-10 Openings in the wall permit sound to pass through it. Block all openings.

SOUND-DEADENING INSULATION

The installation of insulation or sound-deadening blankets in the wall cavity further increases the sound transmission rating (*see* 12-8). The application of a layer of sound-deadening board to the studs before the drywall is installed is also effective (*see* 12-9).

After the wallboard has been installed, sound transmission can be reduced even more by caulking around any wall openings such as electrical outlets and switch boxes (*see* 12-10).

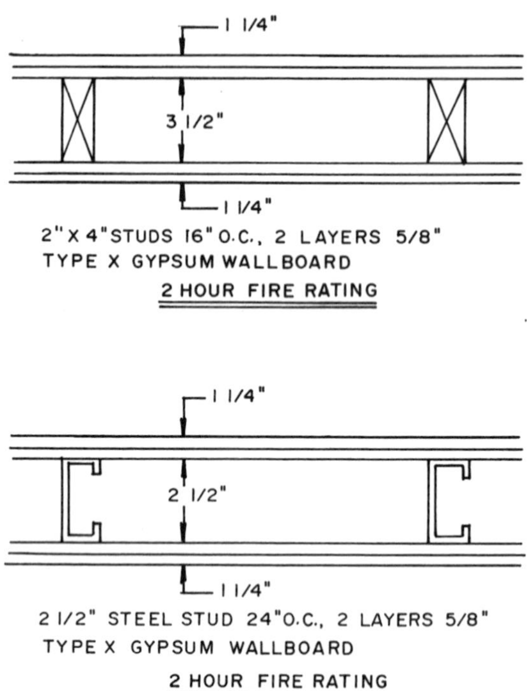

12-11 Fire ratings for two typical wall assemblies.

Fire Control

Since gypsum wallboard does not burn and resists exposure to fire, it is used to protect walls where fire danger exists or where special protection is required by codes, such as a wall between the garage and the house or between apartments. Type X drywall has special fire-resistant properties and is used as the exposed layer on these assemblies. Building codes specify the requirements that must be met. Manufacturers of gypsum products have the results of extensive tests that are used as fire-resistant walls are designed. Two examples are shown in 12-11. Codes also specify the required nailing or screwing requirements. Double-nailing or screwing is commonly required.

Exterior Soffits & Ceilings

A weather-resistant gypsum ceiling board is available for use on soffits and porch and carport ceilings (*see* 12-12 and 12-13). It has many uses on commercial buildings that have exterior exposure but no direct exposure to the weather. This ceiling board is noncombustible and is worked in the same manner is regular wallboard. It can be painted and given a textured finish.

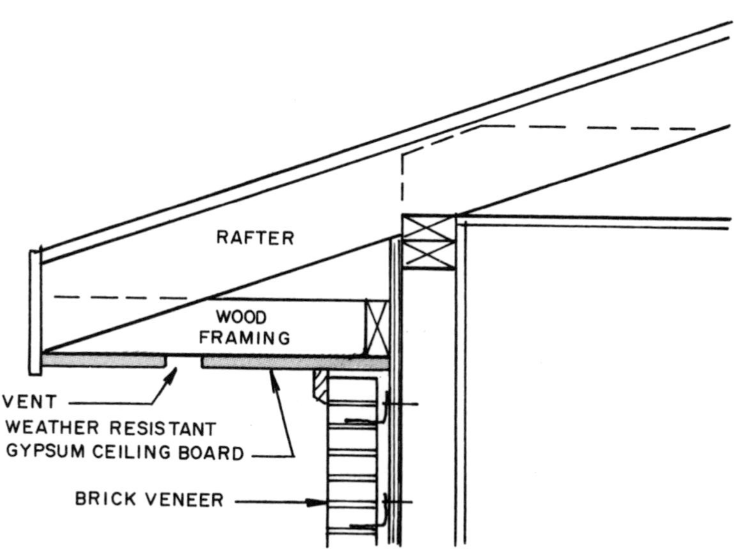

12-12 Weather-resistant gypsum wallboard is used for finished soffit construction.

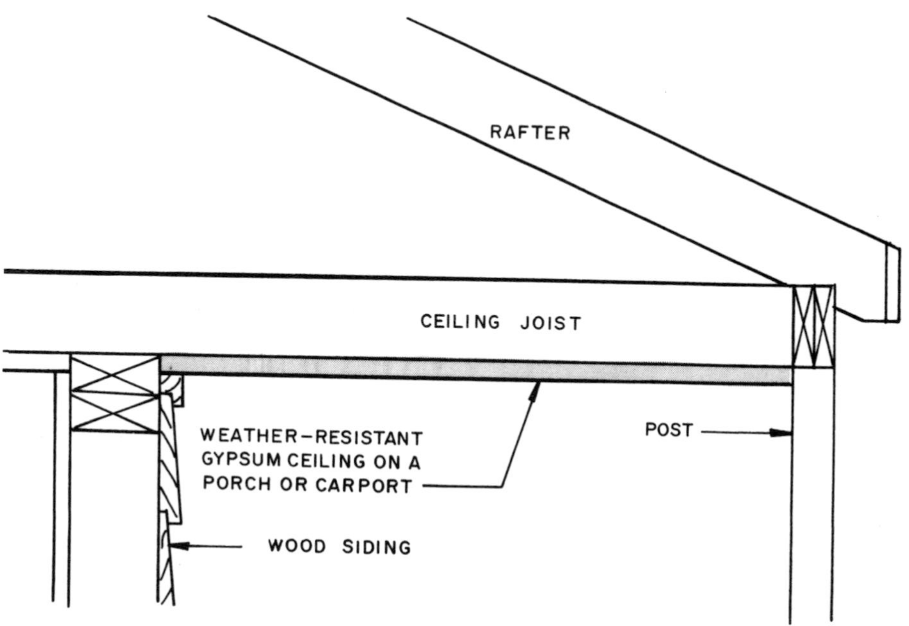

12-13 Weather-resistant gypsum wallboard is used for porch and carport ceilings.

Application to Masonry Walls

Gypsum wallboard can be applied directly to interior, above-grade concrete or masonry walls that are dry. The panels are bonded with a special adhesive available from the manufacturer. The wall should be absolutely flat and any protruding mortar ground away. Holes should be filled with grout or a setting-type gypsum compound. Press the panels against the wall and hold them there with temporary bracing until the adhesive sets.

Below-grade masonry and concrete walls are best covered by furring out the wall with wood or steel studs and installing the drywall in the normal manner.

Application over an Existing Wall

Gypsum wallboard can be applied over an old plaster, wallboard, or wood wall. If the old wall is smooth and sound, wallboard can be applied to it with adhesives. Drywall nails used to hold the panel should be long enough to penetrate the framing about one inch. Screws may also be used.

When the old wall is rough or irregular, it is best to fur and shim as necessary to get a plane surface. Remember to move out and reset electrical boxes so they are flush with the face of the new wallboard.

Glossary

Useful Terms for Installing Drywall

adhesive A compound, glue, or mastic used in the application of gypsum board to framing or for laminating one or more layers of gypsum boards.

angle A corner where two walls intersect.

annular ring nail A deformed shank nail with improved holding qualities specially designed for use with gypsum board.

backing board (1) A gypsum board designed for use as the first or base layer in a multilayer system. (2) A base layer in ceilings for the adhesive application of acoustical tile, (3) A type of water-resistant gypsum board.

backup strips Pieces of wood nailed at the ceiling–sidewall corner to provide fastening for ends of plaster base or gypsum panels.

baseboard Trim that is applied at the bottom of a wall.

beading A condition where flat joints become visible under critical lighting, showing a narrow bead or ridge in the center of the joint. No loss of bond. Synonym for ridging and picture framing.

bed coat First compound coat after taping.

beveled edge The long edge of a sheet of drywall that is tapered to form a recessed area when two sheets abut.

blister A raised loose spot on the tape caused by insufficient compound beneath the tape.

bullnose A type of metal corner bead with rounded corners.

butt joint Joints formed by the mill-cut ends or by job cuts without a tapered edge.

centerline A line used as a nailing guide, running down the center of a wallboard panel.

chalkline Straight working line made by snapping a chalked cord stretched between two points, which transfers the chalk to the work surface.

cladding Gypsum panels, gypsum bases, gypsum sheathing, cement board, etc., applied to framing.

corner bead A metal or plastic angle used to protect outside corners where gypsum panels meet.

corner cracking Hairline fracture or wider crack occurring in the apex of inside corners. Synonym for shrinkage cracking and angle cracks.

depressed nails Depressions in the joint or topping compound that occur directly over the head of a nail. Synonym for dimpled nail heads, recessed nail heads. Sometimes incorrectly referred to as shrinkage.

drywall Generic term for interior surfacing material, such as gypsum panels, applied to framing.

drywall lift A tool used to lift drywall to the wall and ceiling and hold it until it is nailed in place.

drywall taping The application of tape over the gypsum wallboard joints.

edge cracking Straight hairline cracks at one or both edges of the joint tape. Shows through finishing coats and/or painting.

feathering Spreading the finish coats of compound out from the joint to a very thin coating.

feathered edge The thin outer edge of the finish coats.

fire-rated drywall Treated drywall that has a higher resistance to fire than regular drywall.

fire wall Any wall separating two units, such as apartments.

first finishing coat Application of the first coat of joint or topping compound over tape, bead, and nails. Synonym for second coat, filling, bedding, floating, bed-coat, prebedding, first bed.

fur down A drop-down section attached to the ceiling, such as above a set of cabinets.

green board A gypsum panel with a green surface used in areas where dampness may be present.

gypsum board or wallboard Generic terms for gypsum-core panels covered on both sides by paper.

high joint Butt or tapered-edge joint protruding above the plane of the board—also termed crowned.

horizontal application Application of gypsum wallboard with the length perpendicular to the nailing members. Synonym for around the room, across the joists or studs.

joint blisters Looseness of paper appearing after the first finishing coat.

joint compound A compound used for taping and finishing joints in drywall construction.

joint darkening Joint and nail spots that appear darker than the surrounding areas.

joint lightening Joints and nail spots that appear lighter than the surrounding areas.

joint shadowing Joints that appear darker when viewed from an oblique angle, yet show no color differentiation when seen from a right angle. Usually caused by texture variation, low joints, or high joints. Incorrectly referred to as burning, flashing, photographing, and joint darkening.

mud A term commonly used when referring to joint compound.

nail dimpling Depression in the wallboard surface resulting from setting nails with a wallboard hammer.

nail-pop The protrusion of the nail usually attributed to the shrinkage of or use of improperly cured wood framing.

predecorated wallboard A gypsum panel product that has the exposed surface finished when the panel was manufactured.

router A power tool that uses special bits to plunge-cut interior openings within drywall panels, such as for electrical outlets or heat ducts.

score To cut through the paper facing and into the gypsum panel.

second finishing coat Application of the second coat of joint or topping compound over tape, bead, and nails. Synonym for third coat, finishing, finish bed, polishing, feather coat, skimming.

shadowing An undesirable appearance that occurs when the joint finish shows through the surface decoration.

sheen variation Joints or nail spots that appear with more or less sheen than the wallboard.

shrinkage cracking Cracking that occurs with joint or topping compound when applied too thick in one application.

skim coat Applications of a thin coat of joint or topping compound to the entire wall and ceiling after joint treatment. Provides a uniform smoothness of paper and joints.

spotting nails Application of joint-finishing compound to nail heads and dimples. Synonym for spotting and nail coating.

starved joint Depression in the joint over tapered joints. Also seen as depressions on each side of the tape on a butt joint. Synonym for low-point, delayed shrinkage, concave joint.

substrate Underlying material to which a finish is applied or by which it is supported.

tape photographing Outline of tape is visible in corners and flat joints after joints are finished.

taping Application of joint compound and joint tape on gypsum wallboard joints. Synonym for embedding tape, first coat, hanging, laying tape, bedding, roughing, joint finishing.

taping compound A joint compound designed to bond joint tape to the panel.

texturing Application of texture by roller, spray, brush, or other method. Synonym for stripling.

wallboard Another term for drywall.

Appendix A

The Metric System

As the construction industry converts to metric units, drywall panels will be available in metric units. These sizes will be kept very close to the current inch sizes. The spacing of studs and wall height in metric units will also influence the metric wallboard panel sizes. Inch-size panels can be converted to their equivalent metric sizes by using the conversion factors in **Table 1**. This change is referred to as a soft conversion. When true metric design sizes are available it will be referred to as hard conversion. A soft conversion of a 1/2-in.-thick 4 x 8 ft. panel is recorded as 12.7 mm x 1201.8 mm x 2403.8 mm.

The metric system includes all aspects of measurement. The basic metric units, their symbols, and customary measuring system equivalents are shown in **Table 2**.

A table of metric equivalents is presented in **Table 3**; it is useful in the approximate quick conversion of working measurements.

Table 1 Metric Conversion

When you know	You can find	If you multiply by
Length		
inches	millimeters	25.4
feet	millimeters	300.48
yards	meters	0.91
millimeters	inches	0.04
meters	yards	1.1
Area		
square inches	square centimeters	6.45
square feet	square meters	0.09
square yards	square meters	0.83
square centimeters	square inches	0.16
square meters	square yards	1.2
Mass (Weight)		
ounces	grams	28.0
pounds	kilograms	0.45
tons (short)	metric tons	0.9
grams	ounces	0.04
kilograms	pounds	2.2
metric tons	tons (short)	1.1
Volume		
cubic feet	cubic meters	0.03
cubic inches	cubic centimeters	16.4
cubic yards	cubic meters	0.8

When you know	You can find	If you multiply by
Volume (Fluid)		
ounces	milliliters	30.0
pints	liters	0.47
quarts	liters	0.95
gallons	liters	3.8
milliliters	ounces	0.03
liters	pints	2.1
liters	quarts	1.06
liters	gallons	0.26
Temperature		
degrees Fahrenheit	degrees Celsius	0.6 (after subtracting 32)
degrees Celsius	degrees Fahrenheit	1.8 (then add 32)
Power		
horsepower	kilowatts	0.75
kilowatts	horsepower	1.34
Pressure		
pounds per square inch	kilopascals	6.9
kilopascals	pounds per square inch	0.15

Table 2 Metric Units

	Unit	Symbol	Equivalent
Length			
	millimeter	mm	0.039 in.
	meter	m	3.281 ft.
			1.094 yd.
Area			
	meter	m^2	10.763 $ft.^2$
			1.195 $yd.^2$
Volume			
	meter	m^3	35.314 $ft.^3$
			1.195 $yd.^3$
Volume (Fluid)			
	liter	L	33.815 oz.
			0.264 gal.
Mass (Weight)			
	gram	g	0.035 oz.
	kilogram	kg	2.205 lb.
	ton	t	2204.600 lb.
Force			
	newton	N	0.226 lb.-ft.
Temperature			
(Interval)	kelvin	K	1.8 degrees F
(Interval)	one degree Celsius	degree C	1.8 degrees F
Temperature	Celsius	degrees C	(degrees F – 32)·5/9

Unit	Symbol	Equivalent
Thermal Resistance		
	$K \cdot m^2/W$	5.679 $ft^2 \cdot hr \cdot$degrees F/Btu
Heat Transfer		
watt	W	3.412 Btu/hr
Pressure		
kilopascal	kPa	0.145 lb./in.^{2} (psi)
pascal	Pa	20.890 lb./ft.^{2} (psf)

TABLE 3 METRIC EQUIVALENTS

mm = millimeter
cm = centimeter
m = meter

inches	mm	cm	inches	cm	inches	cm
1/8	3	0.3	9	22.9	30	76.2
1/4	6	0.6	10	25.4	31	78.7
3/8	10	1.0	11	27.9	32	81.3
1/2	13	1.3	12	30.5	33	83.8
5/8	16	1.6	13	33.0	34	86.4
3/4	19	1.9	14	35.6	35	88.9
7/8	22	2.2	15	38.1	36	91.4
1	25	2.5	16	40.6	37	94.0
1 1/4	32	3.2	17	43.2	38	96.6
1 1/2	38	3.8	18	45.7	39	99.1
1 3/4	44	4.4	19	48.3	40	101.6
2	51	5.1	20	50.8	41	104.1
2 1/2	64	6.4	21	53.3	42	106.7
3	76	7.6	22	55.9	43	109.2
3 1/2	89	8.9	23	58.4	44	111.8
4	102	10.2	24	61.0	45	114.3
4 1/2	114	11.4	25	63.5	46	116.8
5	127	12.7	26	66.0	47	119.4
6	152	15.2	27	68.6	48	121.9
7	178	17.8	28	71.1	49	124.5
8	203	20.3	29	73.7	50	127.0

Foot and Inch Conversions

1 inch = 25.4 mm
1 foot = 304.8 mm

Metric Conversions

1 mm = 0.039 inch
1 m = 3.28 feet

Appendix B

Industry Trade Associations

Gypsum Association

810 First Street NE, #510
Washington, DC 20002
202-289-5440

Information Bureau for Lath, Plaster, and Drywall

3127 Los Feliz Blvd.
Los Angeles, CA 90059
231-663-2213

Wallcovering Manufacturers Association and Wallcovering Information Bureau

401 N. Michigan Ave., Suite 2200
Chicago, IL 60611

Foundation of the Wall and Ceiling Industry

307 Annadale, Suite 200
Falls Church, VA 22042

Index